TOURISM
TODAY AND TOMORROW

TOURISM

TODAY AND TOMORROW

Edited by
Praveen Sethi

ANMOL PUBLICATIONS PVT. LTD.
NEW DELHI - 110 002 (INDIA)

ANMOL PUBLICATIONS PVT. LTD.
4374/4B, Ansari Road, Daryaganj
New Delhi - 110 002

Tourism: Today and Tomorrow

First Edition, 1999
ISBN 81-261-0446-5

PRINTED IN INDIA

Published by J.L. Kumar for Anmol Publications Pvt. Ltd., New Delhi - 110 002 and Printed at Tarun Offset Press, Delhi.

Contents

Preface

Tourism in the twenty-first century must anticipate a future marked by changing global relationships and societal structures, technological innovations, and growing spatial awareness and environmental concern. Major shifts in the nature and scale of tourism are already in evidence as the industry struggles to respond to a range of forces at work. Change and the change agents involved are powerful and positive forces if harnessed constructively. Rather than opposing change, or merely accepting and accommodating change, the tourism industry must manage change to its advantage and that of the environment which nurtures it.

Endorsement and application of the concept of sustainability and of best-practice environmental management offer compelling evidence of how change can be harnessed to contribute towards the achievement of environmental excellence. Although tourism flourishes best in conditions of peace, prosperity, freedom and security, disturbance to these conditions is to be expected. The industry response must be sufficiently resilient to generate opportunities for the growth of tourism in keeping with the dynamics of a changing world and increasing concern for ecologically sustainable development.

Since the Earth Summit held in Rio de Janeiro in 1992, pressure has grown for the tourism industry to lift its environmental performance in common with other economic sectors, and to work towards ecologically sustainable forms of tourism development. At the same time, planners and developers seeking to create satisfying settings for tourists into the next century must anticipate a world influenced by a new and bewildering array of forces, many of which are difficult to predict. Given such uncertainty, the challenge is to pursue tourism growth in a manner resilient enough to respond positively to a changing global environment and societal structure, while remaining compatible with the principles and practice of ecologically sustainable tourism which will exist for today and tomorrow.

Editor

1

Tourism: Today and Tomorrow

Tourism has a long history. We know of its existence in ancient Egypt and it seems reasonable to assume that travel for pleasure would have been a feature of many past societies where levels of productivity were sufficient to sustain forms of leisure. And Yet, our knowledge is highly biased towards Western and Classical societies and we remain remarkably ignorant about tourism in other past worlds. How, for instance, did tourism evolve in China or parts of India? It seems highly unlikely that tourism was a purely Western invention. This fundamental bias in the historical record is perhaps the most noticeable feature of tourism's past but, even within Western societies, our understanding is highly selective, Much of what we know and think is important about the evolution of tourism is conditioned by particular historical perspectives. The focus of this paper is, therefore, on the historiography of tourism history, as it developed in the past, its present state and its future prospects.

Research into tourism's history has consisted of two main characteristics. The first concerns the distinct themes which have attracted attention. These themes include the I tourism activities of particular groups of people, generally the wealthy, and a concern with the development of particular tourism places such as spas and seaside resorts. This is partly, but not entirely, due to the nature of historical source material which tends to favour the powerful in society. In most cases the dramatic and prestigious episodes have triumphed over the ordinary and regular.

The second characteristic of research relates to the groups undertaking the work. This includes not only professional historians but also social science tourism specialists. In addition, these two distinct camps have been 'Joined by a considerable number of popular writers attracted by the apparent eclat of the subject matter and its nostalgic appeal to modern readers. Each group has brought its own distinctive perspective to tourism's history.

Research into tourism history before the 1970s helped to illuminate three broad areas: travel and tourism in the ancient worlds, Grand Touring in the 17th and 18th centuries and the growth of spas and seaside resorts. A further, closely related field, was the study of changing tastes and fashions for landscape and the arts, which clearly had an influence on tourists' choice and evaluation of destinations.

Some of the earliest research into tourism history was done at the beginning of this century. Ludwig Friedlander, in his study of life and manners in ancient Rome, wrote extensively on travel and the emergence of second home villas for wealthy Romans on the Bay of Naples. This pioneering effort was not really supplemented until the 1960s and early 1970s when Balsdon wrote his major study of life and leisure in Rome, and Lindsay and D'Arms wrote of leisure and pleasure in Egypt and the Bay of Naples. Tourism in the ancient world received its most recent authoritative summary with the work of Lionel Casson who considered its significance in Egypt, Greece and Rome. Classical sources have provided a rich quarry for historians ranging from literary records, inscriptions and graffiti to archaeological remains. The latter have enabled researchers to investigate the size and layout of villas, hotels and restaurants in ancient Rome, whilst the writings of Horace, Virgil, Pliny the Younger and others, provide a vivid evocation of villa life for the rich and powerful.

Most of the research on tourism in the ancient world has been undertaken by classical scholars and has been characterised by a thorough command of source materials and a meticulous approach to the subject. Past research in this particular area means that we know more about forms of tourism in, for instance, ancient Rome, than we do for many later periods of history.

The prestigious Grand Tours of Europe which developed in the 16th, 17th and 18th centuries, were also the subject of early research. Bates and Mead produced detailed studies of British continental travel in the 17th and 18th centuries making use of diaries, letters and journals of the aristocracy and gentry as well as contemporary guidebooks. Continental travel was not confined to the British, however, but it was not until Schudt's work that other nationalities were included in a major review. The role of the Grand Tour in developing aesthetic tastes and creating art collections in Britain has received exhaustive attention front art historians, perhaps reinforcing the image of past tourism as an exclusively upper-class and essentially cultural experience.

Scholarly work on the Grand Tour has always been supplemented by a vast array of popular works. Amusing anecdotes, extensive illustrative material and the nostalgic appeal of a 'golden age of travel', help explain this enthusiasm, These popular books have been of variable quality, though Hibbert's was a good account of some aspects of the tour itself. Scholarly and popular works all shared one characteristic however. They focused exclusively on the attitudes and activities of the tourists themselves. The tour has rarely been placed in a wider social context and the views of the host society remain largely unknown. Even more recent research on the Grand Tour has tended to follow a well-worn path.

Another major theme for past research has been the development of specific tourist locations, especially spas and seaside resorts, These are large-scale tourist forms which have created their own source material and contemporary commentary. A stimulating early work on English watering places was undertaken by Reginald Lennard in the early 1930s based on a close analysis of primary data. The same theme was explored by Carl Bridenbaugh's pioneering research into the spas of colonial America, Broader themes of general tourism were explored by Moir for England and Dulles for the United States. Seaside resort development in England was studied at an early date by the historical geographer F. W. Gilbert, who was notable in considering the wider implications of resorts beyond the comings and goings of I, he rich and influential. During the 1960s, French historians produced a number of papers relating to activities of the English upper classes at French seaside and mountain resorts. As with the Grand Tour, a preoccupation with the lives of the rich, together with entertaining anecdotal material, resulted in a host of popular works on spas and seaside resorts which Walton characterised as 'journalistic in tone and of little scholarly merit.

Standing in complete contrast, however, was the classic work of J. A, R. Pimlott. He produced an outstanding survey of the Englishman's holiday from Elizabethan times to the 20th century. He ranged from spas and seaside resorts to continental touring, from the activities of the rich to those of the poor. He was particularly ingenious in his search for primary data, trawling not only diaries, letters, journals and guide books, but also newspapers, periodicals, official reports, novels and illustrations. For breadth of coverage and research, his book remains unsurpassed.

One other theme that past research has illuminated is that of the aesthetics of tourism; the changing tastes and fashions of the tourists, especially their evaluations of landscapes. Hussey provided an early examination of the rise of picturesque taste and a scholarly analysis of 18th century aesthetic theories was developed by Hipple. A literary analysis of travel by Parks related changing tastes, especially the rise of romantic conceptions, to tourism activity and this was but one of many studies which included the aesthetics of travel.

Three major works moved beyond the aesthetics of tourism to embrace the links with philosophical and scientific movements. Frantz showed how 17th century travellers in Europe, in their tireless accumulation of lists and measurements of all they saw, reflected the scientific inductive philosophies of Bacon and Descartes, Fussell related the 'empirical tourism' of 18th century travellers to the humanist outlook of the Augustan age where the quest was for evidence of enduring, human reason. Marjorie Hope Nicolson, sought to explain the developing taste for mountain and wild scenery in the late 17th and early 18th centuries by the rise of scientific thought. She argued that this new taste, which was to have a profound influence on changing tourist itineraries and landscape evaluations, was due to science changing people's awe for God to an awe for an expanded cosmos which included mountains and other remote areas. Recent work which continues this strong tradition of landscape taste and tourism include Andrews, Lowenthal and Prince and Newby.

Past research into tourism history has thus

developed a number of particular themes. Despite evident strengths in ancient tourism, Grand Touring, spas, seaside resorts and aesthetics, a distorted picture of the past was, nevertheless, produced. Studies tended to focus on the activities of a social elite, especially when they engaged in dramatic and prestigious events. The importance of particular forms of tourism tended to become equated with quantifiable measures such as length of time spent on holiday and the amount of money expended. Thus, the *significance* of tourism in people's lives was generally overlooked. A short holiday, once a year, could be more important for some people than a lengthy winter season in Nice or Cannes for others. The attitudes of host societies and the wider social, economic and political contexts of tourism also received scant attention. Wealthy tourists, and their activities in particular destination areas, created the dominant picture of tourism's history.

The present

There are two notable developments in tourism history research today. The first is the growing interest of social historians in leisure. Historians subsume tourism within the wider arena of leisure and they avoid the awkward and rather artificial breakdown of the subject into either leisure, or recreation, or tourism. Not only has the field been empirically expanded, but historians have introduced a much-needed theoretical and ideological debate into the evolution of leisure. Without engaging in this debate, tourism history would be in danger of becoming merely a superficial preface to contemporary tourism research.

The second major development in tourism history research has been the attempt by some tourism social science researchers to provide an historical perspective on models and concepts evolved for present-day tourism. If these models and concepts were to acquire an acceptable 'depth' of explanation, then relating them to past circumstances would strengthen their claim to validity.

Walton and Walvin and Bailey have provided valuable summaries of the developments in leisure history in Britain since the 1970s and they both identify certain important characteristics. A major focus of historical research has been into the leisure experience of the working class and its transformation in the late 18th and early 19th centuries. From seeing leisure closely integrated with the world of work, historians have debated the extent to which leisure was broken down or transformed under the pressures of urbanisation and industrialisation. Leisure emerged in new ways in the later 19th century ways which included tourism.

As well as emphasising that the working classes also had forms of tourism, social historians have argued the underlying causes of change. Leisure was not just a consequence of the industrial revolution, technological change and class structures. Nor were leisure activities simply passed down from one social class to another. Both Cunningham and Thompson argue that working-class culture had its own momentum and was not simply a passive recipient of ideas from above. Similarly, Thompson has recently shown that 19th-century middle-class leisure practices were not just derived from the upper classes, but evolved in a much more intricate manner that did not adhere to simple class stereotypes. Not only were these social divisions complex, but as Walton, Walton and Walvin and Cunningham emphasise, there were significant regional and local differences in leisure habits in Britain. These important variations in demand areas deserve further exploration.

There has also been a useful debate over the role of transport technology in tourism development. A simplistic view of railways 'creating' seaside resorts is debated by Walton and Simmons. Railways created certain patterns of tourism but growth may have occurred in different ways without them.

These ideas have clear implications for tourism history. So often, a picture is presented of tourism's evolution being driven by changes in transport or the mechanistic process of successive class intrusion. Bailey's view on the evolution of leisure as 'a process that has been erratic, complex and contentious' is a useful corrective to simplistic notions of the evolution of tourism.

Certain social history works have made a major contribution to our understanding of tourism. John Walton's research on working-class tourism in 19th-century Lancashire is notable because he explored conditions in the destination areas but balanced this with the particular circumstances evolving in the generating areas. This even balance is also found in his work on the English seaside resort. Together with McGloin, Walton has also provided a useful critique of historical research techniques. Urban historians have also produced stimulating work related to tourism. Neale's. Marxist perspective on the growth of Bath is a refreshing change to the usual catalogue of famous visitors to the spa, and lie includes a consideration of the wider impacts of tourism including local labour demands. Elsewhere, Borsay and McInnes have debated the emergence of provincial 'leisure' towns in England outside the world of the spas and seaside resorts. This richer and more balanced view of leisure and tourism can also be seen in Haug's study of the effect of tourism on Nice in the 19th century. Using census data, he isolates the main tourist, local middle-class and local working-class areas of the city and considers the unequal provision of services between the wealthy and the poor. For Haug, the rich visitors, so intriguing to others are 'not very interesting individually' but provided the force that caused important changes elsewhere in the area.

The rising interest of social science researchers in tourism history is probably most clearly marked by the collection of writings on the evolution of recreation and tourism in Canada edited by Wall and Marsh, and a special issue of the *Annals of Tourism Research* edited by Butler and Wall. In the former, historical analyses are provided mainly by geographers who are interested in tracing the relationship between people and environments as revealed by recreation and tourism. In the latter, most of the articles are written by social scientists and a dominant feature of the papers is the attempt to use models and conceptual frameworks to organise and inform research. Thus, Meyer-Arendt uses Butler's cycle of tourist area evolution to study the development of Grand Isle, Louisiana, as does Hugill for examining early 20th-century automobile touring in the USA. Wightman and Wall link spa development in the Canadian Rockies to Nelson's framework for studying national parks and Towner relates the Grand Tour to Leiper's conceptualisation of the overall tourism system.

One of the major problems inherent in these attempts is the lack of historical data which enables models to be rigorously tested For example, Butler's model has been used extensively but the absence of consistent and accurate data raises questions about the degree of *post hoc* reasoning involved. The general conceptual frameworks evolved by social scientists are, however, of value in identifying and structuring the complex interrelationships arising from leisure, recreation and tourism and ensuring that an holistic view is taken of processes and outcomes.

What is particularly noticeable about the present

state of tourism history research is that, despite being an interdisciplinary field of interest, there are few substantive links between historians and social scientists. There seem to be no methodological barriers to closer cooperation as both history and the social issues increasingly share a whole range of approaches. And yet, few historians publish papers in tourism journals, and few tourism researchers seem aware of the substantial body of research developed in leisure history, This is a major weakness, because it is often at the frontiers between different disciplines that the most interesting and useful research occurs.

The future of tourism history research will be influenced by a whole range of issues. There are, however, a number of ideas that can be explored. These include: (1) the need for closer interdisciplinary links, (2) the integration of tourism within the wider leisure field, (3) the value of a lifestyle/life cycle approach, (4) the use of an holistic systems approach, (5) the development of non-Western perspectives on tourism's evolution, and (6) the use of a wider range of source material in research.

The need for closer interdisciplinary links has been argued for above and does not need further amplification. Integrating tourism history within the wider field of leisure, recreation and tourism is part of this process. The absence of subdivisions within leisure has enabled historians to research the whole interconnected world of leisure without becoming preoccupied with classifying activities as leisure or recreation or tourism. In North America much relevant research appears under the heading of 'recreation' and communication between disciplines is frustrated by this seemingly trivial difference. Furthermore, as Hughes recently points out, the creation of a separate 'discipline' of tourism owes more to the demands of the 'industry' than to scholarly endeavour.

Tourism history could profitably explore the lifestyle/life cycle approach to leisure. So often, research focuses on particular tourism episodes—going to spas, going to the seaside, going on the Grand Tour rather than considering how these episodes related to other aspects of people's leisure lifestyles. Furthermore, these leisure lifestyles need to be incorporated into the life cycle. How did patterns of tourism change for individuals through their fives? The availability of suitable primary data presents a problem here, but there is a body of information in the form of longterm diaries that enable some research to be undertaken. The episodic approach to tourism history has tended to ignore the longerterm, almost routine practices.

The rhythms and structures of usual life and the role of leisure and tourism within this framework can easily be distorted by a focus on intermittent events. So, we find the Grand Tour taking precedence over the regular migration of Venetian merchants to their country villas. The annual cycle of informal hospitality amongst the gentry of England can be overshadowed by the visits to spas and seaside resorts. The self-help creation of holiday-homes by the relatively poor or the development of a weekend cottage zone around Paris becomes obscured by a focus on Thomas Cook's tours abroad.

Tourism history can be usefully viewed within an holistic systems framework which is related to wider social, economic, political and technological worlds. Research needs not only to consider tourist destination areas and transport routes but also to explore processes in the tourist-generating areas. Understanding the development of Blackpool, Coney Island, Nice or Cannes requires research into conditions in the centres of demand as much as activities at destinations. As discussed above, historians have pointed to important local and regional variations in leisure cultures.

Generating areas cannot, therefore, be considered as uniform regions. Leisure varied not just with social strata but from place to place.

In tourist destination areas, more attention needs to be given to the effects of tourism in creating centres of consumption. Thus, food, fuel and a whole range of direct and indirect services are involved. Tourism history has tended to be preoccupied with the activities of the holidaymakers at the expense of impacts on the host society. Leisure historians have already highlighted issues of power and control of resources and development which can often be usefully related to the balance between core and periphery areas.

The tourism system is dynamic. As well as considering the processes which created particular systems, examining change and continuity in those systems is an important area of research. Were some changes a reflection of technological shifts in transport or due to more deep-seated cultural change? The pace of change also needs consideration. Some systems showed remarkable longterm endurance, such as the allure of southern Europe for north Europeans. Other systems experienced rapid rise and fall. Distinguishing between the more profound influences on change and continuity and the more superficial veneer of fashion remains a major task for research.

Tourism history needs to become more ideologically aware. Many commonly held views derived from past writings are laden with unstated value-judgements. Spas 'declined' when the upper classes forsook them for more exclusive destinations, seaside resorts 'waned' when their social tone altered. No matter that the actual numbers of visitors increased; they were the wrong sort of visitors. This view permeates the idea of the 'golden age of the traveller' before vulgar tourism began and can be traced in modern critiques of tourism. The lack of attention paid to gender is also a reflection of these unstated biases. Women have generally remained hidden from tourism history, whether as tourists or as workers, yet their significance was clearly very great. The rapid expansion of research in this area of leisure history is uncovering a major omission in the historical record.

A further major bias in research was highlighted at the beginning of this paper. The history of tourism is primarily the history of west European (especially British) and North American tourism. As well as dominating empirical research, Western concepts of leisure and tourism dominate the picture. How they have been manifested in other societies in the past remains virtually unknown. It can be argued that correcting this one-sided view of history is, in fact, the main task for future tourism history research.

Finally, some observations can be made about the range of source material used in research. Until now, much of our knowledge has been derived from a fairly limited range of information. The letters, diaries and journals of a restricted group of tourists together with guide books have generally formed the basis for much research in the pre-19th-century era. After that, census data becomes available, and this is supplemented from the 1920s by a growing volume of official tourist statistics. These sources have been reviewed in detail by Pimlott, Walton and McGloin and Towner and so will not be discussed at length here. Rather, three potentially fruitful and under-used sources will be outlined.

For the very recent historical past, the possibilities of oral history are especially attractive. This approach has been used in important studies of leisure in Manchester and Salford by Davies and has also been used in a Scottish context by Blair and Smout and Wood.

Particularly important here is the opportunity to explore the leisure and tourism experiences of a wide range of people and to place these experiences within their everyday lives. Recent work by Cross shows how the mass observation surveys of the late 1930s, despite their methodological weaknesses, can give a vivid insight into attitudes towards leisure in the near past.

Works of fiction, especially novels, can provide valuable insights into the mentalities of a culture and their potential for tourism history was briefly noted by Pimlott in 1947. Nevertheless, no systematic review has been made of the vast amount of material that could be used. Herbert has shown how novels like Jane Austen's can be used to capture the sense of place as experienced by people in the past—a valuable context for understanding their leisure. Jane Austen's books are full of direct references to leisure and tourism in polite society in early 19th century England, as are the earlier works of Smollett, Fielding and Sterne. In later periods, the social novels of Dickens, Trollope and Henry James provide a rich vein of information as do those of H. G. Wells and Arnold Bennett. Bennett's *Anna of the Five Towns* for instance, has a marvellous portrayal of the anticipation and excitement of a first holiday away from home—a visit to the Isle of Man from the Potteries. No statistics can capture that significant event in someone's life, Thomas Mann's *Buddenbrooks* gives us an understanding of the role played by the seaside at Travemunde for the wealthy merchant classes of Lubeck on the north German coast. Further examples are boundless. However, in addition to cataloguing these works, methods of analysis and interpretation have to be devised. Their potential is to provide not only factual details but an appreciation of the role of leisure and tourism in past cultures.

The visual arts are a further source of information that have beep, little used. A major review of visual images in historical interpretation has recently been produced by Haskell which forms a useful starting point for explorations of this kind, For the world of pleasure, visual images may simply be ways of piecing together past activities, whether in paintings, cartoons or photographs. More subtle interpretation is possible, however. Ludolf de Jonghe's *Farewells Before a Country House* for instance, portrays a whole world of 17th-century Dutch leisure culture. For mid-19th-century France, the social art historian Robert Herbert links Impressionist art, leisure and Parisian society together and demonstrates the potential of fusing picture analysis with sociohistorical material in exploring ideas of leisure and tourism in past societies. Thus, literary works of fiction and the visual arts should not be seen as merely surrogates for the lack of tourism statistics in the past. They can, if used with sensitivity, be a way of gaining insight into the world of leisure and tourism in the lives of people in other ages.

2

Tourism and the Environment

This chapter deals with the interrelationships between tourism and the environment. It discusses the awareness of environmental issues, and the need for preventative and remedial action. The chapter also describes the issues related to zoning, planning and land use, and the concept of yield in the physical planning of tourism facilities, It outlines some other issues in facilities planning, and introduces the idea of paying environmental and cultural royalties. The chapter concludes by listing environmental management standards, and a checklist for the preparation of an environmental impact statement for tourism projects. The fulfilment of human needs causes environmental change of some sort. To adapt the natural environment to human existence is part being human. Every time people cultivate crops, divert rivers, construct buildings, engineer new roads, or undertake any development, it rebounds in some way on the environment. The arguments are about whether such actions are detrimental or not; whether the environment is harmed, and whether development is sustainable.

Development cannot mean growth alone. Growth may make some people richer but it doesn't necessarily add to everybody'_ state of wellbeing. Economic development should have broad and interdependent effects which lead to the improvement of life. Are people better off not just in financial terms, but in access to health, to educational opportunities, to housing, leisure options, recreational facilities and so on? In the past, progress was measured principally by GNP *per capita;* a measurement which does not reflect either the distribution of benefits or the quality of life. In an effort to move forward and take a more appropriate view, the United Nations Development Programme (UNDP) introduced its human development index. This index takes into consideration not only the *per capita GNP,* but also people's life expectancy and rate of literacy.

Sustainable means something which can continue. Development should enhance and conserve the world for future generations. There is a danger of using up non-renewable resources while starting off degenerative processes and leaving the world a progressively poorer place.

Trade offs

Every time people act, it usually means that something is gained and something is lost. Environmental issues are largely a question of trade offs; for example, development takes place but resources are used. Access is improved but views are lost or frees are cut down. New factories are created but the air is polluted. Some trade offs when examined may make sense. Other trade offs may be unacceptable. Urgent short-term economic advantage should not be used to justify lasting environmental damage.

In tourism, destroying the resource that attracts tourists, e.g. a coral reef, for immediate economic gain, makes little sense. There are many pressing global environmental issues, for example, global warming, the ozone layer and the use of chlorofluorocarbons, pesticide use, desertification, and the problems of urbanization, air, water, and noise pollution, waste disposal, habitat destruction, soil depletion, endangered species, acid rain, and rainforests, oceans, wetlands, coral reefs, rivers and estuaries. All of these pose many urgent needs.

Costs

Environmental targets often mean either higher costs or short-term losses in revenue. In response, companies draw attention to their responsibility to shareholders. They reason that action is not urgent, and that the threat to the environment is exaggerated. They play for time.. Environmental costs have to be paid. If measures are delayed the costs increase. Costs are of three types:

— The costs which are preventative expenditures are made to prevent specific, foreseeable and negative outcomes. They are costs which should be included as part of a given investment.

— The costs which are remedial expenditures which have to be paid out by someone eventually, to remedy the damage caused by ignoring them in the first place. Those who damage the environment should be penalized and made to pay compensation.

— The costs of causing lasting impoverishment these are costs which are difficult to quantify, but which represent a lasting impoverishment in the quality and variety of life. They are often incalculable.

A responsible attitude recognizes realistically all of these costs. Two decades of turmoil in Cambodia have resulted in the planting of some eight to ten million landmines. It is estimated that the cost of planting a mine is US$15.00, but that the cost of safely removing it is US$1000.00. It is an example of outrageously inflicted damage at little Cost. The cost of repairing the damage is very high, not only financially but also in lost limbs and lives.

Using tourism to justify conservation

If the use of natural resources is denied to people because of conservation, it is likely to mean a, loss of income-earning opportunities. If conservation causes a loss of income, the focal population should be somehow compensated. Tourism may be able to provide this compensation in a variety of ways, It may create jobs as well as opportunities for the provision of various produce and services.

In one area of Zanzibar there is presently only one small hotel. The closest village, some two kilometres away, started to sell sea shells to the tourists. The hotel, to protect the natural environment, urged their guests not to buy the shells. It therefore deprived the villagers of a source of additional income. In compensation, however, all the hotel's staff are employed from the village. The hotel also tries to buy as many supplies as possible from there, and it has counselled the villagers on how to grow various vegetables which it needs for its menus.

In the Himalayan Kingdom of Bhutan one can note the case of Phobjika valley. It is one of the well-known wintering places for the rare black-necked crane. But it is also home to a community which could develop the region by cultivating potatoes a high yielding cash crop. If the cranes are valued more highly than potatoes, then the people of Phobjika need to be compensated.

The game parks of East Africa provide another example. Considerable land is set aside for the parks. However, people may compete with the animals for this land. Poachers may kill the animals, It is only by allocating a proportion of the game park benefits to the local people that their support can be obtained. Such local support is essential for conservation.

These various initiatives illustrate certain principles. One should:

— Recognize that if people's livelihoods suffer, however important the environmental issues, their support and collaboration are unlikely to be given.

— Provide alternative sources of employment, income and/or compensation, using the opportunities offered by tourism.

Environmental measures do not tend to work without the support of the local population. Tourism can help obtain that support.

Tourism's contribution

'Tourism can focus attention on important environmental issues, and can trigger projects which both conserve and enhance the environments, for example:

— It creates an audience for historical and archaeological attractions, and may generate funds for their conservation and upkeep.

— Similarly, tourism develops a flow of traffic to beauty spots which while putting pressure on them, also generates funds for their protection and management.

— Because of the importance of sunshine as one of tourism Is principal themes and motivations, it highlights the seriousness of ozone depletion.

— It draws attention to the issue of biodiversity and the numerous endangered species particularly the more spectacular ones such as elephants, rhinoceros and tigers.

— Because so much tourism revolves around the sea and the marine environment, it draws attention to problems of pollution, destruction of reefs and damage to coral, the plight of dolphins, whales and other marine mammals, and the dangers of overfishing.

— Similarly, it highlights the need to conserve and protect forested areas and wetlands, and stimulates funding for the creation of national parks and reserves.

— Tourism installations often create an example of energy-saving through the use of solar energy, wind-generated power, and natural ventilation,

— Tourism can often use landscaping and improved architecture to reduce the needs for expensive cooling, heating and lighting systems.

— Tourism has often been the predominant influence in the redevelopment and beautification of factory sites, mining areas, and riverside locations, all of which have been abandoned after years of former industrial use.

— Similarly, tourism has enabled the conservation of period transportation systems, old steam railways and sailing ships.

Approaches to cost/benefit analysis

Cost/benefit analysis justifies the use of resources. It attempts to calculate a rate of return for society as a whole. The costs of some resources, such as land or labour, may not be based on market values. If there is no demand for an alternative use, resources can be valued and below normal market prices.

In a situation of high unemployment and underemployment, labour may be costed at below market rates. Similarly, government owned land, undeveloped and without any obvious alternative use, may also be costed at a figure seemingly below market value. This approach is known as shadow pricing.

Similarly, there may be costs due to environmental losses or damage, which may not appear as commercial costs. However, they may be so high that they should prevent any project from going ahead. In calculating a project's rate of return, market prices do not always reflect the true value to society of using resources. This technique makes objective value judgements about the true costs to society, to arrive at the true benefits.

Political decision making often relies on value judgements. The costs and benefits may depend on the opinions of values assigned to decision makers at a given moment. These values may change over time as circumstances and priorities change. In Bhutan, the quantity of water channelled through the country's numerous rivers is known as white power. But to harness all of this power through more and more hydroelectric projects is thought to have too high an environmental cost. The environmental costs are judged to outweigh any benefits from the export of the additional electricity generated.

Environmentally-adjusted domestic product

Until now, environmental costs are not usually reflected in national economic accounting. The use of natural capital is omitted from the customary methods of measuring economic performance. Although many environmental assets are not subject to market transactions, they are being used up and should be costed.

A monetary value is therefore included for all natural capital used and environmental damage suffered. This allows for the calculation of an EDP the Environmentally-adjusted Domestic Product known as the Green GDP. As noted by Glenn-Marie Lange and Faye Duchin sustainable development is said to be achieved if EDP is not decreasing with the passage of time.' As tourism uses natural resources, so it can conserve and enhance them. It depends on the concept and type of tourism, and on the effectiveness of tourism planning.

Zoning, planning and land use

Zoning and planning regulations are fundamental in all development. Tourism should not be allowed to grow in an explosion of random development. Land use planning is essential. It provides a framework for what can be built where, how big, how high, and in what form and style. Intersectoral coordination is essential for effective land use planning. Different sectors compete with each other for space. Interests need to be reconciled to arrive at the best use of different areas.

Part of zoning for tourism can consist not only in designating certain areas and sites for development, but also in indicating their minimum and maximum yield in rooms or beds. A minimum yield is an important concept. It may be wasteful, for example, to take five hectares of prime beachfront land, and build no more than 20 rooms on it (four rooms eight beds per hectare). Yet where land is initially cheap this sometimes happens.

In agriculture one measures appropriate development in terms of sustainable yields; cattle or fruit trees per hectare, tonnes of wheat, tons of potatoes etc. In tourism one should think similarly. If key sites are used to maximize the number of beds up to a certain limit', then this means a better yield for the land area used. It means that less land is needed, more green spaces remain and more land is left free from development.

On a number of small Caribbean islands (where land is a very limited resource) this principle is not necessarily followed. All beachfront land is often developed. While much of it is very low density and no building is above the treetops, it does not always represent the most efficient use of land. In many places one could have achieved the same height restrictions and as many tourist rooms, while leaving more green and empty spaces for the enjoyment of all.

While yields in rooms should not be too low, it is often too many rooms per hectare which is found to be the case. Depending on the resort location and type of development, ratios from 20 to 60 rooms per hectare might be considered, the difference, say, between cottage or bungalow type projects and two or three storey blocks. Yet developers may succeed in putting 500 rooms or more onto a five hectare resort site, and far more on a city centre site.

Land prices are related to permitted height. As height restrictions become relaxed, land prices tend to increase and the buildings go higher. Twenty and thirty storey hotels or more are common in some urban environments. In some areas of the United States, high rise buildings are often favoured while maintaining a low ratio of rooms to the land used. This places a modern multi-storeyed building in a spacious landscaped setting for many a very agreeable planning solution. It may also allow for greater operational efficiency; the services are concentrated more closely together, resulting in the economic use of labour.

Restrictions on the use of land conflict with the idea of an individual's right to own and develop land as he or she chooses. Most societies, while recognizing this right, do not allow it to be exercised in an unrestricted manner. There are clear limits as to:

— the right to develop land or not

— what the land can be used for

— what can be demolished or not

— upper and lower limits on how big, or small the development can be

— the design; the form, positioning, architectural style and height of building

— the setback from roads, other buildings, the shoreline or riverside as the case may be

— regulations governing the buildings themselves

— requirements as to drainage and waste disposal

— requirements about parking

— access and, landscaping requirements, ensuring the right treatment of surrounding areas.

Planning need not be over-restrictive. It will not prevent the individual touches which make a development distinctive. Paint, banners, awnings and canopies, whitewash, sunshades, statues, flowers, shrubs and trees, help to make places feel distinctive, welcoming and loved. In tropical countries the appropriate use of landscaping, with shrubs and flowers, can transform a basic concrete block building into a visual delight.

The system of controls over land should be as transparent as possible. The approval process should be open and participative. There should be open discussions of the issues, time allowed for publicizing decisions, public hearings and the right of appeal and review. The environment and what happens to it involves the society as a whole; everybody can have a say.

Those responsible for the planning of tourism facilities need above all to conform to all related regulations and codes. Beyond this there are some other useful guidelines. Projects should:

— Respect the spirit of the place. Buildings should be congruent with their surroundings. Development should be sympathetic to the local culture and environment.

— Restore old buildings but respect their original use. They should be adapted if necessary, while respecting their integrity,

— Allow high rise building only when it is in keeping with the overall development concept, and when it conforms with local density standards.

— Leave green spaces and animal habitats intact and undisturbed.

— Conserve trees wherever possible, plant flowers, and revegetate any disturbed areas,

— Conceal plant and machinery as well as car parking.

— Leave views unblocked by buildings. If possible, views should be opened up from every balcony, terrace and window.

Visual pollution is often a controversial concept. Some things can be agreed as universally ugly. Others are only ugly as a matter of personal opinion.

Carrying capacity

Carrying capacity was summarized as the point when more visitors would damage the environment or lower people's enjoyment below an acceptable level. Every destination has a limitation as to the total number of people that can visit. It is this limitation which defines the destination's carrying capacity. It can be further broken down into five elements; two are quantifiable and three qualitative.

— *Damage.* The number of visitors without causing measurable damage to the environment.

— *Delay.* The number of visitors without causing intolerable delays in the use and enjoyment of attractions, with people having to queue or wait in traffic.

— *Overcrowding.* The number of visitors without giving a feeling of Overcrowding, so that people are not jostled and squeezed.

— *Image.* The number of visitors in and around a destination without changing its image, and the necessary atmosphere and ambience which form a part of the enjoyment.

— *Reaction.* The number of visitors before there is a strong reaction, on the part of the local population, to the excessive pressures created. A feeling of cultural invasion is provoked when religion, language, heritage and traditions seem threatened.

The current carrying capacity of a place can often be increased through careful planning and management. By improving existing facilities and the organization of tourists, greater numbers can be received in still acceptable ways.

The payment of environmental and cultural royalties

Many natural attractions and cultural attractions can be visited free of charge, or they may only have a nominal entry charge. It may be considered a fundamental human right to allow everyone to enjoy these attractions. It may be a sound principle to give people equal opportunities to visit and enjoy not only their own national heritage but also world heritage. It is the concept of generational equity of passing on a heritage as rich or richer than the one received that underlies much of the philosophy of sustainable development.

However, as noted, the demand to visit a place may exceed the limit set by its carrying capacity. As time goes by, incomes rise, available leisure time expands and tourism increases, so the pressures on places and their carrying capacity grow correspondingly. One way of limiting demand and decreasing this pressure, is to raise admission charges. This excludes all but the people who can afford to pay. This is a policy, however, which appears elitist, favours the well off, and discriminates against the poorer sections of society. Basing the enjoyment of heritage on buying power seems an unfair policy to adopt. Heritage is simply viewed as something to be shared by all. A country may also extend this idea of sharing to foreigners. Nominal entrance fees to attractions may be paid as at home, while the general environment of the country is free. Visitors do not expect to pay for it.

However, should this principle also apply when people from rich countries enjoy the heritage of poorer countries? In such cases, many believe that the constraint of price control need not exist. If you want to go to Bhutan, for example, you have to pay for it. The Government levies a substantial royalty for the privilege of visiting and enjoying the country. Bhutan can be regarded as futuristic in its application of this concept.

— It views carrying capacity in the widest possible sense looking at the assimilation of tourism not only in terms of environmental impacts, but also in terms sociocultural criteria and the potential disruption to the local way of life.

— It chooses, though a poor country, not to develop resources to the detriment of the environment. It levies a royalty for the store of pleasure which it is conserving.

Land tenure

Systems of land tenure are at the heart of any culture. The individual right to own and develop land has represented a fundamental value in many societies. At the same time the acquisition of land by the state, to carry out works which will serve for the common good, has become an important feature of policy and planning. While ostensibly fair compensation is paid in such cases, people seldom like to suffer the loss of their land. In a similar way the restriction of the ways in which land may be used, as already noted, also affects its value. Land is the basic resource for all human activity. As such its ownership and use are not only the basis of economic development, but also lie deep in the human psyche. People's relationship to land the territorial attachment is an integral part of their make-up. Deep down, people often believe that doing whatever they want with their land is morally right.

However, people are told what they can or cannot do with the land. There is the right to appeal, the right to argue one's case, but the overriding rule of law is based on the needs and interests of the community as a whole, Land can only be used by individuals in such ways as to serve the common good.

In many parts of the world, land ownership is often collective by nature. Land belongs to the tribe or the community, to be used and enjoyed by all. Individual use is the subject of group approval.

The regulation of land ownership requires a very effective system of registration, allowing for the efficient transference of ownership in the event of sale, gift or inheritance. Land tenure, the use of land, and zoning and planning regulations are among the most charged of all development issues. Any ambiguity or confusion may represent a major barrier to development. It is essential that the legal system is rapid and efficient, and that any doubts can be quickly removed. It is equally essential that published policies and permitted land use are made widely known.

It is useful to review the range of environmental

management standards now adopted by the European Union.

The eco-management and auditing scheme regulation

This was introduced in July 1993, and compliance is to be voluntary for the first four years. An environmental agency monitors participating enterprises. The enterprise carries out an environmental auditing procedure.

Air emissions

This governs emissions from plants, for transport fleets, and includes substances damaging to the ozone layer,

Amenities, trees and wildlife

There arc numerous national regulations designed to control the reservation and upkeep of amenities, trees and wildlife, Enterprises need to be sensitive to their responsibilities in accordance with local requirements.

Noise

This refers to established standards for permitted noise for various types of plant and equipment including, for example, motorized mowers.

Nuisances

This includes a variety of nuisances affecting the environment, For example, drainage systems, caravans, temporary buildings or sheds, or even vehicles.

Physical planning

The principal provisions of physical planning will cover, according to local conditions; density, height, setback, etc. The assessment of environmental impact has become a prerequisite to obtain planning permission.

Radiation

This embraces all the regulations governing permitted levels of radiation.

Urban renewal

These regulations differ in application according to cover protected buildings, the need for renovation to achieve health and safety standards, and the designation of areas and sites for urban renewal schemes.

Waste

This deals with waste management and includes the disposal of toxic waste. It also covers dumping at sea, transportation of toxic waste and other special provisions.

Water resources

This covers water pollution, discharges, and water quality standards. Inland waters and the sea are both included.

Water supplies and sewage treatment

This covers questions of contamination, and safeguarding the water supply system.

Safeguards as to the proper use of products, the disposal of waste materials, energy conservation, and health and safety regulations are also covered. EU regulation is also expected to encompass packaging, so as to encourage recycling and lessen quantities of waste destined for landfills. Rothery lists a fuller summary of EU provisions.

Voluntary codes

Education and the development of the public consciousness are essential in maintaining environmental quality. This requires that most people observe requirements, complying voluntarily without the need for enforcement.

It is easy to choose between 'have to' versus 'want to. When people want to do something, it is much more effective motivation than when they have to. When people have to, it requires constant supervision and enforcement to ensure that they do. And this is often ineffective. Codes should be agreed after full and detailed discussion of the standards which are in the best interests of all. People will then choose to keep to them. Indeed they will tend to police the sector themselves, and ensure that the codes are observed and standards maintained.

Sensitivity should also be developed towards building conservation provisions which protect historical buildings and heritage sites, and countryside conservation measures which designate national parks, protected areas, and nature reserves.

For the development of designated tourism areas:

— Ensure the participation of the local community in planning approvals.

— Develop areas in strict accordance with the legislation governing all aspects of physical planning.

— Do not demolish any protected buildings or, if possible, any buildings of historical or architectural interest.

— Enhance the distinctiveness and authenticity of the development.

— Make sure that long-term considerations take precedence over the short term.

— Use environmental conservation as a feature of the development.

— Make the development a reflection of local values.

— Minimize all economic leakage; try to develop linkages with local enterprises and use local resources.

— Prioritize job creation for the local labour force.

— Charge the costs of environmental measures, and the corresponding precautions that need to be taken, to the development itself.

— Retain flexibility to review and modify plans in the light of experience.

— Check that the zoning policies and physical plans are achieving the best use and interrelationship of land areas.

— Make sure that the provision of infrastructure is adequate and unobtrusive.

— Check for the introduction of imbalances in the local economy.

Project description

A description of the project which should include the following:

The project concept

Its nature, form, size, category, capacity, and range of activities. Its principal markets and pricing policies.

Location and site

Precise details of the location of the project and its site. Surrounding areas and uses. History of the site. Effect on adjacent and neighbouring land and property. Plan of the site area showing options for future development and expansion.

Design/Architectural solution

Key aspects. Functional interrelationships of areas and buildings. Site limitations. Application of planning regulations and building limitations. Style and image of the proposed scheme. 1 : 1000 scale drawings plus cross sections and elevations.

Construction

Construction methods and timetable. Organization of work, materials and equipment during the construction phase. Site preparation, transportation of materials to the site, blasting, excavation and earth-moving. Disposal of construction spoil. Control measures during construction dust, noise, drainage and runoffs, water pollution, waste disposal.

Planning controls

Conformity with current regulations affecting the project.

Commercial feasibility

Statement of marketing feasibility

Principal market segments to be served and their characteristics. Market assessments and forecasts by each sales outlet.

Statement of financial feasibility

Summary of financial projections, with underlying assumptions and key operating ratios.

Infrastructural requirements

Transport access

Implications and needs. Car parking provisions.

Water *supply*

Demand is the development proceeds. Special needs, e.g. swimming pools, fire fighting etc.

Drainage

Drainage needs, Any problematic aspects. Proposed stormwater drainage.

Sewage treatment

Treatment and disposal. Proposed installations.

Waste disposal

Proposed provisions for waste disposal.

Electricity

Demand as the development proceeds. Eventual annual energy needs. Provision for emergency supply. Alternate energy sources.

Communications

Proposed installations and needs. Demand when project is fully operational.

Social services

Specific requirements and provisions for the tabour force. Housing, health, education and other social services.

Environmental impacts

Change

Change to the whole character of the area. What this represents. Assessment of impact acceptability. Visual impact. Effects on landscape and views.

Pollution

Dangers and safeguards against all types of pollution; water including the sea, rivers, lakes etc., air, noise. Visual pollution.

Coastline

If the project is on the coast, compatibility with overall coastal management objectives.

Flora and fauna

Any danger of damage to vegetation and wildlife.

Waste disposal

Acceptable provisions for all waste disposal.

Traffic and congestion

Any danger of causing a deterioration in local traffic conditions.

Local community

Possible disruptions to the local way of life. Effects on neighbouring building and population.

3

Gender Dimensions of Tourism

In the context of the Greek tourism industry *gender* dimensions have received scant attention. Data availability is poor. The literature distinguishing any gender aspects of tourism, especially from a sociocultural perspective, is minimal. Women are silent in tourism surveys. If we exclude a couple of anecdotal references, gender dimensions have not been discussed in the literature on tourism as an industry or as a consumption sector, on tourism and economic or regional development, on tourism and the tabour market. The following exposition therefore relies on the few specialist works, on passing references in works with a different focus, on the few statistical surveys, and on the personal experience of the author. Tourist arrivals in Greece are currently doubling every five years. The number of annual foreign visitors are as many as the population of Greece - 8,053,052 and 10,264,156 respectively. Other Europeans form the bulk of tourist arrivals, having overtaken Americans in the early 1970s. Among gender dimensions of tourism development examined, types of tabour commitment and cultural tensions in sun and beach resorts have been those most stressed in Greece. The former pertain to informal female work, where tourism creates an invisible 'formal market', especially in the very countries where tourist development is rapid and massive. Cultural aspects have to do with tensions emerging in tourist localities, especially between local and foreign women.

However, tourism 'resources' are heterogeneous, and have several gender implications. Gender divisions are changing. For example, conference tourism, which concentrates in cities, especially Paris and London used to be male-dominated; this is gradually changing, The bulk of tourism, with extreme coastal concentration, has a strong and apparently growing female element. Sunshine beach holidays, urban/cultural tourism, business/ conference tourism, and rural tourism are all to be found in Greece. The Country also presents a typical case study of ways in which tourism, as an industry, redistributes income between North and South in Europe. The predominant tourism types for holidays, especially beach and Alpine tourism, tend to divert visitors from industrial to underdeveloped areas arid between city and countryside, arid promote the economic development d the latter. This underlines core/periphery, North/South, rich/poor binary distinctions, but also the important role of tourism in a spatial depolarisation process.

However, this is where the international/regional comparison must stop. Studies at the regional level indicate that depolarisation is often far from the case. In fact, there are interactions between national and regional development, such as national investment schemes, international currency fluctuations, etc., affecting the regions. In addition, social depolarisation is another matter, since the dividing line between natives and tourists is a class line, and there are sharp class and gender divisions within the tabour force employed in tourism.

At the local level, the redistributive impact of tourism is often reversed or viewed in a completely different light. This is hidden by the insistence of research on tourist arrivals and uneven socioeconomic development of regions of destination of tourists, their transformation through the tourist inflow, their economic and social restructuring, and their protection. This is very important, no doubt; but uneven regional, economic and social development is also evident in the differential access to leisure of residents of various regions, inequalities between regions of origin of tourists and the tensions created in poor localities serving the tourist inflow. These different aspects and binary distinctions will be seen in the following, with special attention given to the gender dimension.

Vacation is a kind of flight from everyday routine, a means to realising dreams, and requires a population working hard to create an ideal environment, Inequality and tension are inherent in such a relationship. As for the definition of female work and leisure and the concepts of work, employment, activity, unemployment, idleness and Inactivity, difficult problems are raised in every social formation and historical period. The limits between work and leisure are clearer for women during the tourist season, and this often creates a tension between groups of women working versus idle women, locals versus foreigners-in tourist resorts. Traditionally, Greece has lived with the divisions of traveller/host, tourist/ servant, movement/ stasis, male/female. In other words, gender distinctions in the past had men as travellers and women as hostesses. This is no longer the case. As women increasingly travel in groups without men, the disturbance of local societies and relationships between women are restructured in a completely different manner.

Access to tourism and leisure

There has been a spectacular growth of international tourists as incomes rise along with leisure time, from 25 million in 1950 to 69 million in 1960, 160 million in 1970 and 280 million in 1982. Tourism consumption contributes to national income, especially in Mediterranean Europe. In 1986, 47.4 million tourists visited Spain, 20 million visited Italy, 6.7 million visited Greece, and 5.4 million visited Portugal. Today 100 million annual tourists arrive in the Mediterranean and the forecasts are that they will have doubled by the year 2000. One of the major destinations may be Greece, which 36 per cent of the Europeans considered attractive for future holidays. This is mainly because mass tourist attractions, which by far outnumber other types of attractions, are sea and sun, as well as skiing conditions. Over half of tourists from the EC take their main holidays at the seaside. Greece, with its 15,021 kin of coastline, of which 3,000 are sandy beaches, and with its 337 inhabited islands, is a major destination. It is a pity that no information on tourist differentiation by age and sex is available, but there seems to be a tendency among visitors from the Mediterranean to travel in couples or families or in mixed company, while northerners are more likely to travel as couples and, increasingly, in groups of women or mixed groups. Among domestic tourists there is a preponderance of women with children, as discussed below.

Seaside tourism is highly seasonal, and this is amplified by the increasing involvement of tour operators in the industry. Seasonality by nation, but not vet by region, has been well documented. In the Mediterranean, 35 per cent of tourists arrive in two summer months, while countries with skiing seasons have double peaks. The lowest degree of seasonal peaking is found in the Netherlands, Germany and the United Kingdom. Spain has a low index, 29 per cent, despite its attraction of mass tourism. In Greece, seasonality is always acute and appears to be increasing, despite efforts to spread activity more evenly by the encouragement of other types of tourism. In 1981, 61.6 per cent of arrivals and 66.7 per cent of overnight stays by foreigners were concentrated between June and September. By 1987 this had grown to 65 per cent of arrivals and 68.5 per cent of overnight stays.

Accessibility to tourism is a function of income levels and free time at the disposal of populations. Tourism is characterised by a positive income elasticity of demand: demand rises are proportionately greater than increases in income levels. High-income countries and regions generate the bulk of international tourists. EC residents are foremost in international tourist activity, representing 180 million tourists a year, with the USA closely following. It has been estimated that EC households spend an average of seven per cent of their budgets on holidays.

However, it was found that 44 per cent of EC residents did not take a holiday at all in 1985. Of these, older people, those with large families and those living in rural areas were the groups most likely to fall into this category. National variations are also significant. Mediterranean countries do not usually generate large numbers of tourists. The OECD analysed receipts and expenditure on international tourism and revealed the highest positive balance to be realised by Spain and Italy, while Germany had the greatest negative balance. In Portugal, only 44 per cent of the population surveyed in 1985 had any paid holidays at all, and half of them were of very short duration.

Within the EC regional disparities are due mostly to poverty: in Portugal, Ireland and Greece, 67, 61 and 55 per cent respectively of non-holidaying respondents in 1985 could not afford to take a holiday. Economic constraints, as well as the problem of leave of absence, affected manual workers. Gender dimensions have not been included in such surveys, but they would probably favour women, as in the case of Greek domestic tourism: as children are given priority in family holidays, they are often escorted by mothers, while fathers remain behind to work during the summer.

Cultural preferences and segmentation

Different places in the Greek islands are particularly attractive for certain nationalities. It has been demonstrated in Greece that tourists have tended to be drawn to particular locations by nationality during the early 1980s: tourists originating in the UK have concentrated in Corfu, those from Western Germany in Crete, those from the Netherlands in Rhodes and Crete, Yugoslavians in Pieria, Austrians and all Scandinavians in Rhodes. This concentration is largely due to decisions by tour operators, besides accommodation available, that is, decisions taken abroad. In fact, tour operators dominate Greek tourism, and the level of dependence of certain localities on particular countries creates high risk at periods of crisis.

On the other hand, cases can be discerned where the destinations of tourists vary according to cultural orientations of the holidaying groups: in international tourism, southerners tend to be drawn to cities, northerners to the countryside and the beaches. It is interesting to note in this connection the positive cultural orientation to urbanism of Mediterranean people, which tends to concentrate their demand in cities and cultural tourism, although Athens does not attract many visitors any more. By contrast, the far more numerous northern Europeans tend to concentrate at seaside and mountain locations for beach and alpine tourism. This can reflect their negative attitude to urban congestion and need to escape to nature and the countryside. In 1982, of the overnight stays of Italian and Spanish tourists in Greece,

26 per cent and 73 per cent respectively were spent in Athens. The figures for French and Belgian tourists were 20 per cent and 1.3 per cent respectively, while the proportion of tourists from all other European countries was much lower at 3.5-8.5 per cent.

Another North/South division can be discerned in the spending habits and preferences in mass tourism. A broad segmentation of the market between two groups of tourists appears to be developing, a factor that Greek authorities are particularly sensitive to. One group, originating in the industrialised regions of the European core, will be much more demanding of tourist services than another group, drawn from the South, agricultural and poor regions. This segmentation of the market is discussed with respect to the economic benefit to localities of destination, and policy is formulated in order to attract richer tourists. However, it can also be seen in another light: the expansion of affluent but also mass tourism, in the end, undermines exploration and the unexpected as one of the joys and advantages of travelling. Especially in Mediterranean countries, independent holiday-takers are increasingly excluded from certain localities of mass tourism and foreign ownership. It is increasingly difficult for domestic tourists to arrange their own holidays independently from commercial networks, or spontaneously, as they behave in several areas of social life.

Their reluctance to rely on travel agents should not be negatively evaluated as a 'lack of professionalism and institutionalism in the organisation of the industry. After all, the right to spontaneity and last-moment choices, the right to wander and discover, should at least be allowed during days of leisure. But it is not. Such an attitude emanates from female approaches to tourism exploration, as one of the best aspects of tourism, is precluded both in localities with mass tourism and foreign-owned areas. Through tour operators, moreover ', foreigners obtain better bargains in local hotels than domestic tourists. Organised package holidays exclude individual tourists from booking accommodation, which is held long in advance by tour operators. In foreign-owned localities, even some beaches are closed to the public. The host populations of many tourist destinations are becoming increasingly excluded from holidaying in their own country. Places are unique; attractiveness and location, physical beauty and cultural tradition are scarce resources, and competition for them is unequal and increasingly excludes low-wage populations and spontaneous tourists. The 'free' market and the monopolistic market in the tourism industry thus create regional polarisation on the demand side.

Local cultural tensions and latent conflicts

Besides the provision of jobs and the stability of the balance of payments between North and South as positive results of tourism, the EC has already stressed closer relationships between states, the contact among people reinforcing European integration. However, things are often not so pleasant in tourist regions. There has been an unresolved controversy about the effects of tourism on local Cultures, arts and crafts. The invasion of foreigners in a locality no doubt interferes with indigenous cultural manifestations, and population succession in rural areas can be a blow to cultural tourism.

The reversal of seasons of work and leisure for the host population and some conspicuous consumption by tourists in poor countries can create grievances against extravagance: in Tunisia, tourists spend in one week what a resident may spend in one year. In Greece the difference is not so sharp, but other tensions mount. On the one hand, there is the relatively well researched issue of the disturbance of local society by daring young foreign women and the tension between them and local women, loyal to tradition, On the other hand, there are the women who search for culture, and ancient and sacred places, as opposed to those seeking pleasure and vacation. As the post-modern condition saturates tourist resorts, several reversals can be observed there, besides that of the seasons of work and leisure. From the point of view of gender relations, there is a stunning reversal of roles in commercialised love. The importance of female prostitution is limited in Greek tourist regions. *Kamakia who* pursue ephemeral relations with tourists in Greece are males, but their role is controversial. While there are examples of male prostitution in other tourist countries, the Greek men sometimes marry their victims'.

This is an aspect of tourism in Greece which has been stressed repeatedly by gender studies, and has been surveyed in Kos, Ios and Serifos. Domestic female tourists know how to handle these men, while foreigners sometimes complain that they are annoyed. Many foreign female tourists, however, tend to behave in a liberated way, often quite different from their attitudes in their countries of origin, influenced by the atmosphere of holidays. Local women, for their part, are not free to express their sexuality. In Kos, they complained about the disadvantages of tourism, and stressed that their social life was disturbed and men were lost to foreigners. Nudist beaches and ephemeral love affairs are invasions detested by women secluded in traditional villages, where there is a shortage of men anyway, because they sail or migrate. Despite its economic benefits, about 35 per cent of both sexes of the sample in the Cyclades islands considered tourism to create 'ethical' problem.

Before discussing gender in the tourist tabour force,

a short discussion of female work in general is necessary, in order to stress Greek particularities. 'Tourism comes somewhere between rural and urban work. In rural areas, despite gender divisions of labour, the forms of male and female employment are closer. Time allocation is governed by the needs of each activity rather than some formal work schedule or timetable. In rural societies., the allocation of tasks is quasi-precapitalist, in that the organisation of work time is subdivided into periods of exhausting work and periods of non-activity. These are natural rhythms, close to nature, which contrast with urban work, where time of work is regular and measured by the clock.

Workers and employees in tourist localities work in the summer and are idle, or take up other tasks, during the winter. This reversal of seasons is especially evident in countries with a high seasonality of the tourist industry, such as Greece. Tourism here re-establishes the dominance of nature and seasons, but in an inverse manner from the one familiar to Western societies: work and overpopulation during the summer, pause and depopulation during the winter. This reversal of seasons involves labourers very unevenly in work, and places undergo massive population fluctuations. It also disturbs everyday life: women must often dismantle their homes every summer to rent out the rooms, often leaving the family to sleep on the terrace. In tourist localities, the tourist/native distinction is a class distinction: the idle class versus the labourers.

Segmentation in the Greek female labour force

The National Statistical Service of Greece first started to classify workers by sex in 1907, when only eight per cent of the labour force was female. The massive integration of women into the tabour market followed the arrival of 1.5 million refugees in Greece from Asia Minor with population exchanges in 1922. There were many women among these refugees, widows and orphans of the war, who were integrated as low-paid but skilled workers in industry, comprising about 26 per cent of the total tabour force. At the time, whole industry groups, such as textiles and carpets, were established in. Greece with female workers whose wages were half or one-third those of men. They were a proletariat in large factories, while men were dominant as petty entrepreneurs; but they were barred from labour unions and unable to organise themselves. Some of them became home workers in the informal sector.

For many Greek women it has been impossible to undertake paid work because of heavy domestic tasks, especially in shanty towns and poor rural localities, and, sometimes, seasonal tasks in tourist regions. This partly explains the low activity ratios in Greece. By 1951, one year before Greek women won the right to vote, their participation in the economically active population had dropped from 26 to 18 per cent but was higher in towns with over 20,000 inhabitants. This remained stable until 1971, but rose to one-third of the active population by 1981. By 1989, women represented 52.3 per cent of the total population and 37 per cent of the economically active population. A rapid growth of female unemployment in the 1980s, brought it to over double the percentages of male unemployment, especially in cities. In the total Greek population, only 48 per cent work, compared with 6071 per cent in the rest of Europe. This is not only due to reduced female activity, but also to the delay of the young in entering the tabour market and the early retirement of elderly populations. Both of these create demanding tasks for women in the house.

For a very long period since the interwar years, the Greek female tabour force evidenced some class homogeneity along the lines of a continuum: all their groupings, whether in services or factories, worked in the worst-paid jobs as junior clerks, manual labourers in factories or the informal sector, and as servants. Though there were some teachers, writers and artists, it was difficult to speak of class polarisation on any broad scale. Dividing lines were between working and idle women, between integrated and marginal labourers, and much less between higher and lower classes. This is no longer the case: the latter division is now very strong and has come to the forefront. The female labour force is much more polarised and segmented than the male one.

At the one extreme, educated women working especially in the tertiary sector in Athens, Piraeus and Salonica increased in number, following the rapid changes in the sex composition of the student population in the 1970s. The massive entrance of girls into higher education affected all universities, especially those specialising in preparing students for employment in the public sector. Liberal professions and entrepreneurial activities are still dominated by *men,* though no longer monopolised by them; women also occupy higher professions, but especially salaried public employment. Occupational mobility is faster for *the female* than the male tabour force. Greek researchers speak of a 'new female middle-class elite and of far strategies to direct women to the public sector, where secure salary, paid leave and holidays facilitate raising a family. Researchers refer to a strategy d investment in 'educational capital' and even speak of 'quasi-dowry', which is more durable and secure than traditional dowry.

At the other extreme, there is the usual lower-paid, exploited female labour force, working in factories and services. Besides traditional manual jobs, new de-skilled ones emerge in the service sector with the generalisation of new technology. Besides Greek women, ethnic minorities, such as Filipinas, Albanians and other Eastern Europeans, arrive to work in urban services and rural temporary jobs, in the informal sector as pieceworkers at home, or as domestic servants. The discordance between census data at place of residence and place of work is an indication of large numbers of women in seasonal activities and the informal sector. In many industries, female workers at place of residence were found to be over double those in establishments for some industries, while the number of men was almost the same during the 1970s. In clothing industries there were 117,00 men and women officially working in factories in 1988, but this amount is estimated to double if pieceworkers, mostly female, are added. Leather and fur, printing, toys, various fitments, etc., are also run by such an unprotected, unstable, seasonal or temporary labour force, unable to unionise. Today informal work in manufacturing industry and services absorbs much of Greek feminist research. A glaring gap in this is the tourist sector, to which *we now* turn.

Employment in activities related to tourism

It is difficult to approach employment in tourism, not least because of indirect employment on the one hand, and hidden, undeclared employment on the other. Attempts have been made to quantify the former. The World Tourism, Organisation suggested that tourism-related jobs accounted for 15.5 per cent of total employment in the 1970s. An EC report estimated that to provided 5 million direct and 1015 million direct and indirect jobs in Europe, which means a multiplier of 2-3. Direct tourist employment is usually considered that in the accommodation sector, hotels, restaurants, transport, recreational and cultural services. The industry is far larger, however. Sectors prospering around tourism range from recreation, tourist attractions, shops, local services, to agriculture, wholesaling and manufacturing.

In Greece, direct employment in tourism was estimated at 23,500 persons in 1966 and later at 26,100 people in 1970. Employment grew largely during the subsequent period. The labour force in hotels and restaurants, recreational and cultural services and transport increased by 59,680 persons in the period 196171, and then again by 88,460 in the period 1971-81 and grew from 6.12 to 10.46 per cent of total employment, with women as a minority. However, these numbers should be used with caution, because of undeclared beds and undeclared employment, especially female. By 1984, employment in hotels alone had risen to 50,000. The 1983-87 five-year development plan estimated total direct employment in tourism would rise to 160,000 people by 1987 at peak period and to 200,000 if indirect employment was added. Among these, 25,000 qualified and 50,000 less-skilled labourers were absorbed in hotels.

The recent availability of data from the 1988 census makes an analysis feasible. Registered employment is only part of the story, but its diachronic development, fluctuations and sectoral structure can lead to certain important conclusions. The sectoral structure of employment in activities related to tourism in Greater Athens and the most important tourist region of Greece, the Aegean islands. Greater Athens is the largest agglomeration, concentrating 30.2 per cent of the Greek population in 1991 and 14.3 per cent of foreign tourist overnight stays in 1987, which are in decline, while the Aegean islands, with 4.44 per cent of the Greek population represent a dynamic tourist area concentrating 30 per cent of overnight stays in 1987, of which 88 per cent in the Dodecanese.

The major complications arise from the fact that all

sectors presented, except hotels, serve local residents as well as visitors. Their degree of inclusion into the tourist sector is different in different localities: in the islands, the small entrepreneurs in commerce insist that their occupations are tourism-oriented. Their main argument is that the largest part of their profits comes from tourist-season sales, and that they would not have opened up at all if tourism did not exist. In Greater Athens, by contrast, such activities serve mainly residents. It is noteworthy that the overall percentage of employment in sectors related to tourism appears the same in both Athens and the Aegean; just over 27 per cent in both regions. Structural differences, however, are evident.

With respect to seasonality, average annual employment represents a smaller percentage of employment in September where seasonality is more marked: the population from outside migrates toward tourist localities to work, or more family members are involved in paid employment during the peak season. The latter culminates in August, which would be a more appropriate month for comparison, but official censuses are carried out in September. The highest seasonality is observed in Aegean hotels and restaurants, recreational and cultural services and agencies renting goods and property. Seasonality in the same sectors is more acute in the Ionian Islands and less so in Crete. As for Greater Athens, even the hotel sector does not evidence any remarkable seasonality, In more specialised surveys, however, employment in hotels and restaurants has been found to be highly seasonal,, unlike that in transport, recreation and Cultural services. Seasonality of employment in hotels In 1969-78 studied on the basis of data from the Hotel Employees Insurance Fund, was not found to improve over time. Fluctuations were almost negligible in larger cities, but important in certain tourist towns and small seaside settlements.

With respect to gender, sectors run by women in Greater Athens to the largest extent are the personal services, a case which is different in the Aegean islands. By contrast, restaurants and hotels are more male-dominated in Athens than in the Aegean or in Greece as a whole. The participation of women is also high in retail commerce, especially in Athens, where this sector is addressed at residents to a larger extent than at tourists. The comparison of employment data collected at place of residence and place of work offers further conclusions as to the extent of the informal sector and its gender dimensions. As mentioned above, the population census reveals women more involved in the personal services than the census of establishments, which means that they are more involved in the informal economy in this sector, while there is greater male involvement in the case of hotels and restaurants.

Finally, with respect to growing/declining sectors in 197888, an unprecedented growth in agencies renting goods and property should be stressed: employment in this sector has grown by 17.6 per cent annually in the Aegean, and 14.2 per cent in Athens. Restaurants and hotels are rapidly growing in the Aegean but less so in Athens. In this city the tourist wave is in decline, as amply demonstrated by the negative growth rate of hotel employment. Employment in transport also declines in Athens while growing in the Aegean.

A very interesting contrast involves recreational and cultural services: this sector increases rapidly in Athens, apparently for the resident population, while it declines in the Aegean. This virtual collapse is vividly demonstrated by the fact that while there are huge hotels not a single theatre or library exists. Window-shop building addressing the needs of tourists, abound in the island of Kos.

Social polyvalence and segmentation

Double job-holding, underestimated in official statistics, or what can be characterised as multiactivity or 'pluriactivity' or 'social polyvalence', is very widespread in Greece. In 1984, 5.1-9.4 per cent of the economically active population used to have a second job, and these rates did not oscillate much in 1983-86. A 1988 survey on multiple employment indicated very high rates of second job-holding among rural rather than urban populations; the former have been five times as high as the latter in all of Greece, and high rates are also evident in the Aegean islands, where 51.6 per cent of women and 52.6 per cent of men working in agriculture hold a second job, usually in seasonal tourist activities. If it is taken into account that interviewees are usually working in secret, the rates must be higher than shown in the tables.

Although pluriactivity is stigmatised by the Greek authorities, especially for reasons of tax evasion, and by political parties for the informal work arrangements it implies, it does not necessarily have a negative impact on the level of regional development. Job creation in multiactivity regions often brings about the repopulation of certain rural tourist areas, diffuse urbanisation along the coast and in the islands, as encountered in Mediterranean Europe during the late 1970s and 1980s, or diffuse industrialisation.

Jobs in tourism can be classified as seasonal/all-year, formal/informal, part-time/full-time, family-labour/wage-labour, voluntary/waged labour, manual/non-manual, skilled/ unskilled, etc. While indirect employment may be highly skilled and well rewarded, direct employment is usually inferior, with seasonal, part-time and unskilled jobs amounting to 98 per cent of employment in tourism. Pluriactivity usually combines with seasonality agriculture or industry in the spring or winter, services for tourism combined with part-time agriculture in the summer. Social polyvalence, informal work and gender divisions constitute the main elements in household strategies, which aim at increasing income sources of poor households, especially in multiactivity regions. Tourism has been found to broaden the economic base and open up employment prospects in some regions, while elsewhere, 'monoculture' of tourism has been found to dominate regions of destination.

Aversion from traditional activities was found during a survey in the Cyclades islands in Greece, and preference of the young for tourism-related jobs, involving easy profits and less effort: 75 per cent of the young in Ios took jobs related to tourism, and 65 per cent of entrepreneurs were under 35 years old.

Female employment in the tourist sector is increasingly segmented, as in the labour market in general, but with much larger numbers in the lower-paid and manual jobs servants, cleaners, craftspeople, who have no ambition for a career but work out of economic need. There are only few women office employees and specialists, while in transport and communications women appear in 'occupations with gender', such as stewardesses, catering and ticket salespeople, rather than pilots or managers. An additional axis for segmentation is the preponderance of small-scale family tourism, reproducing informality, and contrasting with organised tourism, where contractual bonds predominate, even where seasonality is acute.

Jobs in the accommodation sector are gendered, and male female in the Greek language shows this clearly, as in new-technology sectors. Bedmakers, cleaners and servants are women, especially in the small-scale informal sector, where such Jobs in unrecorded rooms come 'naturally' as an extension of domestic work. In the organised tourist sector, women maintain the 'housewife' role in hotel employment— in Chalkidiki, about one-third are now paid for what used to be regarded as inferior work, such as cleaning, and acquire economic independence. Female employment in that area is 47.4 per cent of the total, and a strict differentiation by gender is evident: women as above, men as gardeners and drivers, while waiters and the administrative staff are more mixed, with a male majority. The attraction of 'housewives' into tourist employment has been encouraged by the Greek government since the mid-1970s. In the informal rented rooms sector, on the other hand, a division of labour reappears according to gender: women take care of the guests and rooms, and men collect clients at the port, negotiate prices, and, where the rooms are declared, contact the authorities. In family taverns and restaurants, men manage the business and do the accounting, children set and clean the tables, and women cook and wash dishes.

Legal and illegal exploitation of property

The main difficulty in the above quantifications stems from illegal exploitation of property and informal work, especially during the peak season. The quality of jobs in tourism is controversial, not only because of seasonality, but also because of informalisation and hidden employment in the para-hotel business, *paraxenodocheia.* '*This* stems from the exploitation of small property during the peak season in tourist localities. It is important from every point of view, because it has been calculated that in the Greek islands over the tourist season, for every formal overnight stay there are three informal ones; and it is important from a gender point of view, because these businesses are often run by women.

The accommodation sector is polarised to varying degrees in various countries. In Italy the small-scale sector is dominant, with 250,000 different enterprises and family effort in the fragmented tourist industry, so that tourism is actually integrated in most local economies. An obvious contrast is Spain, with multinational and foreign capital involvement predominant in the industry. In 1969-78 the average size of hotel and restaurant establishments in Greece grew from 2.21 to only 2.50 employees per establishment and that of recreational and cultural services decreased. By 1988 there were 2.45 employees per restaurant/hotel. Greece promoted small and medium capital in the 1980s, with some negative side-effects as a result. It was more recently realised that this sort of antidote to mass tourism promoted informal and unauthorised development, amateurism and environmental deterioration by the concentration of several small businesses in specific areas.

Dualism can be found within the very same region. The accommodation sector in this region was severely polarised between large hotel complexes, built especially during the period of the 'colonels' junta' in Greece and small rooms of the informal sector. Another comparative study of tourism in the Greek islands found a more beneficial impact of tourism in larger islands with more diversified economies and limited leakage effects. In small islands, it was found to dominate the economy and to lead to unstable, short-term and dualistic development.

It is difficult to generalise about gender characteristics of real estate owners, and it seems that the exploitation of property for tourism and recreation is very often undertaken by male entrepreneurs in Greek tourist resorts. But there are some traditional bonds worth stressing, and they all relate to the institution of dowry. This has been a form of family contribution to young couples by the bride's family, 18 which was abolished by the PASOK legislation on family institutional arrangements in 1983, but only formally. For a very long period, land plots or houses were a popular form of investment by rural families, often as dowry to daughters, and sayings were channelled to cities, to the point where a peculiar matrilocality developed: a large number of real estate owners have been female, because of dowry, reproducing conditions of spatial inertia of women in urban neighbourhoods. An unpublished 1986 survey by EKKE found that 25 per cent of owner-occupiers in Greater Athens had acquired their houses through dowry, parental donation or inheritance, while 41 per cent and 29 per cent respectively had purchased or built their houses on plots, 35 per cent of which had been acquired through parental donation.

Conditions are different for rural land, which has usually been passed through inheritance, where male family members have had priority, except in certain Cyclades islands. In the past, peasants used to let their property as they migrated to cities. As soon as they were established, and as demand for their rural land by domestic and foreign tourists rose, they used to sell it and buy urban property as residence or dowry. Today, however, tourist areas are starting to form an alternative to urban-oriented investment. Land appreciation because of rising tourist demand forms an important source of income for the host population. Already by the early 1960s there were increasing land transactions along the Greek coast, while the share of plots sold increased personal income from 53 per cent in 1958 to 16.8 per cent in 1971-73.

As new types of tourism emerge, time-sharing and second homes dominate the market and visitors are succeeded by owner-occupiers in certain tourist resorts, where retired populations buy out land and traditional houses. Local landowners do profit initially from land sales to developers or individuals. They are lured by the high prices offered, choose to sell, and often sub-divide their property for speculative purposes. After this, however, the landowners in such tourist regions are mostly absentees and export local income in the long term. Prices soar, real estate markets emerge which are inaccessible to domestic buyers, agricultural land changes into residential, and excessive and fragmentation often emerge which are inaccessible to domestic buyers, agricultural land changes into residential, and excessive land fragmentation often emerges with resulting environmental problem problems. Population invasion/ succession processes also follow.

Alonnisos, Myconos Paxi, small islands near Paros and Naxos, and other islands in Greece, are cases in point. A survey in the land registry during, the mid-1980s indicated interesting differences between tourist and less tourist-oriented islands. In the former, exemplified by Ios, real estate prices are 45 times as high as in Serifos. Several seaside plots have passed to foreigners, and there are three times as many foreign buyers in Ios than in Serifos, as well as many Athenian entrepreneurs opening up bars, taverns and shops. Serifos by contrast, a less tourist-oriented island, has attracted returning migrants and Athenians for the purchase of a second residence. Another interesting finding is the secrecy of transactions with foreigners, with the use of names of companies located in Greece, or locals as a front. In some peripheral localities where sales to foreigners are prohibited, a new parasitic occupation has emerged, acting in transactions as a 'front'. This illustrates the difficulty of the study of such phenomena and the discovery of any gender dimensions.

Population succession often results in social segregation between outsiders and tourists on the one hand, and inhabitants on the other. Overcommitment of resources to tourism is balanced out by preservation of natural beauty, which higher-income groups preserve with great care, and the reduction of acute Seasonality in some of the areas sold to retired foreigners.

In such areas and mass-tourism localities, population pressures cause shortages of technological and social infrastructure. It is difficult to quantify summer versus winter population in coastal areas, but in some Greek islands the population can rise fourfold or more during the peak summer season, without a corresponding rise in public services. For example, the population of the Cyclades islands in 1981 rose from 88,500 in spring to 205,000 during peak season, or more if seasonal labour migration and tourists sleeping in informal lodgings or even on beaches are counted. Infrastructure becomes overloaded and the public sector suffers from limited number of doctors, pharmacists, municipal and public servants. Such services do not increase in the summer in proportion with the additional population and activity. In the initial stages, mass tourism may create jobs and an intensification of agriculture. Later, however, negative consequences are felt, by overcommitment of resources to tourism. As there are critical numbers of tourists which can be integrated into regional structures and localities, the number of tourists in attractive sites may exceed the tourist carrying capacity of a region. Congestion and later desertion may follow. The EC has recognised overcrowding, over-exploitation and depletion of resources for tourism in many regions. With the entrance of large and multinational entrepreneurs, land use conflict also arises. Various economic activities, especially agriculture, industry and tourism, compete for 'optimum' sites on the coast, limited water supplies and often limited labour reserves Certain activities may be destroyed by tourist development, which are basic in certain regions in the long term for local employment.

Women in alternative forms of Tourism

Although in general most tourist regions occupy leading positions in listings of per capita income, the host populations sometimes realise that tourist development does not contribute to their wellbeing. The domination of tour operators in some areas reduces the locally remaining income: in 1983, each tourist paid an average of $625 per trip, and Greece only received 4050 per cent of this sum. Besides complaints about the limited income remaining in the locality, as in Chalkidiki, the host populations may object to the conflicting land uses tourism implies, or stress other priorities set by the community. Most social mobilisations in the Greek countryside, were conflicts between groups of residents with contradictory interests. The community was all but unanimous about environmental protection and tourist development: some groups mobilised in favour of alternative activities, such as manufacturing industry, which are contradictory to tourist development, but bring more employment and income to the locality. Usually, however, there is a favourable attitude towards tourism, because of its perceived economic benefits, irrespective of questions of locally remaining income.

Gender dimensions are difficult to discern here, but another form of grass-roots action is significant. Agro-tourist cooperatives have been set up and run by peasant women. Their conception came from the General Secretariat for Equality, which wished to promote development and interaction between local and foreign women, as well as domestic tourists. Loans to renovate houses were approved to peasant women and they were later taught how to manage an enterprise. The first cooperatives emerged in Ampelakia, Petra, Pyrgi,

Arahova Ag. Germanos and Marona. Others followed, combining hostels and restaurants with handicraft enterprises. Peasant women with economic independence were becoming so emancipated as to storm the kafeneia, the male-dominated coffee shops of Greek villages, and sometimes exclude men from them. Besides tourists, now also local women are entitled to leisure and social interaction, which they combine with work in the cooperatives.

This is an optimistic point on which to conclude a study of the gender dimensions of Greek tourism, instead of the usual deploring of womens' cultural inertia and their informal labour commitment and exploitation. This chapter has stressed acute class boundaries created by tourism in certain areas, work/leisure conflicts and segmentation in the female labour force. Classes of tourists, foreign and domestic, and classes of the host population, complicate the issue, but the basic division between people at work and people at leisure cannot be overcome. Even in Athens, beautiful sites like the Acropolis, Plaka, Greek and Roman Agoras, but also squares, hills, Piraeus ports and the coastal walks, are taken by tourists from spring to autumn, and almost no Greek is spoken there, while the natives used a congested, traffic jammed, unfriendly, often hostile, city, with precariously built streets and offices. Dividing lines between natives and tourists are more acute in the Third World, providing a context for gender divisions. As more people have access to cheap tourism, however, tensions are eased and polarisation is 'limited to specific localities.

4

Tourism Demand

The chapter goes on to discuss whether tourism is supply or demand led. It then explains different levels of demand, and the concept of price elasticity of demand. Structuring the demand for tourism is discussed, and the chapter moves on to explain various approaches to market segmentation. The chapter concludes with visitor surveys and market information systems.

The marketing concept can be expressed very simply as the matching of the product with the needs and desires of the market. People should be offered what they want to buy. One must also develop the right product at an acceptable price. Potential buyers have to be told that this has been done. Then they have to see the product in the right way and they have to be stimulated to buy it. Finally its purchase has to be made as easy as possible.

The key to successful marketing ties in understanding the market and creating the products to satisfy its needs. To know what people want requires the analysis of two types of data:

Who are the people who travel?—what are their characteristics? e.g, social class and profile, age, sex, marital status. Second, what are the motivations of these different groups?—what do they want? what are they looking for?—why are they travelling?

It is important for the GTA, in collaboration with the private sector, to adopt a complete marketing, role Apart from promotion it should play a key part in product development. It should also act as the catalyst in the formulation of the destination's marketing strategy. And it should also monitor the effectiveness of sales programmes, lending its support as necessary. The term marketing is best understood in a wide context embracing market product development, promotion and sales.

Why people travel

People travel for two reasons:

— by obligation
  having to go somewhere on business, or feeling an obligation for religious reasons, or for reasons of family or friendship, or for medical reasons.

— for pleasure
  choosing to go somewhere for pleasure the pleasure, for example, of rest, adventure, escape, discovery, excitement, sport or romance, or any other pleasure seeking motivations. These may differ from person to person. Taken altogether they comprise leisure tourism.

The purposes of travel were listed according to the WTO. They were: leisure, recreation and holiday; visiting friends and relatives; business and professional; health treatment; religion/pilgrimages; and other. Travel for leisure is central to our understanding of tourism. It is linked to the growth in leisure which has accompanied social and economic progress. It is a major contributor to contemporary culture, a part of any modern concept of individual freedom of expression, and the subject of intensive and competitive international market forces. Travel for leisure as a broad category can be broken down into mainstream tourism, special interest tourism and alternative tourism,

Mainstream tourism

Although the overall market may become more diverse, its mainstream changes little. This solid major market segment, by far the largest, is made up of people looking for rest and recreation. They want comfortable holiday hotels and other types of smart tourist accommodation on a beach or elsewhere. Many may prefer to be in a resort complex offering a full range of shopping, recreation, restaurants, entertainment and other facilities and services. This is the traditional holiday market which changes only according to contemporary fashions, tastes and values. It can be segmented mainly on the basis of nationality, social class, spending power and age.

Special interest tourism

The following are examples of special interest markets.

— Nature tourism in all of its specialized forms

— Trekking

— Fishing

— Cultural interest in various specialized forms

— Photography

— Deep sea diving

— While water rafting

— River cruising

— Adventure tourism—based on camping expeditions

— Game watching

— Youth tourism—outdoors and adventure

These markets are formed through the common special interest possessed by the people who make them up, It is this interest—this motivation—which is more important than other characteristics e.g., age, Cultural background, etc. A passion for archery, or photography, or ornithology, or deep sea diving, or military history or archaeology, may unite a highly heterogeneous group of people with otherwise dissimilar backgrounds and characteristics.

Another market may be composed of naturalists. These may be people with a passion for such subjects as ornithology, etymology or botany. In a similar way, hobbyists can be divided into a wide range of segments, for example pastimes like painting, photography or ceramics. Another segment of the market may be looking for soft adventure. This kind of holiday will capture excitement and thrills, while providing a certain level of security and comfort, for example a safari staying at comfortable game lodges or a canoeing trip, again with good food and comfortable accommodation.

Hard adventure is quite different. It will have elements of hardship and apparent risk to go with the thrills, Another segment may be composed of the sports enthusiasts eager, for example, for new golfing, tennis or fishing experiences.

Alternative tourism

It can be questioned whether alternative tourism should exist as a separate category at all, or whether it should just be included as another special interest segment. Tourism marketers tend to talk about the new traveller. The new traveller is described as better educated, more culturally aware, more environmentally and culturally sensitive, and more curious and analytical,

Such people are looking for an alternative to the mainstream trends of the large Mass tourism markets. They do not want large, modern hotels constructed and equipped according to international norms. Alternative tourism is usually based on small locally owned accommodation units, very much a part of the local community and reflecting local values and ways of life. Alternative tourism seeks to feature and protect local Culture, and to involve the community in such ways that local people benefit fully. It is a tourism which aims to be better assimilated and more supportive of local needs and aspirations.

Alternative tourism promotes local cuisine, the use of local materials and handicrafts, and the development of a whole range of other participating tourism services, e.g. local folkloric performances, trekking, handicrafts demonstrations, and cultural and recreational activities. It also fosters the creation and development of tourism enterprises operated and owned by local people.

Is tourism demand or supply led?

In business travel, or visiting friends or relatives, or going on pilgrimages, or for health reasons, or for conventions, the traveller's destination tends to be preselected by the purpose of his or her journey: going to New York on business, going to Lourdes on pilgrimage, going to Florida to see one's mother, going to Singapore to participate in a convention, or to Zurich for a particular medical treatment.

As already noted, these kinds of travel tend to be motivated by a sense of obligation. This obligatory travel is obviously driven by demand, The number of pilgrims is generated by the strength of a particular religion. There is a correlation between business traffic, economic growth, trade and commercial activity. Visiting friends and relatives is related to the ethnic ties between communities in different countries.

By contrast, travellers motivated by pleasure are free to choose their destination There is no obligation to visit a particular place, except perhaps for people who may own a holiday home there. It is a question of choice, People choose the destination which, they believe, will best meet their needs. One can go anywhere. In this sense tourism is supply led. It is the destination with the most attractive product which draws the visitors. Obviously, unless a destination possesses the natural, scenic and cultural attractions, it is difficult to create a demand. In this sense tourism is, always supply led. A place has to be attractive to even consider developing leisure tourism.

For a destination to be demand led given that it has the right natural and other attractions requires a marketing approach. This means the complete analysis of all marketing opportunities, and the selection of certain markets. It means the development of an appropriate product to satisfy these markets, with the pursuit of particular types of tourist.

However, the capacity must then exist (in both resources and professional knowledge and skills) to create and operate facilities of the required category and standard to satisfy these tourists.

Sometimes marketing strategies are chosen which are not workable, given the level of local skills and know-how. It can be seen that tourism is led by both supply and demand by both the product and its markets.

Levels of demand

One can talk of four levels of demand basic, displacement, created and future. The basic demand is an existing demand which is not being completely satisfied, for example, there is a demand to stay in a destination but there are still too few hotels. Displacement demand occurs when people are persuaded to stop using one product in favour of another product which better fulfils their needs, for example, new and better hotels are opened in one destination and displace demand from other destinations. Created demand is when the creation of a new product creates a demand which did not exist before, for example, new hotels in a certain destination create a completely new demand. Future demand will be brought about by future changes and developments, for example, by increases in standards of living, by economic growth, increases in population, and by a general growth in tourism. Future demand eventually becomes a part of the basic demand.

These levels to demand are well illustrated, for example, by the countries of South East Asia. The basic level of demand has tended to exceed the supply of the right kinds of facilities. Rapid regional growth has brought future demand on stream at a steady rate. As countries have added facilities, so they have displaced demand from other destinations. Arid they have created demand particularly from short haul tourism within the region.

Total demand consists of different groups of people, with different preferences, tastes and spending power. There may be lots of different market segments each seeking a particular product with distinctive characteristics. Demand has to be analysed and the market for a destination segmented accordingly. The product should then be developed to meet the various needs of these segments. This means that the product will be segmented in a matching way. Each product segment may have distinctive characteristics and pricing to match fully the needs of its corresponding market segment.

Elasticity of demand

Sometimes when prices are lowered it results in people buying more. Sometimes it has little effect. When the sales of an item are very sensitive to any changes in price, demand is said to be price elastic. When sales are insensitive and demand remains the same, it is price inelastic.

Even small changes in price may result in a substantial effect on demand (elasticity), while quite large changes may have little effect (inelasticity). Leisure travel of the popular mainstream type tends to be price elastic. In contrast, business travel people must travel regardless of cost tends to be price inelastic.

The price elasticity in relation to marginal costing and the need to fill up empty space at the last minute, is an important factor. When prices are greatly reduced to encourage last minute travel, the market tends to respond quickly. However, price is also linked to the image of a product The value attached to a product, its prestige and desirability, may depend largely on how much one has to pay for it.

Marginal cost is the cost of producing one more unit or as is the case in tourism, of accommodating or serving one more visitor. If the cost is low it may be tempting to cut prices to fill up space on aeroplanes and in hotels. Such a strategy takes advantage of the price elasticity of demand, However, it may also cheapen the product, undermine the image, and antagonize people who have paid full price.

Structuring the demand for tourism

Countries market a tourism product according to its diversity. The product may subdivide into many different places and experiences. Separately these may attract both large and small markets domestic and international.

When confronted with this complexity of products and markets, there is a need to try and structure them in a sensible way. Large countries have a very diverse tourism product indeed appealing to a huge spectrum of market segments, one can almost say a continuum of segments, for example, countries such as France or Italy.

However, to make sense of large countries they may have to be broken down into regions, areas, counties, provinces, cities, towns and resorts. Each one has first to be studied separately. They are then all brought together and viewed as a whole.

The product is differentiated according to market segments. And markets are segmented according to the entire range of products offered. This is how supply and demand are matched.

Each market segment has to be well understood and analysed according to its characteristics. As noted, product segments are discussed in the next chapter.

Market segmentation

Each market segment represents people with different characteristics and needs. Segments then sub-segment and sub-segment on down according to these criteria. For example:

— Nationality or place of cultural origin, and gender

— Stage of life

— Social grade

— Psychographics

— Motivation and interests

— Mode of travel/distance travelled

If one was selling clothes people's physical characteristics would matter. Are people tall or short, fat or thin? If it was shoes, do they have big or small feet, and what shape are their feet? If it was golf gloves how many are left handed or right handed. How big or small are their hands? Markets can be segmented in any way, using any criteria, that make sense in identifying the characteristics and patterns of consumer behaviour and needs.

For example, American women, single, between 30 and 40 years old, in the professional group, successful, innovating individuals, who play tennis and golf. A particular resort specializing in these two games might target this market segment. 'There are three basic reasons for segmenting markets:

— to develop the product to satisfy specific needs

— to identify where and how to sell the product

— to judge if and how to mix different segments together.

The following describes typical sets of criteria in the segmentation of markets.

Nationality and gender

It is obviously important for a resort to know whether visitors are, for example, Japanese, French or Italian. Each nationality has its own language and many distinctive preferences and patterns of behaviour.

A particular resort or hotel has to judge the extent to which it can mix nationalities. Few studies have been done which can assist operators in this decision. Operators go by experience. They know that if they exceed 50 per cent of resort or hotel capacity for one nationality alone, say Japanese, it may be difficult for other nationalities to blend in. Many consider that 50 per cent is already too high. It is sometimes held that once 50 percent is exceeded it is better to aim at 100 per cent for the one nationality. Doing this however, makes the resort dependent on one market only. This has obvious dangers.

Similarly there may be dangers in mixing sub cultures from the same country. There has to be a good understanding of the ways in which groups of people differ and how well they will mix together. People from different regions, with variations in educational and cultural levels and incomes, may not go well together. It may depend on the precise proportions arid the nature of the holiday. Gender is also an important variable, Men and women may have some different travel preferences and needs, These 'nave to be, identified.

According to each nationality, and market, people may also have a different order of priority in the way which they choose to spend their disposable income.

Stage of life

An important criterion in the segmentation of markets is found in people's life cycle. The following is a typical breakdown based on the period of life reached and the likely travel preferences.

Teenagers	Mostly single, not yet in employment, dependent on parents, little disposable income. Adventure and discovery travel, action and fun packed.
Single in employment	The bachelor stage, young, single. Still adventure and discovery travel, action and fun packed. But with more sophistication.
Newly married	Young, no children—little disposable income available.

	Family type holidays at an integrated resort.
Family and babies	Youngest child under—six little disposable income.
	Still a family type holiday often with repeat holidays to the same resort.
Family with young children	Youngest child over six start to be a little better off.
	Still at a resort but more diversified holidays, doing more things.
The broken marriage	Divorced, single parents or just remarried, still with dependent children and little disposable income.
	Short breaks, modest holidays, resort destinations,
Family with older children	Getting older and still married or married again, children still dependent.
	Parents possibly holidaying alone.
	Diversified holidays; perhaps multi destination, likely to pursue special interests.
Alone again	Older and married, children have left home.
	A variety of diversified holidays e.g. cruises and

	tours and still pursuing special interests.
Survivors/widows and widowers	Single again and alone. Travelling on tour in groups or clubs often for special interest.

These stages of life give a broad indication only. There are many exceptions; for example, people who choose not to get married or not to have children. Such people are likely to be better off financially. There are various similar approaches to the classification of the stages of life as, for example, by Kotler. Age exercises many other influences on a person's motivations. Needs and tastes will change at each stage of life. Young single people want to do different things to older married couples with children, and elderly people will have developed altogether different preferences,

Social Grade Groupings

The following breakdown, from the Institute of Practitioners in Advertising, is now used as the Social Grade Profile of the UK's National Readership Survey sample and serves as an example of social grade grouping.

The basis of this social grading was originally based on the Head of Household concept, but this has now been changed to Chief Income Earners. This has had the effect of shifting the social class profile more up market. People's incomes help to indicate the price they may be able and willing to pay for a particular product. Some groups, however, may be willing to pay different proportions of their discretionary income for travel. Pricing policy may be developed accordingly. Generally, however, one does not segment markets according to price level; one prices according to each market segment.

The marketing mix as a whole is formulated to target particular segments.

In most countries there are numerous sources of demographic data characterizing segments of society according to criteria such as age, sex, occupation, educational level, income and place of residence. Alone these data allow for crude segmentation only, representing an inflexible way of categorizing society. Marketing specialists have tried to identify more complete ways of explaining consumer behaviour, and have used psychographics. This is a technique which relates personality to social values and lifestyles.

Psychographics

Different psychographic profiles may describe inward and outward looking people, adventurers and play-it-safers, leaders and followers and so on. Some of the thinking described may be useful to apply. It may also be based on studies with some validity, and it may increase understanding of the particular appeal of various tourist experiences.

Sometimes, however, the concepts tend to be too glib and fail to recognize all the complexities of human behaviour, People categorized according to one particular profile, may suddenly demonstrate a range of behavioural inconsistencies, They do not always behave as they are supposed to behave.

The main examples of the psychographic approach are:

— Stanford Research's Values and Lifestyles Programme (VALS).

These are four value groups divided into nine lifestyle categories—Survivors, Sustainers, Belongers, Emulators, Achievers, 1-am-Me, Experiential, Societally Conscious and Integrated.

— Yankelovich Clancy Shulman's Monitor.

These, are seven lifestyle categories Self-explorer, Social Resister, Experimentalist, Conspicuous consumer, Belonger, Survivor and Aimless.

Both these approaches have been widely used internationally. In the United Kingdom, Young and Rubicam's 4Cs—Cross Cultural Consumer Classification reflects the VALS approach. It uses the following categories and groups.

Three basic categories:

Survivors
Internal values
External values

Beth Salmon covers these various systems in her short guide *Psychographics and Lifestyles*. She points out that they have many common threads. 'The major inner-directed/outer-directed axis always seems to be present; the 4Cs 11 "succeeders" and "reformers" seem to bear more than a passing resemblance to Monitor's "conspicuous Consumers" and "self explorers"!

She indicates that most systems have some sort of mass market moral majority at their core. Whether they call them belongers or mainstreamers is riot of crucial importance. In tourism, as noted, it is this mainstream demand which sustains most destinations.

Motivation and interests

Travel motivations and interests can be summarized as: leisure, recreation and holiday; visiting friends and relatives; business and professional; health treatment; religion /pilgrimages; and other. Linked to motivations and interests are peoples' needs and preferences. What do they like and what don't they like? What particular product features are they looking for?

Mode of transport/distance travelled

People will choose to travel by air, sea, rail or road, and they will travel independently—alone or with family or friends or in groups.

Access can usually be described as follows:

— Long haul access by air 6000 kilometres or more usually more than about seven hours flying time.

— Medium haul access by air between *3000* and *6000* kilometres from, about four hours flying time up to about six to seven hours.

— Short haul access by air under 3000 kilometers or up to about three to four hours flying time. This will usually include the major regional markets.

— Access by train mostly national or intraregional.

— Access by road also mostly national or intraregional from neighbouring countries.

— Access by sea mainly from neighbouring and other countries in the region. This does not include cruise ships.

Tourists can be differentiated according to the mode of transport chosen, the distance travelled and whether they are travelling independently or in a group.

The complexity of human behaviour

The various means of categorizing tourists illustrate the complexity of human behaviour, People share the common characteristics of the species. Beyond this, however, they appear to be infinitely variable. As noted, some of the differences originate in their genetic make-up and sex, some in the major cultural influences that play upon them, some in their age and marital status, some in their previous education and experience, some in their economic and social status, some in their spiritual and inner life, some in their simple likes and dislikes, their interests and passions, and some in a variety of other ways. It is important to keep analysing demand. To be sensitive to every clue about behaviour, and to never stop asking questions. One needs a constant flow of market information; keeping track of people, of who exactly they are, and what exactly they want and need.

Some of the psychographic ways of classifying tourists may seem, at times, to be too superficial or fanciful. However, they are still helpful in the review and discussion of tourist behaviour and in shaping future research projects.

Successful segmentation, enabling clearly defined marketing targets, is assisted by interconnecting various kinds of data and criteria. As data is built up age, nationality, gender, occupation, income, motivations and interests, needs and preferences, lifestyles, stage of life, etc. the picture formed becomes clearer and sharper and more particularized.

Visitor surveys

Visitor surveys are conducted to supplement the market information obtained from routine tourism statistics. In designing a survey questionnaire, the following points should be noted:

— The purpose should be explained and people thanked for their participation.

— The meaning of questions should be clear and free of any ambiguit.

— It has to be easy to understand and complete.

— It should be well laid out, organized into clear sections, printed in large clear typeface allowing plenty of space to write answers and comments.

— It should be presented in a logical sequence.

— Questions should not lead the respondent, i.e. suggest or imply an expected answer.

The length of a questionnaire depends partly on the time people have to complete it. It also depends on people's goodwill and the time they are prepared to spend. If tour groups are being asked, they will generally spend some time in the departure lounge before their return journey. They may have to sit and wait for as long as 30 minutes—given that last minute or duty free shopping has been completed. This may be the ideal time to complete a questionnaire.

Ideally each questionnaire should be collected and checked by a survey assistant. Any part not filled out or not clear can be clarified immediately with the respondent.

The design of the questionnaire will also depend on the survey methodology and the size of the sample. As noted, the questionnaire has to permit the collection of accurate and useful feedback. But it must also facilitate the subsequent correlation and analysis of the data. The more extensive the comments and assessments made by respondents, the harder this is. But it is often worth the effort. It will provide more complete answers about the respondents.

— Not only who they are and what they do

— But also where they stayed

— How long they stayed

— What they did

— Where they went

— How much they spent

— And what they liked or didn't like and why.

It is this last assessment which is essential in improving and developing the product. There are usually no other reliable sources for data on tourist expenditures. Banks and currency exchange agencies can give some data on foreign exchange earnings but not enough to build up an accurate and complete picture.

Surveys can help identify and define market segments. Knowledge has to be built up on each market segment, to provide information on how to develop the product and how to promote and sell more effectively. When segments are lumped together the value of a visitor survey is seriously diminished. However, it may not be practical to define and isolate segments in too detailed a way.

The sampling method used can take account of a number of the major variables, for example, seasonality and time of the year, the nationality of visitors, age, and whether travelling independently or in a group. With mainstream leisure tourism there may be quite pronounced differences between people of different nationalities" cultures. And there will obviously be major differences between age groups. Some market segments can be determined by the reason for travel; for example, it is easy to identify and survey separately business and official travellers and visiting friends and family traffic.

Special interest visitors and people coming for health reasons can easily be surveyed separately since they will normally be found together in their related centres. It is also easy to identify backpackers and to keep them apart in a separate survey category, if possible it is always best to separate different nationalities. Sampling has to be done in such way that results are representative of the total number of people under study. The likely error or deviation in survey results also has to be calculated. A random sample means that everybody in the universe under study has an equal chance of being included. If the sample is to be structured according to particular groups, a stratified random sample may be used. Generally the more visitors surveyed, the more reliable the results. Surveys where people themselves choose whether to respond or not, such as guest comment cards in hotels, do not arrive at a reliable sample, Respondents are self-selected and therefore not sufficiently representative.

Market information systems

A market information system, also to be discussed in later chapters, is essential, It is a system established to study market characteristics and trends. The results of desk research and data collection, the analysis of tourism statistics, and the findings from visitor surveys, will feed into this system. There are many published sources of data, for example, the results of country-specific studies and analyses of particular market segments. These are often prepared and published by specialized research companies. The travel trade press should also be followed closely to monitor various trends and new developments.

It is possible to subscribe to a clippings service which will identify and clip all press items of particular interest. Through its statistics, surveys, and market information system, a GTA can be expected, in close collaboration with the private sector, to follow all marketing trends. It should be able to keep in focus the various characteristics of its markets and visitors. However, a GTA would not normally be involved with research of a psychographic nature. This might be carried out by advertising agencies, tour operators or even large hotel companies. These various enterprises will be interested to establish a correlation between choice of holidays, destinations and facilities and particular lifestyles and profiles. Such studies may help to give a clearer idea of who buys what and why, enabling promotional and sales efforts to be better directed. Motivational research of this kind is often carried out through group discussions and indepth interviewing.

Where research is carried out by private sector interests, they should be encouraged to share the results with the GTA. While marketing information may give companies a competitive advantage, the GTA represents the interests of the sector as a whole. One should try to reconcile any conflict between these two sets of needs.

Household surveys are conducted in many countries to establish consumption patterns and trends. Some surveys concentrate on travel and tourism, for example, the United Kingdom Tourism Survey organized by the four UK national tourism boards.

Tourism demand has grown rapidly throughout the 1970s and 1980s, with world international tourist arrivals increasing from 160 million in 1970 to 405 million in 1989. This growth has not been steady, and in fact for the years 1982 and 1983 a decline in tourist arrivals was recorded. However, in general, tourism demand has stood up well to economic pressures: for example, international tourist arrivals continued to grow in the mid-1970s in spite of the massive oil price rises and supply shortages that occurred. After sluggish growth followed by decline in the early 1980s (the 1983 level of world international tourist arrivals was below the 1980 level), the growth in tourism demand recovered and indeed accelerated over the 198688 period.

International tourist arrivals grouped by region in 1988, together with the regions share in world international tourist arrivals. It can be seen that Europe dominates in terms of international tourism, attracting 64 per cent of world arrivals. The Americas attract 19 per cent of world arrivals, and are followed by East Asia and the Pacific (11 per cent), Africa (3 per cent), the Middle East (2 per cent) and South Asia (1 per cent).

Although Europe and North America together account for approximately 80 per cent of worldwide international tourist arrivals, their market shares have declined during the 1970s and 1980s at the expense of developing and newly developed countries, particularly those in the East Asia and the Pacific region. Factors that have contributed to the increased market share of this region include the opening up of new air routes, the provision of relatively cheap inclusive tours and the massive increase in outward international tourism from Japan over the period, which has resulted in increased intraregional tourism. Most international tourism is intraregional— it originates in countries of the same region but this varies considerably with the destination region under consideration. For example, whereas about 80 per cent of arrivals in Europe and North America are intra-regional, this figure reduces to about 25 per cent for Africa. This partially explains why Europe and North America have high market shares of world arrivals the high levels of disposable income in Europe and North America facilitate international tourism, most of which takes place within the regions. However, country size and ease of Access to other countries also affects the level of international tourist arrivals. Thus, a substantial part of the discrepancy between Europe's market share and that of the Americas may be accounted for by the following:

1 Europe contains several relatively small countries.

2 Much intraregional international tourism within Europe takes place between neighbouring countries with common land borders.

By contrast, the USA is an enormous country with great variation in Climate, scenery, facilities, and so on. Hence, a domestic trip within the USA, which involves crossing a state boundary, may well be the equivalent of an international trip within Europe. The size and varied nature of the USA compared with individual European countries result in much USA domestic tourism being the equivalent of much international tourism within Europe.

The major tourism generating countries are ranked according to international tourism expenditures in Table 3.3. In 1987 West Germany was ranked first with a total expenditure of more than $23 billion, followed by the USA, the UK, Japan and France.

The major tourism receiving countries are ranked according to international tourism receipts in Table 3.4. In 1987 Spain was ranked first with total receipts of nearly $15 billion, followed by the USA, Italy, France and the UK. The USA, UK and France thus feature in the top five countries as both origins and destinations when demand is measured in terms of tourist expenditures/receipts, whereas West Germany and Japan (countries characterized in recent history by current account surpluses mainly achieved through the export of manufactured goods) are primarily generating countries, and Spain and Italy (traditional Mediterranean destinations) are primarily receiving countries.

Purpose of visit

The definition of 'tourist is wide-ranging and when tourism demand is broken down according to purpose of visit, the following categories can be identified: holidays, business trips, visits to friends and relatives (VFR) and miscellaneous visits. About 70 per cent of world international tourist arrivals are for holiday purposes, and of the remaining 30 per cent of tourist trips approximately one-half are made for business purposes.

Holidays

Holidays are the most important tourism market overall. This market is characterized by freedom of choice on the part of the individual in terms of selection of destination, transport mode, and so on, and by strong competition among the various ' segments of the tourism industry (including the destinations) that supply the market. Unlike, say, business travel, where the existence of business contacts largely determines the destination to be visited, in the case of holiday tourism the individual can select from among a wide variety of destinations; thus considerations such as price become very important. Holidaymakers can be divided into those who are conservative and risk-averse and those who wish to try something new and are willing to accept some risk. The conservatives tend to take the same type of holiday year after year often returning to the same country once they have found one they enjoy (and even to the same resort or hotel), whereas the risk-takers seek out new experiences in terms of climate, culture, scenery, and so on.

Many different types of holiday exist. For example, in terms of the mass-market, Mediterranean destinations offer 'sun/sea/sand' holidays (where the norm is to lie on a beach), whereas Austria and Switzerland offer lakes and mountains holidays, which concentrate on scenic attractions in the summer and skiing holidays in the winter. There are now also many 'exotic' long-haul destinations on offer to places such as South America and Southeast Asia, where the emphasis is very much on experiencing something different. A range of special-interest holidays also exists pony-trekking, rambling, cycling, yachting, bird watching, farm tourism, canal cruising, and so on. The short-break sightseeing holiday is also proving increasingly popular.

Business trips

Business travel is an important segment of the tourism market, and in certain sectors it plays the major role. Although only about 15 per cent of tourist arrivals are for business purposes, tourist spending on a business trip is likely to be much higher than on a holiday, so the contribution of business tourism to the total will be higher in value terms. Furthermore, as far as transport is concerned, business travellers comprise a disproportionately high proportion of air travellers (of the order of 50 per cent), and as far as accommodation is concerned they comprise a disproportionately high proportion of hotel guests, particularly in the four and five-star range where the figure is of the order of 60 per cent.

The business travel market is characterized by relative lack of seasonality, last-minute booking and inelastic response to price. To the extent that seasonality exists at all, the demand for business tourism is likely to be lower at times of peak holiday demand, because the businessmen themselves may well be on holiday. An important attribute of short business trips is that they usually take place during the week, so hotel accommodation tends to be little used for business purposes at weekends. As business travel is often large town/city-oriented, hotels in these business centres usually offer very attractive rates at weekends to encourage holidaymakers to stay. The facts that many business trips are booked only a short time ahead and that business travellers usually wish to spend the minimum amount of time away on their trips to achieve the required results means that business tourists require maximum flexibility in particular, they do not want restrictive conditions attached to flight tickets and are prepared to pay a premium for this. Furthermore, they usually require good quality accommodation, both in order to be able to function well and also to create the right image with the business contact being visited.

A particular form of business tourism is conference/congress/convention tourism, and considerable attention has been focused on this form of tourism in recent years with the development of large purpose-built conference centres in many cities and seaside resorts. However, most conferences take place in hotels, and educational establishments (universities, colleges) also play an important role. Conference tourism is not as pre-determined as other forms of business tourism, in that the conference organizers can choose the location for the conference on the basis of facilities, price, and so on. Thus conference destinations are in strong competition with each other to attract conferences. Friel identifies the following criteria, which are considered desirable if a conference destination is to be successful:

1 It should be attractive to tourists.

2 It should have a variety of meeting facilities.

3 It should have a range of good accommodation. 4 There should be good access by air/road/rail.

5 There should be a civic commitment to hosting delegates.

6 There should be a coordinated approach to destination marketing and visitor servicing.

Visits to friends and relatives

Tourists visiting friends and relatives tend to spend much less per day while in the destination than do holidaymakers. They often stay with their friends/relatives and, therefore, do not make use of commercial accommodation. Similarly, daily expenditure on food and drink in restaurants, etc., is likely to be considerably lower than would be the case for holidaymakers. However, VFR tourists often stay longer than holidaymakers, and thus the total trip expenditure may, in some cases, be higher for the former than for the latter category of tourists.

Furthermore, VFR traffic almost certainly generates additional local resident spending on food, drink, attractions, and so on. In addition, although daily destination expenditure is likely to be relatively low, the VFR component of the tourism market still needs to reach the destination and is likely to use similar means of transport to holiday makers. In fact, tourists visiting friends and relatives may face higher travel costs than those incurred by inclusive tour holidaymakers, who benefit from the bulk-purchasing power of tour operators.

Miscellaneous visits

This purpose of visit includes tourism for reasons such as study, health, religion, shopping and to attend sporting events. Miscellaneous visits form a small proportion of overall tourism demand, but for certain destinations they can be quite important. For example, visits for religious reasons are dominant in the case of Vatican City, and visits to spas for health purposes form a significant segment of tourism demand in certain European countries such as Germany and Hungary.

Seasonality in tourism demand

'Seasonality' refers to the tendency of tourist flows to be concentrated into relatively short periods of the year (Allcock, 1989b) In Europe and North America, for example, the summer months of July and August are when a large proportion of the population goes on holiday. This is mainly due to natural features such as climate (the best holiday destination weather often occurs during these months), but also partly due to institutional features such as restrictions on when employees may take holiday leave and school holidays.

In recent years ski holidays have grown enormously in popularity, which spreads the tourist season into the winter months for appropriate destinations. Furthermore, many holidaymakers now go on 'winter sun' holidays. Sesonality causes particular problems for employment, in that workers employed in the tourism industry for part of the year may have no opportunities for employment during the rest of the year, and this may cause resentment among employees. In addition, the seasonal nature of employment inhibits training and career progress. Seasonality can result in overcrowding and overuse of facilities in destinations during part of the year, while for the remainder of the year facilities may be considerably under-used or not used at all, resulting in inefficient use of resources and loss of profit potential.

There are four principal strategies for managing seasonality: changing the product-mix, market diversification, differential pricing and encouragement/ facilitation by the state of the staggering "of holidays. Changing the product-mix involves the creation and marketing of new different attractions; thus, a summer beach resort may set out to attract the conference trade in the off season, or it may decide to stage some special event, or to promote special-interest holidays that would be appropriate out of season.

The construction of all-weather facilities, such as covered leisure complexes for year-round use are a means of extending the season. A highly successful example in Northern Europe is the development of Centre Parcs, where accommodation is clustered around an all-weather leisure area incorporating wave-pool, water slides, and so on. Diversification of the market to reach new potential customers may also be used successfully to counteract the effects of seasonality North Americans, particularly from the northeast of the USA and Canada, have been travelling to Florida for winter holidays for some considerable time. The desire to escape the harsh winters for the warmth and sun of Florida has been a strong pull, and many retired North Americans spend several months there each winter. More recently, however, Florida has been marketed as a summer destination to UK residents, and the British have travelled there in increasing numbers. Pricing policies can also be used to reduce seasonality. By the introduction of price reductions in the off-season, tourists can be encouraged to take holidays during this period. Similarly, if tourist resorts become overcrowded during peak periods, price rises can be used to reduce the seasonal congestion. State-initiated measures to stagger holidays can also be successful in reducing the seasonality problem for example, the staggering of school summer holidays over a longer period and the encouragement of the staggering of industrial holidays.

In spite of efforts to reduce seasonality in tourism, only limited success has been achieved. The prime importance attached to the weather by many holidaymakers means that only a certain amount of flexibility is possible.

Tourism demand functions

Tourism demand functions embody the relationship between the demand for international tourism and those factors that influence this demand. They are economic relationships that, when estimated, permit the impact of each of these factors on tourism demand to be identified. Clearly, the group of variables that influences international tourism demand will depend upon the purpose of visit under consideration. For example, the demand for business travel will depend upon where major business centres are located, whereas the demand for visits to friends and relatives will depend upon where close historical, cultural, etc., ties exist, which give rise to the location of friends/relatives in foreign countries. As by far the majority of international tourist trips take place for holiday purposes (approximately 70 per cent), and it is only for holiday trips that individuals are completely free to choose the destination, transport mode, and so on, we shall just concentrate on demand functions that explain the demand for international holiday tourism.

Demand variable

The demand for international tourism is measured in terms of the number of holiday visits from an origin country to a foreign destination country, or in terms of holiday expenditures by visitors from the origin country in the destination country. As the level of foreign tourism from a given origin is expected to depend upon the origin population (the higher the number of people resident in a country, the greater the number of trips taken abroad, ceteris paribus), the demand variable is usually expressed in per capita form. Occasionally, however, population features as a separate explanatory variable rather than demand being expressed in per capita form.

Income

In general, income is included as an explanatory variable. Income usually enters model as origin country real income per capita (corresponding to the specification of demand in per capita terms). As holiday visits are under consideration, the appropriate form of the variable is personal disposable income.

Own price

Price is usually included in demand functions. For

international tourism there are two elements of price: those costs incurred in reaching the destination, and those costs to be met while at the destination. Transport cost can be measured by using representative air fares between the origin and destination for air travel and representative ferry fares and/or petrol costs for surface travel,~ Transport cost should enter model in real terms in origin country currency.

It may be possible to measure the cost of tourism in the destination by a specific tourists' cost of living variable if appropriate data available. Otherwise, the consumer price index in a country may be used to represent tourists' cost of living; and Martin and Witt have shown that this is likely to be a reasonable proxy for the cost of tourism variable. Tourists' cost of living should be specified in real terms in origin currency. It is sometimes suggested that exchange rate should also appear as an explanatory variable influencing, international tourism demand; although exchange rates are already incorporated to some extent in the other price variables, in practice people may be more aware of exchange rates than relative costs of living for tourists in the origin and destination countries, and thus pay considerable attention to this price indicator.

Substitute prices

Economic theory suggests that the prices of substitutes may be important determinants of demand. Potential tourists compare the price of a foreign holiday with the price of a domestic holiday in reaching their holiday decision. However, they also compare the costs of holidaying in a particular foreign destination with the costs involved in visiting other foreign countries. Thus, substitute travel costs and substitute tourists' living costs may be important determinants of the demand for international tourism to a given destination from a particular origin. Substitute prices can be accommodated in model through the inclusion of:

(a) a weighted average substitute transport cost variable, and

(b) a weighted average substitute tourists' cost of living variable.

The weights should reflect the relative attractiveness of the various destinations to residents of the origin under consideration, and are often based on previous market shares.

Dummy variables

Dummy variables can be included in international tourism demand, functions to allow for the impact of 'one off' events. These are specially constructed variables, which take the value when the event occurs and 0 otherwise. For example, the 1973 and 1979 oil crises are likely to have temporarily reduced international tourism demand on account of the resultant uncertainties in the world economic situation. Tourism flows to Greece were lower than expected in 1974 because of the heightened threat of war between Greece and Turkey as a result of the Turkish invasion of Cyprus. When governments impose foreign currency restrictions on their residents, this is likely to reduce outward tourism, as was the case, for example, in the UK during the period late 1966 to late 1969, and foreign currency restrictions can also alter the distribution of foreign holidays. Measurement of the impact of mega-events (such as the Olympic Games) on tourism flows through the use of dummy variables has been discussed by Witt and Martin.

Trend

A trend term may be included in international tourism demand models if it is thought relevant. This mainly represents a steady change in the popularity of a destination country over the period considered as a result of changing tastes, but it also captures the time-dependent effects of all other explanatory variables not explicitly included in the equation, such as changes in air service frequencies and demographic changes in the origins.

Promotional activity

National tourist offices often spend considerable sums in foreign countries on promoting the particular country as a tourist destination, as do carriers, particularly airlines. Hence, promotional expenditure is expected to play a role in determining the level of international tourism demand and thus should feature as an explanatory variable in the demand function. The appropriate form of the variable is promotional expenditure for the destination in the origin, expressed in origin country currency and real terms.

A major problem regarding the inclusion of promotional variables as determinants of tourism demand relates to difficulties in obtaining the relevant data. A further problem concerns the form of the relationship; the impact of advertising on tourism demand may be distributed over time, so that advertising in a given period is likely to influence not only demand in that period but also in subsequent Periods, although the effect will diminish with the passage of time. In addition, the effectiveness of a given level of advertising expenditure in influencing the level of international tourism demand may vary across media.

Lagged dependent variable

A lagged dependent variable is sometimes included in tourism demand functions to allow for habit persistence and supply rigidities. Once people have been on holiday to a particular country and liked it, they tend to return to that destination. Furthermore, knowledge about the destination spreads as people talk about their holidays and show photographs, thereby reducing risk for potential visitors to that country. In fact, this word of mouth' recommendation may well play a more important role in destination selection than does commercial advertising.

Supply constraints may take the form of shortages of hotel accommodation, passenger transportation capacity and trained staff, and these often cannot be increased rapidly. Time is also required tc build up contacts among tour operators, hotels, airlines and travel agencies. Similarly, once the tourist industry to a country has become highly developed it is unlikely to dwindle rapidly. The hotel industry will have invested large sums of money in the country and tour operators will have built up contacts there.

Estimation and testing of demand functions

The tourism demand function may be estimated by regression analysis using historic data. The empirical results obtained show the estimated quantitative relationship between foreign holiday demand and the influencing factors. The estimation process is as follows:

1 Specify the demand function in mathematical form (say, linear, or more commonly log-linear).

2. Assemble data relevant to the model.

3. Use the data to estimate by regression the quantitative effects of the influencing variables on demand in the past.

4. Carry out tests on the estimated model to see if it is sufficiently realistic.

When the tourism demand function is specified in log-linear form, a resulting characteristic is that the estimated coefficients may be interpreted directly as elasticities. It is necessary to evaluate the parameter estimates obtained in a regression model in terms of both sign and magnitude in order to determine whether these estimates are theoretically meaningful. Economic theory imposes restrictions on the signs and values of the parameters in demand functions, and the estimates need to be examined to see whether they satisfy these constraints. For example, foreign holidays are 'superior' goods and thus a positive income elasticity is expected. In fact, most foreign holidays are regarded as 'luxuries' and in such cases the magnitude of the income elasticity is expected to exceed unity. Similarly, the own-price elasticity of demand should be negative and cross-price ties for substitutes positive. Changes in consumer tastes may move towards or away from a particular holiday and therefore the variable could have a positive or negative coefficient. The Promotional expenditure and lagged dependent variable coefficients are both expected to be positive. If an estimated parameter has an 'incorrect, sign or does not satisfy the restrictions on magnitude it should be rejected, as it is theoretically implausible. In general, an unexpected parameter sign or size is the result of deficiencies in the model.

The empirical results may also be evaluated in terms of statistical measures of accuracy and significance of the forecasting equations. For example, the t test can be employed to examine the hypothesis that a particular explanatory variable coefficient is significantly, different from zero, or whether the estimated value may simply have been generated by chance. If the hypothesis that a coefficient is equal to zero is true, then the corresponding explanatory variable does not influence the dependent variable and should be excluded from the tourism demand function. However, when a parameter is not statistically significant, this does not prove that there is no relationship between the explanatory and dependent variables; the insignificance of the parameter may be a result of statistical problems. Prior belief plays a vital role in the decision regarding which explanatory variables should be retained in the equation in view of the statistical evidence. If there are strong theoretical grounds for expecting a particular explanatory variable to influence the dependent variable and a 'correct' coefficient sign is estimated but the parameter is insignificant, the explanatory variable should not be eliminated from the equation, as weak support has been obtained for the hypothesis. If the correct sign is estimated for a coefficient and it is statistically significant, this provides strong support for the hypothesis that the variable has an impact on the dependent variable.

Empirical results

The magnitudes of the various elasticities are of interest. For example, if the demand for tourism is price inelastic, then a price reduction reduces total expenditure on tourism and a price rise increase expenditure. If, however, the absolute value of the price elasticity exceeds unity (that is, demand is price elastic), then a price reduction increases expenditure and a price rise reduces expenditure. Clearly therefore, the impact of a price change on total expenditure on the tourism product depends critically on the magnitude of the elasticity.

Martin and Witt have estimated model for tourism, flows from four major generating countries West Germany, USA, UK, France to their important destinations, using data for the period 1965 to 1980. It is clear that the importance of a particular variable in explaining tourist flows varies considerably with the origin-destination pair under consideration. Building models for USA outward tourism proved difficult, with the result that several of these are rather simplistic, and in general contain fewer explanatory variables that the models for UK outward tourism. The main factors affecting tourism demand by USA residents appear to be income and absolute costs. Most overseas holidays seem to be regarded as luxuries with high income coefficients. The exception is Italy, which may be on account of strong ethnic/family ties or the pull for Roman Catholics to visit the country in either case such motivations would tend to cause these visits to be necessities rather than luxuries. The price elasticities vary considerably. In terms of tourists' living costs, tourism demand is price elastic for travel from the USA to France and West Germany, but price inelastic for travel to Canada and the UK. In terms of transport costs, demand is price inelastic. In the models explaining UK outward tourism, not only do the costs of competing holidays play a more important role than for the USA, but also the exchange rate now enters into some models. The 1974 oil crisis appears to have had a marked impact on international tourism demand by UK residents, featuring in five out of six models, and the currency restrictions appear to have affected those destinations with relatively high tourists' living costs (as expected). All income elasticities exceed unity with the exception of Greece, which has a surprisingly low coefficient value. The coefficients estimated for tourists living costs suggest that demand is price elastic for travel from the UK to Greece and Italy, but price inelastic for travel to Austria, France and West Germany. Air travel costs do not feature in the models, but the estimated surface travel cost elasticities show that demand is price elastic for West Germany and price inelastic for Greece, Italy and Spain.

Long-term influences on tourism demand

Major demographic changes are taking place in the main tourism generating countries, and this is likely to affect both the volume and types of holidays undertaken. For example, in general an increasing proportion of the population will consist of retired people couples with young children, and a declining proportion will consist of young singles. Also, changes in consumer preferences say, away, from sun/sea/sand holiday may have a profound" towards activity holidays such as rambling impact on tourism demand over the long term. Clearly, substantial' ' changes in the amount of holiday entitlement will also influence the level of demand.

Tourism forecasting

It is widely recognized that one of the most important functions of the manager at all levels in an organization is planning, and planning creates a substantial need for forecasts. Reliable forecasts of tourism,~ demand are essential for efficient planning by airlines, shipping, companies, railways, coach operators, hoteliers, tour operators, food and catering establishments, providers of entertainment facilities, manufacturers producing goods primarily for sale to tourists, and other industries connected with the tourism market. Such forecasts are also of great interest to governments in origin and destination countries, and to national tourist organizations.

Both the need for forecasts and the importance of reliable forecasts have been stressed by several authors working in the tourism field. For example, Wandner and Van Erden point out that:

> Since governments and private industry must plan for expected tourism demand and provide tourism investment goods and infrastructure, the availability of accurate estimates of

international tourism demand has important economic consequences.

Also, Archer states that:

No manager can avoid the need for some form of forecasting: a manager must plan for the future in order to minimize the risk off, failure or, more optimistically, to maximize the possibilities of success. In order to plan, he must use forecasts. Forecasts will always be made, whether by guesswork, teamwork or the use complex models, and the accuracy of the forecasts will affect the quality of the management decision.

He goes on to point out that:

In the tourism industry, in common with most other service sectors, the need to forecast accurately is especially acute because', of the perishable nature of the product. Unfilled airline seats and unused hotel rooms cannot be stockpiled and demand must be anticipated and even manipulated.

Considerable benefits derive from an accurate forecasting system. If forecasts of tourism demand are too high, then firms in related industries will suffer; for example, there may be empty seats on aeroplanes and coaches, empty rooms in hotels, unoccupied apartments, unused hire cars, and so on. It is likely that in general capital investment will be excessive, the labour force will be too big and excess stocks will be held of goods normally sold directly to or used by tourists. If, on the other hand, forecasts of demand are too low, then firms will lose opportunities: for example, there may be insufficient hotel accommodation or too few flights to cater for all those wishing to visit a certain area at a given time. Even if supply can be expanded to a limited extent at short notice, this is likely to impose additional costs on firms as, say, less efficient aircraft are used, and excessive overtime is worked. A broad range of techniques is available for demand forecasting in tourism and the main quantitative methods are now reviewed.

Univariate time series methods

Univariate time series methods are non-causal quantitative techniques, i.e. they assume that a variable may be forecast without reference to the factors that determine the level of the variable past history on the forecast variable is simply extrapolated. Univariate time series methods determine future values for a single variable through a process of identifying a relationship for past values of the variable. Thus, a great problem with forecasting by extrapolation is that it presupposes that the factors that were the main cause of growth in the past will continue to be the main cause in the future, which may not be the case. In an industry as highly volatile as international tourism, and one that is influenced by so many factors, trend extrapolation is a technique that should be used with extreme caution. It is rarely possible to justify time series models on the basis of theory. The reasons for their use are essentially pragmatic: they often, generate acceptable forecasts at low cost. Furthermore, univariate time series methods may be used where causal models are inappropriate on account of lack of data or incomplete knowledge regarding the causal structure.

Although time series extrapolation models are 'naive' in the sense that the impacts of the forces that determine the behaviour of the time series are not taken into account, they often predict relatively" well. Several of these methods are considered below:

Moving average (arithmetic)

The arithmetic moving average forecast is very easy and cheap to compute; the data for previous periods are added together an divided by the number of observations to give an average figure, and then as a new data point becomes available this is included in the set the oldest observation is removed, and a new average is calculated.

For seasonal data with seasonality of s periods (for example, quarterly data has four-period seasonality), a moving average s periods long is free of seasonal effects. The moving average forecast for periods $t + 1$, $t + 2$, etc., is given by:

$$F_{t+2} \sim= F_{t+1} [x_t + x_{t-1} + ... + x_{t-s+1}]/s$$

where

X_t is the value of a time series in period t

F_{1+j} is the moving average forecast of x_{t+j} (i.e. the forecast for periods ahead), and

S is the length of the seasonal cycle.

The moving average model attempts to estimate the non-seasonal portion of a time series. It is not applicable to series containing steps or trends, as these would cause the moving average to lag behind the movement of the data. Thus, for example, if tourism demand were increasing the method would underforecast.

Exponential smoothing

Exponential smoothing models provide a relatively simple set of forecasting methods that tend to perform well in practice. The single exponential smoothing model in effect attempts to reduce forecast error by correcting last period's forecast by a proportion of last period's error:

$$F_{t+1} = F_t + k(x_t - F_t)$$

where

x_t is the value of a time series in period t

F_{t+1} is the single exponential smoothing forecast of xt+, (i.e. the!, forecast for one period ahead), and

k is a constant, such that $0 < k < 1$.

Equation states that the forecast for period $t + 1$ is given by the forecast for period t plus a proportion (k) of the forecast error for period t. This equation may be rewritten to give:

$$F_{t+1} = kx_t + (1 - k)F_t$$

Single exponential smoothing methods are only applicable to stationary series, i.e. to data without steps, trend or seasonality components, and with constant variance. For non-stationary series other exponential smoothing models can be used. Adaptive smoothing models can accommodate sudden upward or downward steps in a series; Brown's double exponential smoothing model can be used for time series containing a trend, and the Holt-Winters' double exponential smoothing method is specifically designed for time series exhibiting seasonality (in addition to a trend).

Trend curve analysis

Trend curve analysis is widely used in tourism forecasting situations. In general, regression analysis is used to find a curve of best fit through time series data, which is then projected forward into the future. Trend curve analysis is relatively quick and easy to use and, using transformations, can be employed to produce forecasts from data showing a range of patterns, for example, straight line progressions, exponential growth, or patterns that display a gradual approach to a saturation level.

Decomposition methods

The observed values of a time series are usually the result of several influences, and here we are concerned with isolating and measuring those parts of the time series that are attributable to each of the components. Customarily, time series variations are considered to be the result of three or four basic influences: secular trend, seasonal variations, irregular or random changes, and possibly cyclical fluctuations.

The classical decomposition approach assumes that the observation of the time series at period t, x, can be represented as:

$$X_t = T_t \times S_t \times I_t$$

where

T represents the trend value

S represents the seasonal component

I represents the irregular (unpredictable) component, and

t represents the time period.

Sometimes an additional longer-term cycle component is added to the classical decomposition model, but often this factor is ignored. This can be justified if there are insufficient data to detect it, which may well be the case with tourism series. Classical decomposition is best suited where trend or seasonality, and preferably both, are marked.

An alternative (though considerably more complex) approach to decomposition is provided by the Census XII model originally devised for the US Bureau of Census. This extends the basic decomposition model of equation by allowing the trend term T_t, to be non-linear.

Box-Jenkins univariate method

The Box-Jenkins univariate forecasting method is a highly sophisticated technique and is rather more difficult to apply than the other univariate time series methods considered. The models usually incorporate auto-regressive and moving average terms; the autoregressive component implies that the forecast variable depends on its own past values, and the moving average component implies that the forecast variable depends on previous values of the error term. These autoregressive integrated moving average (ARIMA) models are very flexible they can represent many types of stationary and non-stationary time, series. Furthermore, the models contain few parameters. The Box-Jenkins model-building approach can provide relatively accurate forecasts, but it involves complex mathematical and statistical algorithms, and subjective judgements on the part of the modeller. Experience is an essential prerequisite for improving the final models in the analysis of a time series and thus for successful application of the technique.

Causal quantitative techniques

Multiple regression methods

The econometric approach to forecasting international tourism demand involves the use of regression analysis to estimate the tourism demand function or, more generally model and then combining the estimated relationship with forecasts of the explanatory variables to generate tourism demand forecasts. A major advantage of econometric forecasting is that it explicitly takes into account the impact on demand of changes in the causal variables. Furthermore, econometric models may be used for active forecasting, that is, to assess the consequences of possible changes in the causal factors. An additional advantage is that econometric forecasting provides several statistical measures of the accuracy and significance of the forecasting equations.

Econometric models, however, may be inappropriate in certain cases and are generally more expensive than non-causal models. Econometric forecasting also requires considerable user-understanding in order to develop the correct relationships. A major problem in attempting to generate accurate forecasts of tourism demand with econometric models is the difficulty of obtaining accurate forecasts of the variables that influence demand: income, inflation, exchange rates, and so on.

Box-Jenkins multivariate method

The Box-Jenkins multivariate approach to forecasting is considerably more complicated than the Box-Jenkins univariate method. It is a causal forecasting method in that other variables are allowed to influence the forecast variable. As with the Box-Jenkins univariate method, the model incorporates autoregressive and moving average terms, and complex mathematical and statistical algorithms are involved. However, the existence of more than one time series results in additional modelling problems. Again, experience is essential in order to apply the technique successfully.

Box-Jenkins multivariate models may be viewed as extensions of the multiple linear regression model. For example, if there are just two explanatory variables, then the linear regression model

$$Y = b_1X_i + b_2X_2 + U$$

where

Y is the dependent variable

X_1, X_2 are independent variables

U is an error term, and

b_1, b_2 are parameters

may be modified as follows:

1 The terms b_iX_i, $i = 1,2$, can be replaced by transfer function Models which permit present and past values of X_i to influence Y;

2 The error term can be allowed to follow an ARIMA model.

The multivariate Box-Jenkins model corresponding to the regression model is thus

$$Y = Y_1 + Y_2 + Y_n$$

where

Y_1, Y_2 are the input components of Y, such that Y_i = TF_i (X_i), i = 1,2 (*TF* denotes transfer function) and

Y_n is the noise component, such that $Y_{n'}$ = ARIMA (*U*).

Y is therefore the sum of components that are not directly observed, but are determined in the process of fitting the model.

There are many methods that can be used to forecast tourism demand, and selection of an appropriate technique will depend upon the requirements of the forecaster.

For example, a company in the international tourism industry can use an econometric forecasting system to explore the consequences of alternative future policies on tourism demand, which is not possible with non-causal models.

A small-scale questionnaire survey of tourism practitioners was carried out by Martin and Witt, and the results suggest that the main forecasting techniques used in the tourism business are moving average, exponential smoothing and multiple regression.

Moving average is the most popular technique for short-term forecasting, and multiple regression for long-term forecasting; these methods are both highly popular for medium-term forecasting. The only other quantitative forecasting method in general use among tourism practitioners appears to be trend curve analysis.

5

Timeshare Tourism

It is hard to imagine a tourism activity of greater contradictions than timeshare: a 'bad press' in many countries, with a correspondingly poor public image, yet delivering by far the highest consumer satisfaction rates when compared with most holiday products. But despite both image problems and widespread recession in many markets, timeshare sales continue to be big business. Since the early 1970s, the timeshare industry has grown steadily. In Europe, the growth rate has been between 12% and 15% year on year over the past five years—totally outstripping the growth of the rest of the European travel and tourism sector.

Between 1980 and 1992, the number of timeshare resorts increased by almost 600% worldwide; annual sales of timeshare intervals increased by more than 300% worldwide; annual gross sales volume increased more than 650%; roughly 3.3 million timeshare weeks were purchased, representing a total sales volume of almost $4 billion, Based on this data, timeshare sales are predicted to reach £30 billion over the next 12 years.

More than 2.5 million households all over the world now own timeshare, in almost 4000 resort properties. Over 2600 of these resort properties are 'affiliated' to the RCI exchange system. Given that the average size of household is 3.5 people, a quick calculation reveals that more than 8 million people take timeshare holidays each year. That is a significant number in the tourism industry. Indeed, to take the UK as an example, people travelling on timeshare holidays abroad now equate to 9% of British package holidaymakers going abroad.

History and development

If you play golf, you do not need to buy a golf course to indulge in the sport: you join a club and play when you want to. The principle of timeshare is very similar.

The concept of holiday timeshare started in the late 1950s, with an idea conceived by a Swiss, Alexander Nette, and put into practice in a hotel which he ran in Ticino. The idea evolved into Hapimag, a Swiss-based company, which offered its shares for sale, the proceeds of which were used to buy holiday properties throughout Europe. The ownership of shares conveyed the right to use the holiday properties on a regular basis. Hapimag is now a successful business with more than 90 000 shareholders and 45 holiday resort properties throughout Europe.

In 1967, an enterprising hotelier at Superdevoluy in the French Alps started what has become the more common form of timeshare—the sale of right-to-use 'fixed' weeks in the hotel for holiday purposes—sold with the slogan 'stop hiring a room, buy the hotel, it's cheaper!'

At that time, however, the idea did not spread any further in Europe. As so often happens with Europe's creative ideas, it took America's entrepreneurs fully to exploit the potential of timeshare.

Property developers in Florida in the early 1970s were enjoying a sales boom in holiday condominiums and proceeded to plan and build a vast inventory of condominiums for subsequent sale. The second major oil crisis of the mid-1970s hit the American economy hard and condominium sales collapsed almost overnight. Developers looked desperately for new and creative ways of selling their empty properties. They discovered holiday timeshare and thus began the evolution of special marketing and sales techniques which require the sale of one apartment 50 times over—for each week of the year.

Salesmen soon came up against a particular problem: while the potential client liked the timeshare accommodation and the resort on offer, he did not like the prospect of having to return to the same place at the same time for his holiday year after year.

At the same time, in Indianapolis, Jon and Christel DeHaim had begun a private 'swap' system with their friends, trading weeks in each others' holiday homes. When this swap system was applied to the timeshare idea, the timeshare sales problem was solved. Thus, a company called RCI was founded in 1974 as a timeshare exchange organisation to enable purchasers of timeshare to exchange the weeks they owned each year for weeks in different resorts. A second exchange organisation, Interval International, came along two years later. Between them, these two companies acted as the catalyst which started a boom in timeshare sales in the USA during the following 10 years.

Meanwhile, in 1974, the UK's first timeshare development was begun quite independently by a British entrepreneur, Frank Chapman. This was the Loch Rannoch development in Scotland, completed in 1976. Without any clear sequence of events, timeshare developments began to emerge in France, Italy and Scandinavia. The European timeshare industry was born.

By the early 1980s, the timeshare boom in Florida and other US holiday destinations was reaching its peak.

As a result, a number of experienced and successful marketers came to Europe and persuaded owners of holiday resort properties in the Algarve and the Canary Islands to try the concept of timeshare, and began selling mainly to British holidaymakers.

For 20 years now, timeshare sales have shown a quite amazingly consistent upward trend as the business has spread to all four corners of the world.

In the USA, the entrepreneurial beginnings are being followed by the entry into the business of operators with a more established profile. As the largest and most mature market in the world, the USA is now seeing less spectacular growth, but the image of the industry has become better established, strict regulation has been introduced and the industry has learned to live with the consequences. Some of the very well known names in the international hospitality industry have moved into timeshare—bringing with them a welcome air of respectability and stability, with established brands and substantial credibility. So it is that major hotel chains such as Marriott, Hilton, Sheraton and Radisson have moved into timeshare, as indeed has the Walt Disney Organisation with its Disney Vacation Club at Walt Disney World in Orlando.

Marriott is now one of the largest sellers of timeshare in the world, estimated to have sold $160 million in 1993. Hilton Hotels is now developing a series of hotel-related timeshare resorts in the USA, under the banner of the Hilton Grand Vacations Club. The first of these is a purpose-built timeshare resort next to its existing hotel and casino properties in Las Vegas.

Europe is the second-largest market area in the world for timeshare sales. The European timeshare business had its roots in Britain, since the

Englishspeaking entrepreneurs who started the boom sold mostly to British holidaymakers in the Canary Islands. The Canaries certainly still contain the highest concentration of timeshare development in Europe. The largest number of European timeshare owners is British, but other markets in Europe are now growing rapidly.

Germany is Europe's second-largest market after Britain. The size of the population and its propensity for travel and holidays make this a fertile marketplace—though growth has been somewhat slowed in recent years owing to economic and political circumstances.

A welcome resurgence in the long-established French and Italian markets over the past three years has seen a significant increase in timeshare resorts in both countries—though the French are showing a greater inclination than before to buy in traditional holiday areas such as Spain.

Spain itself saw phenomenal growth in domestic timeshare ownership from 1990 to 1992, with the number of owners escalating from 3000 families in 1990 to 23 000 by the end of 1992. The trend has been similar, though less dramatic, in Portugal and a domestic market is emerging in Greece. The Scandinavian markets have been hit by severe recession and have not realised their potential, but smaller markets like Switzerland and Austria are showing promise.

As in the USA, wellknown names are giving credibility to the business in Europe: Barratt in the UK; the giant Metro group in Germany, known for its chain of cash-and-carry stores as well as its wide-ranging investments in European tourism; France's Club Mediterranee; the Banco Bilbao Vizcaya in Spain (a recent entrant into the business); the Berlusconi group in Italy; and the giant Sol hotel group in Spain, which has announced that it is to begin its entry into the timeshare market through two of its Melia resort hotels.

New opportunities for further growth of the timeshare business are appearing with the liberalisation of the various countries forming Eastern Europe. A number of marketing companies are already selling Spanish and Canary Islands timeshare weeks to East Germans, Hungarians and Poles—and even to residents of the former Soviet Union. What is more, timeshare resorts are being developed in these countries: a new resort is being planned in Moscow; several are coming on-stream in Hungary. Turkey is another country with huge potential, given its population of 60 million, including a well-off middle class, and its increasingly important role in European tourism.

Timeshare has been popular in South Africa for many years and this is therefore one of the maturer markets. The penetration of eligible households rate is high. Despite that fact, and despite political and economic uncertainty, sales are still being achieved at a reasonable rate, with a turnover of $60 million in 1993.

The image of the industry has improved markedly since the introduction by the self-regulatory Timeshare Institute of South Africa (TISA) of a five-day cooling-off period which came into force on 7 October 1992. This has had the effect of reducing the level of presure by sales people on consumers without affecting sales dramatically.

New resort development is now slow. RCI affiliated five new timeshare resorts in 1993 and expects a similar trend to continue during the first half of 1994 when a number of new developments are expected to come on-stream., particularly in the area of the Western Cape, where demand exceeds supply some two and a half times over. Latin America

Having spread to Mexico in the mid 1970s, as American holidaymakers in Mexican resorts proved willing buyers, timeshare in Central and South America is at last taking off in a number of countries. Mexicans themselves have discovered the concept, to the extent that some 125000 Mexican families are owners. About 50% of the available tourist beds in Cancun are now time-shared and the Mexican Ministry of Tourism has recognised timeshare as an important contributor to the national economy.

As buying power recovers in the rest of South America, its sheer size means huge openings for timeshare. By the end of 1992, Latin America had nearly 500 timeshare projects, with significant developments in Argentina, Venezuela, Brazil and Chile. The development curve is currently much steeper than in the early years: Venezuela has developed 60 timeshare projects in five years while it took Mexico 13 years to reach the same total. Mexico now sells more than 100 000 weeks a year and Venezuela almost quadrupled its annual rate of sales between 1990 and 1992 from 13 000 to 50 000 weeks. There are now timeshare projects in Peru, Costa Rica, Uruguay and Chile and projects are under consideration in Ecuador and Columbia.

The last link in timeshare's global chain of active leisure markets is the Asia Pacific region. This developing region has, since the late 1980s, seen a tremendous growth in leisure spending and tourism, and timeshare ownership and resort development is expected to follow the wave of tourism growth as it has in other markets.

The market for timeshare in Asia is still very new, but many feel it is ready to grow rapidly as one of the 'hot' new timeshare markets for the future. Timeshare resort growth (outside of Japan and Australia) will have doubled annually during the last two years as demand for resorts in or close to key urban destinations, such as Singapore, Bangkok and Hong Kong, or well-established holiday locations, such as Bali, is being driven by both existing timeshare owners in Europe, the Americas, Japan and Australia and the growing affluence of indigenous travellers.

Unlike the other markets of the world, Asia Pacific is already seeing more sophisticated companies and hotels participating during the early growth stages. On the other hand, the condominium developer is still able to sell all he can build in a very active and speculative real-estate market. The growing middle class in east and south Asia will continue to fuel this region for many years to conic.

Australia, which led timeshare growth through the 1980s is currently showing little progress on account of the recession there and high administrative costs related to strict regulation. Australian developers and industry specialists are looking towards Indonesia as a new frontier and catalyst for timeshare growth in Bali and Jakarta.

India is potentially one of the world's biggest timeshare markets, since some 20 million households have been identified as eligible buyers. In addition, it is expected that a number of nonresident Indians, such as those living in the Gulf area, Europe and the USA, will be interested in buying timeshare in their home country.

India's first timeshare resort was opened at Kodaïkanal in 1988, by Sterling Holiday Resorts Ltd of Madras. The same company now has nine resorts with eight more planned by 1995. In the past year, around 10 12 new companies have emerged in various parts of the country. Those wishing to enter the holiday timeshare market include some wellknown names in the Indian business world, such as Oberoi hotels and Mahindra Holdings.

A fundamental justification of the planned growth of the tourism industry is its ability to stimulate local economies. This objective is especially true of the timeshare industry.

The World Tourism Organisation and many national tourism organisations around the world recognise the contribution which timeshare is making to the tourism economy of many countries. The benefits of timeshare have been acknowledged by the National tourist bodies of Spain, Portugal, Greece and France. In addition, the head of tourism at the European Commission has publicly demonstrated his support for the industry, recognising how timeshare helps to meet the objectives of his unit in terms of quality of tourism, extension of the traditional season and the higher economic stimulus compared to traditional holiday products.

A considerable amount of research has been carried out, all of which demonstrates that timeshare has a positive economic effect in the areas where resorts are developed, creating jobs in both the construction and operational phases of resort building and attracting to the area relatively affluent and high-spending visitors throughout the extended season.

The financial contribution made by timeshare developments to their local economies includes sales of timeshare, maintenance fees, local taxes, the purchase of travel facilities and the payroll on-site. The developments create permanent full and part-time jobs on-site, and temporary jobs are created in the community.

A review of timeshare in Europe, commissioned towards the end of 1993 by the European Timeshare Federation concluded that 700000 European owners of timeshare generate some £3387 million a year in visitor revenue, and that the timeshare industry sustains at least 20000 full-time equivalent jobs in Europe.

A report carried out for the then Canary Islands Timeshare Resorts Association demonstrated clearly the economic benefits of timeshare to the islands, both in terms of expenditure in development of the timeshare units and of expenditure in the islands by timeshare owners. The ıeport showed a total investment in construction of 67273 million pesetas (£373m); in promotion and advertising of 79850 million pesetas (£443m) and a visitor spend of 25 152 million pesetas (£139m).

The report showed that 239550 households purchased timeshare properties in the Canary Islands; the average number of families owning timeshare intervals in each unit was 30 (some would own more than one week). Given that the size of the party using the timeshare interval on each occasion was at least 2.5, that means some 598875 timeshare visitors travelled to the Canary Islands in 1990.

Owners in northern England resorts spend some £714 per annum on their timeshare holiday. From this beginning, Ernst & Young went on to say, around 42000 timeshare holidays ate taken in British resorts annually, generating almost £30 million of visitor expenditure. Applying conventional multipliers, under which one full-time equivalent job is created for every £20000 of expenditure, this implies that timeshare sustains 1500 full-time equivalent jobs in this country. However, this takes no account of the jobs created as a result of the initial injection of spending arising from the purchase price paid for the timeshare unit, which amounted to £6380 on average in the north of England. We estimate that over the past ten years this has added a further 13

400 full-time equivalent jobs which can be associated with British timeshare resorts, and that on current growth trends this figure will increase by a further 3000 jobs a year as a result of new owners buying in new and existing British resorts during the remainder of the decade. On this basis, timeshare would be responsible for supporting up to 50 000 full-time equivalent jobs in Britain by the year 2000.

In California, the timeshare industry generated about 1.2 million room nights of occupancy in 1991, involving about 515 000 occupants; was responsible for 6735 full and part-time jobs and $91500 of expenditures per unit.

The Canadian economy benefits from timeshare to the tune of $124 000 of expenditures per unit and 4872 full and part-time jobs. In Puerto Vallarta, Mexico, a contribution of $241000 of expenditures per unit plus 3950 jobs are attributable to timeshare.

Most timeshare resorts (except in Italy which generally has relatively short summer and winter seasons) sell 50 weeks of timeshare throughout the Year, therefore ensuring visitor levels year-round.

Even if the owner is unable to take up the option of using his week's ownership, or wishes to travel elsewhere, the exchange system, like that operated by RCI, ensures that a timeshare owner from elsewhere will probably come and use the accommodation.

Ragatz Associates' studies of Mexico, California, Hawaii and Canada show that the number of repeat visits made to a destination by timeshare owners is significantly greater than for other forms of holiday.

Within the UK, the even distribution of timeshare occupancy levels exceeds 70%. This compares favourably with serviced accommodation (hotels have barely exceeded 60% in the 1990s) and is much greater than self-catering accommodation (where second-home occupancy rates are around 10-15% per annum).

In the maturer US market, timeshare occupancy rates exceed 85%. These higher occupancy rates are especially beneficial in traditional resort and holiday areas, as opposed to urban locations, because of the reduction in the seasonality of local employment.

The peak season is also extended. Timeshare developments in capital cities can have 100% year-round occupancy levels. In England, 68% of resorts have a peak season running in the five summer months of May to September inclusive; and in Scotland the pattern is the same, with over half of resorts having an additional two and a half months between February and mid-April for skiing.

A study of timeshare-related tourism in Malta shows the effect of timeshare development on the island's tourism statistics, both in terms of increasing visitor numbers and of extending the usual summer high season into a five-month shoulder season, together with an active winter season. Tourist arrivals to the island rose from 746 000 in 1987 to over 1 million in 1992, an increase of 34%, and occupancy levels rose to 70% following the conversion of several of the island's hotels to timeshare.

The same author identifies similar benefits in Mexico where the stay of Mexican hotel visitors in most coastal destinations averages about 3.5 nights and that of foreign visitor four to five nights. Timeshare, with a typical minimum guest's stay of seven nights, produces an extension to the average tourist's stay and the prospect of repeat visits. A further study of Mexico, specifically of

Puerto Vallarta concluded that average occupancy of timeshare accommodation was 75% compared with 46% for the local hotel industry. Similar studies showed occupancy rates in Canada of 80% and in California of 82%.

Improving the quality of accommodation

Timeshare developments are usually built to a higher specification than most other types of tourist accommodation. They are often built in secluded areas and are designed to blend in with the local countryside. Environmentally, one timeshare unit used for 2550 weeks during the year is less damaging than the 1020 holiday homes that would be required to meet the same demand on a whole-ownership basis.

Research shows that consistent quality of accommodation is an important reason for buying and is a factor which is becoming increasingly important to the sophisticated consumer. It has been acknowledged that a timeshare is probably the most expensive item that many families would buy after a house and a car. They therefore expect to receive value for money, often manifested in the quality of the accommodation, the location and setting and the overall facilities.

Timeshare developers, owners' committees and the exchange organisations all have a longterm interest in maintaining the quality of resorts, not only to protect the values of the initial investment but also to ensure ongoing access to the flexibility of the exchange system.

At RCI, requests are matched for holiday exchange accommodation on the basis of the quality of the holiday weeks deposited by the timeshare owner. It is clear that an owner at a top-quality resort will tend to get top-quality exchanges, while owners at more modest resorts would receive exchanges of an equivalent quality.

RCI operates a sophisticated system of customer feedback to monitor the quality of its affiliated resorts and to encourage the pursuit of the highest possible standards.

On returning home from an exchange holiday, RCI's customers (they are 'members' of RCI's holiday club) are asked to complete questionnaires, rating the resort they have just stayed in across a number of key factors: check in/out; hospitality; quality of unit; quality of resort; and housekeeping. All the data is analysed and a set of a monthly ratings derived for each resort affiliated to RCI, These ratings are sent to the resorts for their use in quality control. The company's 'resort recognition programme' results in the conferring of awards—'Gold Crown Resort' or 'Resort of International Distinction'—on those resorts which consistently receive the most positive feedback from RCI members who have stayed there on exchange visits.

Recognising the growth and impact of timeshare, a number of jurisdictions have enacted, or are about to enact, legislation to embrace the timeshare concept.

The entrepreneurial spirit which has done so much to advance the rapid growth of timeshare has also led in certain instances to unacceptable practices, particularly regarding sales and marketing. It is this, rather than any unsatisfactory aspect of the product itself, which has tarnished the name of timeshare in many parts of the world. It is therefore these practices which legislation has sought to tackle in the interest of consumer protection.

The seminal consumer protection legislation was the Florida law, introduced by the State of Florida in 1983 shortly after the timeshare industry became established and used as a model by almost every other US state. This landmark legislation, regarded as draconian, included provision for a mandatory 'cooling-off period' of 14 days, during which the prospective purchaser can cancel the purchase agreement.

In Europe, the picture is mixed according to jurisdiction, with the European Union awaiting, at the time of writing, a directive which will govern the sale of timeshare in all EU countries. The draft directive includes the basic principles of a cooling-off period after purchase and a restriction or ban on the acceptance of cash deposits during the cooling-off period. In the shortterm, the directive when implemented is likely to dampen sales volumes for a while. However, timeshare has proved itself to be an infinitely adaptable business and there can be no doubt that companies will come to terms with the new legislative parameters in the marketplace, provided that the final legislation is reasonable and well-balanced. The current 13 national timeshare trade associations throughout Europe have formed the European Timeshare Federation (ETF) which has been putting the industry's case to the authorities in Brussels.

A further measure which will affect many jurisdictions is planned legislation in the Isle of Man. Many timeshare resorts in Europe selling under the 'club trustee' legal structure, of which there are about 200, are governed by Isle of Man law because the trusts used for this effective consumer protection vehicle are based in the Isle of Man. A new bill expected in autumn 1994 will also incorporate a cooling-off period and a limit on deposits as well as measures relating to the provision of consumer finance. It is likely that the Isle of Man government will keep the provisions of their law in line with those of the EU directive.

Most European countries currently do not have specific laws covering the sale and operation of timeshare. In these jurisdictions, developers, and all of those connected with the industry, find their own ways to reconcile the legal aspects of their projects with any existing laws on the sale of property.

In France, ineffective legislation has tended to stunt the growth of the business to some extent. In Austria, Switzerland and Denmark the law prevents land or property ownership—and therefore timeshare ownership—by nonnationals. The timeshare industry in Denmark is lobbying the government to halt this restriction, which would open up new opportunities for the otherwise stagnant timeshare market. In Austria, a review of this particular piece of legislation also looks likely.

In Spain—a major market for European timeshare resorts sold to a range of nationalities—a draft law to regulate timeshare sales has been in the hands of the Ministry of Tourism for some time, but is unlikely to be passed in advance of the EU directive.

A stringent new Portuguese timeshare law was passed in August 1993. Long and complex, it is aimed both at curbing hard-sell techniques and at dealing with the financial problems of some major Portuguese resorts. Unfortunately, it had the instant effect of severely curtailing timeshare sales. The likely future consequence of this legislation could be to halve the number of new resorts able to undertake timeshare development.

In the UK, a Timeshare Act came into force in October 1992, introducing a mandatory cooling-off period of 14 days—and virtually nothing else. While the industry as a whole acknowledges the need for a cooling-off period to curb the worst excesses of the hard sell, 14 days is thought to be unnecessarily long. The UK Act singularly failed to protect the consumer in any other way, such as by insisting on full disclosure to the purchaser of the exact nature of the timeshare week being purchased.

It is inevitable that the introduction of legislation will put a brake on growth for a period. In some cases, those sales people active in markets which become regulated move out and go elsewhere; Eastern Europe, for example, currently provides rich pastures. In other cases, the growth of the timeshare business will slow down considerably. A report for the European Timeshare Federation found that the sales volume in the UK timeshare industry was halved in the first 12 months after the introduction of the Timeshare Act, with cancellation rates increasing two to threefold and only a handful of the previous 60 off-site sales offices still doing business.

Despite certain misgivings concerning the effect of legislation in Europe in the short term, there is no significant factor in sight which would seriously dampen the growth of timeshare sales on a global basis within the foreseeable future. The significance of the timeshare industry is increasing rapidly and the trend is set to continue around the world. In the next few years, analysts believe that timeshare may grow up to 10 times faster than the tourism industry as a whole.

A report carried out in the UK for RCI identified a number of socioeconomic trends, including trends in the pattern of holiday-taking, which bode well for the future of timeshare. The report forecasts a modest recovery of consumer spending in the 1990s, with spending on leisure likely to grow slightly faster than consumer spending as a whole. A more numerous, active and affluent group of people aged 45-plus will also have the advantage of being the first generation to benefit in any general sense from inheritances resulting from the fact that their parents were property owners.

Furthermore, the report points out that holidaymakers will be taking more initiative in organising their holidays, seeking more excitement as well as benefiting from longer holiday entitlement,

In 1990, Projection 2000 forecast continuing growth for timeshare in the late 1990s, stimulated by more frequent holiday-taking, the maturity of the exchange mechanism, relatively lower air travel costs and the inheritance factor. The same report recognised vast untapped potential across Europe.

RCI has a longer list than ever before of timeshare developers wanting to affiliate new resorts to its exchange programme. A number of untapped markets are emerging within which timeshare is burgeoning: Israel and the Middle East, Eastern European countries, India, South America, the Far East and South-East Asia.

Even within established markets there is astonishing potential for future business. Joachimsthaler's study earmarked Germany as one of Europe's most important markets. Predicting a penetration rate of 5% of all German households likely to be interested in owning timeshare, Joachimsthaler estimates that 573 000 households will have bought timeshare in the next 20 years, equivalent to a market value of more than 11 billion DM. In the short term, recession and the economic problems associated with German reunification have meant that the rate of growth has slowed over the past year. Nevertheless, the longterm outlook for Germany remains strong. Economic difficulties aside, reunification has significantly increased the total potential.

Growth in France will be slower but still significant, with an estimated 260 000 new French owners likely to buy timeshare over a 20-year period.

The UK market is expected to be worth some £385 million per annum in new sales by 1997. The growth of various European markets means that the dominance of the UK is gradually declining as the business matures and growth becomes slower while other markets in Europe catch up.

The advent of new products, bringing greater flexibility to the industry, will further increase future business levels. 'Classic' timeshare has to date been handled in one-week fractions. However, with the trend in the holiday market moving more towards short breaks—long weekends and midweek breaks—there is some demand for a system of 'holiday points'. By buying groups of points instead of units of time, timeshare owners are able to decide how many days' holiday to take at any one time, and are able to trade up or down in both size of unit and season, by 'spending' more or fewer of the points they have purchased. Points systems have been in place in South Africa since 1987, operating a variety of flexi-swap, repackaged weeks, multi-ownership and resort ownership systems.

Such systems will lend themselves particularly well to hotel groups, several of which have already been mentioned. There is no doubt that the entry of these well-established companies into the timeshare business is important both for the image of timeshare and for future timeshare development.

It is very likely that several other major hospitality companies will enter the timeshare business in the next five years. Nor is there any doubt that these international companies will extend their timeshare product to other parts of the world in due course.

Further prospects are being created as an ever-wider range of companies enter timeshare: banks, financial services companies, industrial conglomerates, media companies and a pension fund are just a few of the sectors which have taken on timeshare interests in the recent past.

The business of timeshare has already proved itself not just resilient to recession but particularly able to adapt to crisis. The flexibility of the business means it can be a source of solutions to problems in other areas. Consequently, many new timeshare developers now entering the business are doing so because they cannot sell their holiday developments for whole ownership or because their hotels are in a distressed state.

Despite worldwide recession, timeshare has proved that there is always a market for the right sort of holiday product, especially since there is a growing tendency in the mind of the customer to regard holidays not as a luxury but as a necessity.

The one fact which is likely to restrict growth in Europe in the short term is the advent of new legislation in the European Union. But there is little doubt that the industry will adapt to the new climate and will forge ahead after a period of readjustment.

In other parts of the world, the possibilities are virtually endless. Timeshare is clearly a force which is changing the way many people plan their holidays. It is improving the quality of holidays and therefore increasing consumers' expectations. As it continues to grow, so the influence of this extraordinary business on the rest of tourism will increasingly be felt.

6

Tourism—the Next Generation

The term 'virtual reality' (VR) was first coined by Myron Krueger in the mid-1970s to describe a theoretical approach to understanding the human/computer interface.

Today, the VR concept has emerged and stands as the vanguard of a new technological revolution. Describing VR, Kuffel observed, Virtual reality grabs your imagination by the throat. This is the final frontier for silicone junkies, a place which never existed and yet there it is right in front of you—and behind, below and above. This is the looking glass through which Alice fell'. Whether creating new worlds, or recreating 'real world' environments, VR technology is likely to have a major impact on the future tourism industry. It may potentially redefine the nature of tourism as we understand it today.

Technology has already had a dynamic effect on the tourism industry. For example, computer systems were installed in many tourism operations, with their main function being to support the frontline staff in carrying out their jobs. These systems were designed to make improvements in clerical and administrative efficiency, and as Gamble noted, 'the only difference being that they [computers] work at electronic speeds'. These early systems focused on the main data-processing functions, such as input, storage, and retrieval of large amounts of information. Consequently, these systems became prominent in reservation departments and accounting offices, where there was a large amount of data to be processed. Despite the technology playing an essentially passive role, operators gained substantial improvements in efficiency and in many cases this resulted in competitive advantage over other tourism suppliers.

As the price of technology has fallen, and the processing power of computers has improved, the relative competitive advantages have been slowly diminished. Consequently, suppliers have looked to new technological developments to maintain their position in the market. A new generation of systems have evolved, which are now playing a more significant role in operations and management of the whole tourism industry than their predecessors. The position of computer systems has changed from playing a largely passive and supporting role, to a more strategic and proactive role.

The central focus of present and future technology developments lies within communication systems. Computerised reservation systems (CRS) which were instigated by the airlines, now provide many tourism suppliers with an increasingly global distribution of their products and services. In fact, it is argued that the dramatic impact of CRS is actually redefining the marketing and distribution channels of tourism products and services. In many cases the early investment in CRS created substantial competitive advantages for the owners of the CRS. In the case of American Airlines, through its CRS system (SABRE), it has created such a large competitive advantage, that the CRS division now generates more profit for the company than the airline division.

Poon also highlights that the tourism industry is impacted by a complex system of information technologies (SIT). She points out that the SIT affects four components of the tourism system; these are the delivery of tourism services, the management of tourism, the marketing of tourism, and producer /consumer relationships. It can thus be deduced, that the whole tourism industry is, in some way, affected by, or entirely dependent on, developments in information technology. Williams goes further by suggesting that information technology is the dependent factor for business survival in the tourism industry of the future.

As communication technologies continue to evolve, there will be growing impacts from technology on different sectors of the tourism industry. Developments such as artificial intelligence, electronic data interchange (EDI), and ISDN technologies are likely to play key roles in shaping the future tourism industry. For example, ISDN technology is creating some exciting opportunities with the ability to transmit graphics and digitised images (video images) over long distances. The major CRS companies are already investing in and researching into the potential of ISDN. American Airlines' SABREVISION, has started an initiative in this direction, by combining the pictures and video images of destinations, with the availability and price information of the CRS. Other CRS companies are sure to follow this latest development.

Obviously, the continued pace of rapid technological change creates a dilemma for operators and suppliers. While, on the one hand, it creates new opportunities, on the other hand, it makes existing technologies obsolete, which creates investment and cost difficulties. The potential competitive advantages gained may be short-lived, or even nonexistent, which then questions the need to invest at all. However, Shafer makes some relevant observations. To many tourism professionals the past seems immaterial and the present obsolete. Technology—

in the form of new innovations, information, techniques, procedures, and/or equipment—has accelerated the pace of change within the tourism industry to the point where the future seems to arrive faster every day'. Thus, it is clear that advanced technologies have become an integral part of the tourism industry, and will play an increasingly prominent role in the future.

Despite the recession in the Western industrialised countries and Japan, international tourism is still growing at a faster rate than international economic growth. Between 1970 and 1990 tourism grew by nearly 300% and it is expected to grow by half as much again by the end of the century. In 1991, 450 million tourists travelled internationally; but this only represents 8% of the world's population. Looking at the world in population terms, in 1992 the world's population stood at 5.4 billion people. It is expected to grow to 7.1 billion by 2010, and 8.5 billion by the year 2025. Most of this population growth will be in Asia, and it is estimated that Asia will represent 60% of the world population by the end of the century. Asia is also the fastest-growing economic region of the world. As Andrews pointed out, 'By almost every yardstick Asia has become home to the most impressive economic growth in history'. With such economic growth predicted, tourism is set to enjoy further increases. In east Asia and the Pacific, tourism growth is already surging, with tourism arrivals there growing by 8.2% in 1992, well above the world average. It has been noted by some observers that it is not beyond the realm of possibility that by 2010, China's travel market could be larger than the USA. Meanwhile, with the recession failing to dampen the demand for travel in the developed industrialised countries, the tourism industry seems well placed to take advantage of the economic upswing. The future longterm growth of the tourism industry, from a demand point of view, looks promising.

The developments of new transport technologies have allowed us to travel further, faster. Each new technological breakthrough, has allowed us to make another leap forward in our travel patterns. However, it is already clear that the world's tourism infrastructure is being increasingly stretched and overloaded. As Cleverdon observed, 'the scale of growth in tourism will place great pressure on the facilities and amenities required by tourists'. Currently, many countries are facing large budget deficits, and the sheer scale of the required infrastructure projects is becoming too' financially daunting.

Whether it is in industrialised countries, or in developing third world countries, traffic congestion appears to be a worsening problem. Furthermore, with the majority of European and American airports already reporting congestion problems, and forecasting even more difficulties in the coming decades, long-distance travel may already be losing its allure. As the main generating tourism markets are becoming increasingly sophisticated and demanding, potential tourists are already looking at alternatives to long-distance travel.

It may not be surprising to see, that alternatives to the 'actual' travel experience already exist—for example, substitute and surrogate tourism. Substitute tourism has existed for some time and can be defined as where 'one destination takes the place of another destination'. For example, The English Riviera concept was created and marketed by the Great Western Railway (GWR), to offer a British substitute to its continental rivals in France and Italy. Similarly, Montreal in Quebec, Canada, has marketed itself as a French-speaking substitute destination to Americans, who are unwilling or unable to travel all the way to France.

Surrogate tourism on the other hand, can be defined

as, 'a whole travel experience, where tourists make trips to imitations of actual destinations or to fictitiously created places or events'. For example, Disney's EPCOT offers an imitation of the Eiffel Tower in Paris, and it also offers created experiences such as its 'Star Tours' to outer space.

Predicting the future, Anthony Smith, President of Magdalen College, Oxford, sees two parallel trends of opposite kinds that are converging to impact leisure and entertainment, and consequently the tourism industry. On the other hand, the development of largescale public events with impressive venues and media aided by technology that can deliver convincing representations of historical, contemporary or fantasy events. On the other hand, he saw people demanding more choice, and becoming more comfortable with interactions with technology. He observed that,

> If you attempt to link these two tendencies—the public spectacle and the capacity for individual choice—you arrive at a medium of dial-up virtual techniques to gain access to an intangible but wholly enthralling experience, giving the solitary individual the feeling of being present at a spectacle in the illusory company of a large number of others. Somewhere in Japan you may be sure that someone is thinking hard about VOD (video on demand) and VR (virtual reality).

VR or cyberspace as some prefer to call it, has become a recent 'buzzword' amongst computer technology academics and industry practitioners alike. It has been identified as one of the most exciting technological developments of the future, where different experiences can be created through the use of computer-mediated imaging and graphical environments. Potentially, there are an infinite number of 'experiences' which VR technology can create. Recent literature on VR has discussed the many implications of the VR experiences for the psychological and sociological impacts on human behaviour.

Early developments in VR were closely linked to the film and entertainment industries, especially the computer and video games market. Film distributors and producers have experimented with various imagining technologies in the quest to offer the 'complete' or 'whole' experience for consumers of entertainment. Advances such as 3-D glasses, sound and high-quality imaging technology within cinemas have emerged and production teams have recently created some amazing computer-generated graphics and special effects in movies such as *Star Wars* and *Jurassic Park.*

VR will provide an experience which is beyond the normal capabilities of an individual. It will enable participants to enter computer-generated environments that offer three-dimensional perspectives through the use of sound, sight and touch technology. VR uses a selection of different hardware and software technologies to create the simulated experiences which the participant actually believes are in fact real. For example, participants will soon be able to enjoy the VR experiences such as flying an F-16 jet fighter, or playing a round of golf at St Andrews, all within a realistic, but simulated environment.

Although there are many questions which remain to be answered about VR, there are several features which can be clarified. Firstly, a VR experience is a simulation, it is not 'real', but for authenticity and immersion it should look or feel 'real'. Caneday notes that VR is oxymoronic, that something must be virtual or real but not both. This raises some interesting philosophical questions, such as what is and what is not a 'real' experience in this world? However, these are questions beyond the scope of this chapter. Heim argues that human imagination is the key difference between reality and virtual reality, suggesting that, 'virtual reality needs to be not quite real or it will lessen the pull of imagination... which allows us to take what we read or hear and reconstitute the symbolic components into a mental vision'. He also states that, virtual realities may be all the richer for preserving some relationship to a real world without however becoming boring or mundane'. It is this difference between a real experience and a VR experience which is in fact the attraction of VR. Similarly, Walser argues that 'the whole purpose of cyberspace technology is to trick the human senses and sensibilities, to help people believe and sustain an illusion'.

Secondly, VR acts as an interface between human beings and technology. As Kuffel notes, 'much as the Macintosh operating system and now Windows for PCs made computing easier for computer semi-literates, virtual reality has the potential to expand the relationship between humans and computers into three-dimensions'. Spring agrees claiming that 'virtual realities represent a natural evolution of interface design with increasing control of the interface being placed with the computer system'. VR is thus helping to overcome some of the barriers between human uses and applications of technology in the world.

The final important component of VR technology is that it serves as a massive information processor, which creates pictures and visual images of information for users to understand the data being presented. It has been found that 'the human mind can assimilate about 100 bits of information per second from text, but takes in about one billion bits per second merely observing the world. Virtual Reality seeks to open the text bottleneck, by describing complex information visually'. The use of pictures, images, graphics, sound and interactive environments can create much more meaningful information and better understanding for participants.

The technologies involved in producing VR experiences include a combination of visual, audio and kinetic effects. The core of every VR simulation is a large database which stores the relevant data. A powerful computer with a sophisticated graphics capability is then used to create the virtual world, in three dimensions, and presents the data precisely as required.

As technology costs decrease and computer power increases, the development of VR experiences is coming much closer. The quality of computer-generated visual images has improved enormously over the last few years, with graphics, animation and digitised video images having clearer resolutions than ever before. This imaging technology is continuously improving and will play a key role in future VR developments.

The use of high-definition television (HDTV) offers an insight into the quality of computer-generated images of the future. The technical capability of HDTV is 1920 pixels per line for 1000-line resolution. This creates superb quality pictures which, 'have more depth, definition and texture. The colours are richer... it presents imagery so clear it's startling'. HD imagery will have a strong emphasis in the creation of future VR experiences. Similarly, the quality of digitised sound has improved dramatically with compact disc (CD) quality now possible in many computer simulations. As the quality of visual images and sound improves, the degree of immersion and realism in the VR experience will be enhanced.

VR technologies differ considerably from the technologies used in simple computer games and advanced motion pictures, through their interactive capabilities and kinetic effects on the human body. A series of different sensory effects can be created to allow the VR participant to interact with the technology in different ways. Props, such as joysticks and steering columns, have been developed to create realistic kinetic effects. Currently, most VR developments have focused on a variety of head-mounted displays (HMD), which allow a person to look around in a virtual room by simply turning the head. A sensor detects head movement and the direction of the eyes, and the software reconfigures the vision being seen by the participant. As these head-mounted displays evolve, they are becoming increasingly portable and user-friendly. Recent technologies are even more advanced, such as the 'dataglove' and 'datasuit' which are still under development, but will be able to detect movement of the arm and, eventually, whole body movement.

Other VR technology designs have centred on the 'pod'-based enclosed shell. Here, the participant enters into a semi-closed environment, such as a flight simulator, in addition to wearing an HMD. In the future, advances of VR technology may include developments such as sensory floors, which can detect the location and body position of the participant. Another important upcoming development is where multiple participants can share the same VR experience. Maloney notes that consumers want more out of the 'experiences'—group participation, control and intellectual stimulation will be more important than sensory overload. These technologies will create even more realism for the VR experience, which is likely to speed up VR's commercial availability.

Towards a paradigm for the complete virtual reality experience

As technologies have improved, the degree of realism in

VR is even closer to becoming the next best thing to the real experience. However, it is important to isolate the VR experience from the simple simulations and video games, which have so far been developed for the home computer market and amusement arcades. The complete or true VR experience includes several features.

There are several components of the VR visual experience which must be incorporated into the complete VR experience. Spring notes, 'fundamental to much of the virtual reality work is research on visualisation—the animated display of symbolic information in the form of concrete objects and physical relations'.

Rheingold has suggested that interaction in VR is vital to give the feeling of presence. Interactivity, which is based on the degree of control the participant holds in the experience, is probably the key differentiating factor of VR from early gaming simulations. Spring notes that interactivity arises from the naturalness of user involvement and whether it is artificial or natural. The development of kinetic sensors and graphical manipulators have helped to create realism and naturalness in the interactive experience. Heim notes 'the degree of realism is in principle unlimited. This very realism may turn to irrealism where virtual worlds are indistinguishable from real worlds, where virtual reality gets bland and mundane'. Coates argues that at present 'we are able to create and enjoy images, but we are beginning to go beyond images used passively'.

Despite being in the early stages in the development of VR technologies, it is possible to see heavy investment in its future from major companies such as Sega and VP Industries. At this stage, there are seen to be some weaknesses with VR technology, especially with some of the visualisation features, such as graphics quality. However, there is a general optimistic consensus amongst industry practitioners and academics, that the technology is rapidly improving and the true VR experience is likely to be available not too far into the future. VR technology will eventually allow the participant to visit existing environments or, as in the case of 'Alice in Wonderland' stories, create totally new realities and worlds. Looking to the future possibilities of VR, Welter pointed out that VR participants, 'can touch, pick up, and manipulate virtual objects in the computer with their hands. They can fly or ride bicycles in the sky. They can hear cars whizzing by them.... These aren't pie in the sky. The adventures of Alice may no longer be fiction'.

Already applications of VR technology are being touted in the tourism industry. For example, Sega plans to develop 50 theme parks in Japan over the next few years with the aim of 'making its attractions interactive, letting people shoot and steer to give them the incentive to try again'. Similarly, Disney are promising to use VR technology in their proposed historical America Park outside Washington, DC. As Robert Weiss senior vicepresident of Walt Disney Imagineering pointed out, 'We can make you a civil war soldier.... We can make you feel what slavery was like during that period, and what it was like to escape on the underground railroad'.

Looking at the future role of theme parks, Jones and Robinett acknowledged that 'When one looks ahead at the large number of tourists who are expected to travel to new destinations (particularly within the Asia-Pacific region), there will be increasing pressure on sensitive environmental and social resources at the destination'. The tourist system is going to have a more difficult time in meeting these demands. Furthermore, as tourists become more sophisticated and mature, it is arguable that they are becoming more dissatisfied with the full 'actual tourist experience' and are instead opting for the 'surrogate travel' experiences that the 'let's pretend worlds' can offer. As Stipanuk points out, 'the tourism experience is potentially fragile and vulnerable to events which might fracture this experience... tourists wish to have safe and secure experiences'.

As further pressures are placed on the tourism system, it is perhaps likely that tourists will become increasingly disenchanted with the tourism experience because of the gap that often exists between their expectations and reality. Surrogate travel, within the security of some form of location-based entertainment (LBE) centre is one way of ensuring the best tourism experience is 'guaranteed'. Bruce supports this, claiming that 'with the developments in communication technologies it may be that the amount of movement of people will start to decrease. Instead business people may well hold teleconferences, and other potential travellers will take instant trips with audio visual images'.

Once the cost of VR further decreases, it will be possible to enjoy the experience from the comfort and familiarity of the home environment, much as Anthony Smith predicted. As Caneday goes on to point out, it will allow travellers to participate in their fantasies through VR with 'the dream of making worlds, of visiting environments and living inside stories, without leaving the living room'.

7

Tourism Planning and Development

The need for planning arises whenever some rational thinking is required to arrive at a choice among a set of limited means so that certain ends are satisfied especially when the means are substitutable among themselves. In other words planning essentially attempts to allocate scarce resources between different competing uses with a view to maximising output, income and employment and to ensure the balanced growth of different sectors. Such planning may be at an individual level or at a firm level or at an industry level or for the economy as a whole. There are broadly two economic systems prevailing in the economy--*Planned economy* and *market economy*. Planned economy is one in which each production unit (or a firm) uses only the resources of men, material and equipment allocated to it by quota and disposes of its products to persons or firms indicated to it by simple order. On the other hand a market economy is controlled by the forces of market, like demand, supply, prices, transport, etc. Plan can be applied to any type of economic system, whether centrally structured or built up of many units of purely market economy character. The different institutional frameworks will lead to compulsory planning under the first system and to indicative planning under the second.

Planning for tourism

In the field of tourism, the need for planned development is of paramount importance. Many countries in the world especially the developing countries have lately realized the importance of tourism and the benefits which it brings out. The use of macro-economic planning techniques for tourism sector are however relatively new. The planning methods for national economic development which have been largely utilized since the end of the World War II did not always cover tourism development as a particular field. The increasing significance of tourism as a source of income, employment generation, regional development and as a major factor in the balance of payments for many countries has been attracting increasing attention on the part of many governments as well as others with an interest in economic development. Thus, tourism development became more and more a particular field of research in the economic planning undertaken by many countries. As far back as in the year 1962 the Secretary General of the United Nations had declared: "Impressive unanimity has been achieved regarding the potential value of development planning".

The United Nations Conference on International Travel and Tourism held in Rome in 1963 emphasised the need for planning in tourism and made several recommendations. Some of the important recommendations that the United Nations Conferences made in the area of need for development plan in tourism were as follows:

(i) that the governments of developing countries should give high priority to projects concerning the development of tourism in their respective countries;

(ii) that the governments of developing countries should consider the possibility of seeking the assistance of the United Nations Special Fund for Regional and Subregional Surveys of existing and potential tourist resources and for the preparation by experts of tourist traffic estimates and forecasts, with a view to the establishment of short-term and long-term plans for the development of tourist facilities and plant.

The conference endorsed the relevant comments of the Group of Experts who bad pointed out that tourism was expanding swiftly as world economy improved and more and more travellers sought new places to visit. It further stated, that, to the extent permitted by its economic resources, a country should see a steady growth in the number of new tourist resorts developed. Existing possibilities of attracting tourists--mountaineering, winter sports, fishing, hunting, beaches, spas, national parks, game sanctuaries, national monuments, sites and shrines, folk traditions and customs, pilgrimages, festivals and sporting events--should likewise be developed and protected. Stress was laid on the importance of ensuring protection, not only for monuments, archaeological remains and buildings or historical, cultural or architectural importance, but also for the customs, traditions, art and folklore of indigenous peoples. The conference also agreed that a developing country which proposed to set up a national tourist organisation should consider obtaining a preliminary survey in order to assess clearly what positive tourist attractions the country already had, what potential tourist attractions existed, and how they could most effectively be developed within the limits of the funds available.

The recommendations had far-reaching implications as far as planned development of tourism was concerned. All member states and the specialized agencies of the United Nations were called upon to consider and implement as appropriate the recommendations contained in the report of the conference. The recommendations of the conference were of particular interest to those countries which were just beginning to develop tourism. Until quite recently tourism was principally a feature of, and was largely confined to the developed countries. Many of the developing countries saw the possibilities in tourism development. Encouraged by the conference recommendations, many developing countries introduced tourism development programmes.

The United Nations Conference on Trade and Development (UNCTAD) in the year 1965 also emphasised the promise which tourism held out for the developing countries. For some countries, tourism offers a major opportunity since it provides employment for many, it stimulates investment and is an important source of foreign exchange. The third International Union of Official Travel Organisations (IUOTO) Travel Research Seminar held in Prague, Czechoslovakia, in 1964, examined in great detail the many problems involved in the development of tourist industry and concluded that planning whether at national, regional or local level, was indispensable. It concluded that all tourist planning should be based on two types of preliminary surveys: (i) detailed survey of the characteristics of the area being considered for development and, in particular, of its tourist resources; (ii) studies of future customers based on surveys and forecasts.

Careful planning is a prerequisite for complete success of any programme. The haphazard development in many countries had made the planners aware of the need for planning of tourism development based on scientific research. Any country, whether it already has an active flourishing tourist industry or is thinking of developing a tourist industry has to decide on many crucial issues before launching a tourism development programme. The agencies responsible for tourism development have to consider the various issues. The official government agencies especially in the developing countries have to be extra cautious as they cannot afford to waste scarce resources on developmental plans which do not bring benefits. The governments in these countries have to decide on the following issues:

(i) rate of growth of the tourism sector, whether it wishes to encourage mass tourism or develop it more slowly, gradually and selectively;

(ii) the importance of the tourism sector to the national economy and how its development and growth is to fit in with the plans for national, regional and local development;

(iii) the respective roles which it assigns to public and private sector in the development of the industry;

(iv) the respective roles to be played by domestic and foreign capital. Whether the foreign investments are to be encouraged in case the country's financial resources are limited;

(v) decision as to whether the tourist industry should be treated in the same way as other industries or whether the peculiar character of the industry warrants it being given special treatment;

(vi) decision as to whether tourist industry is to be developed on a continuous long-term basis or only as a short-term arrangement to overcome the trade deficit.

The Organisation for Economic Cooperation and Development (OECD) in a seminar held at Estoril, focussed its attention on all the above issues. According to the report "much of the discussion turned on the fact that tourism is by its nature somewhat different from other sectors of the economy, since it is an industry based on movement of people rather than goods. For this reason it is particularly susceptible to subjective considerations quite apart from the play of the economic forces. Political and social pressures, psychological attitudes, changes of fashion may all influence the course of tourism development markedly and unpredictably. It is essential therefore that tourism industry should be as flexible as possible to be able to adapt to changing conditions and requirements". The discussions at the OECD seminar also drew attention to the fact that tourism involves several considerations which are essentially of non-economic nature. The report of the seminar stated: "Tourism often has significant cultural implications (for example, the restoration of ancient monuments); aesthetic (the preservation of beauties of landscape and the safeguarding of the nation's heritage); social (the provision of recreational facilities for the health and welfare of the people); and political (the improvement of international understanding)".

The fact that tourism is by its nature somewhat different from other sectors of the economy makes it more necessary that there should be careful planning. This is much more important for the developing countries which cannot afford to waste scarce resources. The various issues involved in the planning and development of tourism especially in the developing countries show how necessary it is for these countries to adopt growth plans in this specific branch, duly relating to their political and economic institutional framework. Just as a country will adopt a monetary policy, a policy of agriculture, of public works, of health, of transport, etc; as different elements of its national economic plan, so it should on the same grounds, adopt a specific policy of tourism development.

Coordination in planning

The peculiar characteristics of tourism make it particularly beneficial in terms of general economic development. From this follows the necessity of adopting a development policy, which will take into account all the country's economic sectors which have a direct or indirect interest in its expansion, On the other hand, tourism, as an integral part or specific sector of the general plan of economic development, can only prosper within the context of the country's overall progress even though it calls for its own particular policy. Tourism like other economic activities flourishes best when it fits into a context of general economic policies and programmes designed to lead to the optimum growth of the economy of a country as a whole. This calls for coordination. Coordination between tourism planning and the general plan must therefore be based on coordination of effort in all the sectors concerned. Tourism policy must therefore be a global policy of development, taking into account the important implications, affecting the progress of this activity. In addition, the overall tourism development plan must take into account the social and cultural components of the phenomenon, for these also acquire prominence in the development process.

The planning of tourism, whether at the national or the regional level, must be regarded as an integral, and therefore coordinated part of the country's general economic and social planning. This coordinated approach has a direct bearing on the success of the tourism industry, more so in a developing country. It is also to be remembered that tourism is not one business but involves many industries and a whole range of complex processes.

A plan for tourism can only survive and serve its stated purposes, if there is coordination among all the processes. A first requisite is the need to ensure that the government organs specifically responsible for the tourist sector play their important role, which is that of cooperating with all those governmental departments responsible for other branches concerned with the expansion of tourism. The essential aim of the tourist plan is to arrive at a balanced growth of demand and supply. In other words to arrive at an optimum harmonization of the interrelations between the two poles of market, while avoiding the creation of serious economic, territorial or social imbalances. Hence, the basis of planning in a sector must be viewed globally and mutually arranged with country's economic and social development and with the overall policy of planning for the territory in which the location of tourist centres assume primary importance.

The planning process

A process for tourism planning or the subjects of analysis of a plan of tourism development must be correlated with all the elements noted above. in order that they can achieve an optimum level of expansion without creating serious imbalances of various kinds. If a country, region or an area possesses attractions and provides some hospitality for prospective tourists, tourism will probably develop. If this tourism development is to benefit the host area, formal forward-looking planning is essential. If tourism planning is to happen in a specific area. someone or some entity must stimulate and enunciate the original idea. This basic inspiration must be shared by some entity which holds controlling interests and responsibility for the resources to be utilized by the tourism industry. This principle holds true for planning a programme of any scope or dimension. For instance, there may be an existing resort, hotel or industry in a region. The stimulus may be realization that there is potential for growth if only existing facilities can be expanded or new ones generated. At the other extreme, an area may have potential but underdeveloped resources. No matter what the situation, for effective tourism planning, there must be active involvement and participation by persons or entities controlling the essential resources.

A description of various planning processes or analysis of a plan of tourism development is very essential. A description given here can only be briefly indicative and is limited to mere suggestions of the topics or the steps without entering into detailed analysis. The plan must take account of these various processes in quantitative terms, if it is to outline the optimum objectives to be attained in a given period of time. The objectives must be related to those of the overall economic development plan. The key steps, or phases in planning can be as follows: (a) assessment of tourist demand and supply; (b) establishing objectives; (c) territorial planning; (d) basic infrastructure; (e) financial planning; (f) human resource planning; (g) administrative structure; (h), marketing and promotion; (i) monitoring progress; and (j) the time factor.

Assessment of tourist demand and supply

One of the early steps in planning is gathering information on the things the way they are and on the potential available for desirable growth. One of the main problems in investigating the potential of tourism can be the simple lack of information. Recording of information and the development of statistics is therefore of utmost importance. The important initial steps in evaluating a potential for tourism development lies in determining present status. An analysis of the present structure of demand and supply in tourism is a precondition of any other estimate. This information base is a prerequisite for initiating tourism planning programme. In the first place there must be a survey of the tourist attractions of various types which the country has to offer. Without a full study of the attractions a country possesses, it is not possible to plan for future expansion. It is therefore, of fundamental importance that a very careful assessment be made of all attractions--physical, cultural, historical--that a country possesses.

Peters lays down a number of principles on which assessment should be based. First, it is highly desirable that the attractions should be developed progressively throughout the entire country so that tourism. is spread as widely as possible. In this way the benefits which accrue from the industry are also widely spread and most parts of the country benefit. Secondly, areas and attractions which are singled out for special development should appeal to the widest possible cross section of tourists over the longest possible season. By adhering to this principle, overdependence upon a particular season of the year will be avoided. Thirdly, priority should be given to those attractions which can be most easily and most successfully developed. Those attractions which can be based upon the existing infrastructural services should be given priority as these would require less finance. Fourthly, since it is very difficult, rather impossible to develop all the potential attractions at the same time, it is important that similar or competing attractions should not be embarked upon until the volume of visitors can justify them. Finally, it is important to know that the tourist is usually looking for something new, he desires new experiences, different environments, new thrills, etc. Any country possessing attractions which are unique or out of the ordinary should attempt to capitalise on these for they are likely to have a great drawing power.

Demand must then be estimated, for both national and foreign tourists. Both internal and external data on tourism activities affecting the area under consideration should be assembled. This task should use published statistics on travel and tourism which are readily available from international and regional organisations. In addition travel and accommodation statistics can be assembled from the region under study. Next the tourist supply must include all the different types of facilities additional to various types of accommodation establishments. Special attention must be given to the seasonal factor, i.e., the annual fluctuations in the demand as related to the country's tourist attractions.

Establishing objectives

The initial data or the information thus gathered should develop a composite picture of what tourism can do for and to a particular area. In order to relate these projected results to a decision on whether to proceed with tourism development, there must be a basis for comparison. This basis is the cumulative set of objectives which should be developed concurrently. Basically, objectives for tourism should be a subset of the overall objectives (either implicit or documented) for nation, the economy, the people and the social structure within an area. There are however, no hard or set rules as to what the objectives should be. In general, however, tourism objectives should deal with growth leading to increased standard of living, employment levels, opportunities for intellectual growth, enhancement of the investment potential in an area or country. Cumulatively, tourism objectives should describe the set of conditions under which a favourable decision should be made.

If the data indicate that reasonable objectives for tourism development can be met, this will generally lead to a decision to proceed with a conceptual planning study. As a basis for moving ahead with a conceptual planning study, a request for proposal (RFP) should be prepared. This is a detailed description and a set of guidelines for the study which will be used by prospective organisations as a uniform basis for submitting proposals. As a first step towards preparation of conceptual plan for tourism development, a market study and resource analysis should be performed. The market study begins with a determination of the type of tourism business which exists and can be expected. Market study provides the basis for conceptual planning. The conceptual plan provides a general view of the future tourism development programme and the steps necessary to achieve targeted results. The various steps involved in conceptual planning, once the market survey has been performed, include:

(i) Statement of objectives; (ii) Selection of site; (iii) Requirements of various facilities; (iv) Supplementary attractions; (v) Land use allocation and control; (vi) Budgets; and (vii) Legislative requirements.

Preparation of a master plan is another important step in planning. Master planning is a process for completing and detailing additional work on the portions of the conceptual plan which are approved for farther development. The differences between conceptual and master planning lie largely in the level of details involved. Where conceptual planning, for example, might indicate the need to expand airport runways and terminal facilities, master planning would go into specifics oil land and construction.

Territorial planning

The need will arise of locating each pole of tourism development 80 as to fit in with the general policy of territorial planning. Particular attention must be given here to natural and cultural assets of the country, while avoiding the damage which results from an unbalanced exploitation of their economic value.

The need for tourist territorial planning must be reconciled with the limits in pace of industrialisation and urbanisation which, even though complementary to tourism, can constitute a serious danger to it. It will also be necessary to plan further tourism development in the selected zones in order to avoid excessive concentration in one area.

Basic infrastructure

If a tourism development programme is to succeed, it is necessary to provide life support through a number of infrastructural facilities and services. Infrastructure elements comprise the system of services and utilities which are necessary to the operation of a tourism destination. The estimation of the basic infrastructure required for tourist expansion accordingly becomes a key economic factor in proceeding to the active phase of implementation. This infrastructure will be either specifically tourist in nature, e.g., transport, or more general, such as energy producing units, and will in any case vary with the type of tourism envisaged. The requirements for infrastructure will vary for different areas. The requirements for example will be different for a mountain resort and for a tourist pole adjacent to some cultural attraction. The requirements will be for both tourists and local residents. AS various agencies are responsible for development of infrastructure services, coordination is very essential. Without coordination, different elements of infrastructure may infringe upon each other resulting in wasteful expenditure. Specific areas of infrastructure are power, water, communication, sewage and drainage, roads and highways, parks, recreation and health care facilities.

Financial planning

Financial planning is very essential for a successful tourism development plan. Before any major attraction, facility or destination gets into full swing, considerable expenses are involved. There follows the study of a vital element in tourist development, that is, the financing of both infrastructure and superstructure. Assessing the cost of the project is relatively easy when compared to assessing benefits. There may be a choice of locations or a choice of techniques. Estimates must be made for each choice within a feasible range. Each proposal must be assessed separately to establish its feasibility, cost-benefit and degree of priority in making a plan. Agencies concerned with the development of an optional national investment programme should compare investments in tourism facilities and related infrastucture with alternative investment opportunities in other sectors. In World Bank Group Operations, this comparison is attempted on the basis of economic rates of return for defined investment proposals. In evaluating tourism investments the World Bank Group pays very close attention to the projected financial results. In general, tourism projects financed by the World Bank Group are justified in terms of both their economic impact and their financial viability.

In the case of those countries which already possess an active tourist industry or have potential for increased tourism development, finances for investment will usually be available readily. However, in the case or developing countries, which are anxious to develop tourism, due to financial constraints, the provision of adequate resources of capital may be difficult. The development of tourism sector will be only one of the number of options for development before a government, since government resources will inevitably be inadequate for all the competing claims upon them. In view of this the proposed investment in tourism must be justified in terms of its anticipated contribution to the economic development of the country.

Except in centrally planned economies, such as in countries like U.S.S.R., Poland, Yugoslavia, public investment will be suported by private investment as happens in the mixed economies like France, Italy and India. The government may take the initiative in project development, but it will expect private investment support. If the government is anxious to develop and promote an active tourist industry it will help the private investor to the maximum extent. This can be done first, by creating a favourable climate for investment and, second, by assisting private investor to consider tourism development as an attractive investment proposition. This could be done by way of offering special financial inducements such as subsidies, tax concessions, preferential rates of interests, credits, special facilities for purchase of land, etc. All these investment incentives in some form or the other encourage private investment in tourism sector.

In addition to the public and private finance, foreign capital also plays an important role in tourism development programmes. Attention will have to be given to financial means and facilities designed to attract foreign capital. A basic obligation at this stage will be the calculation of the output capital ratio, which will depend for the most part in the external economies which can be achieved. Foreign investment is usually welcomed by many developing countries, largely because of their own acute shortage of capital resources.

Human resource planning

Efficient and professional management is an obvious prerequisite of successful tourism development. Of equal importance, however, is the quality of staff training, which is often relatively neglected during the early stages of tourism sector development. Tourism basically being a service business, a developing destination must take the necessary steps to build a pool of efficiently trained people to fill various jobs which will be created subsequently. A variety of jobs will have to be created to look after and manage various tourist services. Special attention, therefore, will have to be given to needs in manpower and personnel to be trained and rendered qualified for the various tourism professions. Special care has to be taken to ensure that there will be no shortage of trained manpower in case there is expansion of facilities and services. In the case of a developing country, it will also be appropriate to study at this stage the volume of manpower required for activities complementary to accommodation industry, in particular in the commercial sector. In planning for human resources development, programmes should be established to screen and train prospective employees so that they could acquire both attitudinal as well as technical skills. Attitudinal characteristics contribute to an employee's success in tourism position and include pride, flexibility, adaptability and judgement. Technical skills required include facility and equipment operation and maintenance, financial management, food and beverage production and service, personnel management and administration and system analysis and design. In order to determine the need for various personnel required, a staff planning exercise may be done. This involves a series of steps which include job analysis, preparing job descriptions, job specifications and preparing staff forecasts. This sequence of activities leads to a detailed forecast of exactly what types of persons, with what specific qualifications and skills will be required at all major facilities within the tourist destination. All this helps in determining the development of requisite education and training programmes within the country for local residents. This will also help in determining whether there is a need for trained personnel from other countries and also whether local people are to be sent for training elsewhere.

Administrative structure

Next comes the necessity of setting up an adequate administrative organisation to look after various aspects. If a tourism programme is to succeed, the responsibility of success must be assumed by some entity in the form of an organisation. This organisation should have a charter and resources appropriate to carry out various functions. Many countries have established special departments or agencies to manage and coordinate tourism programmes. Depending upon the economic, social and political structure in the country, the tourism organisation may be a governmental department, a semi-governmental agency in the form of corporation supported by government but operating outside its organisational structure. It may also be a private-sector organisation with government support and recognition. Whatever form the tourism organisation takes, it needs to exercise its authority and responsibility in the sphere of tourism development. The administrative organisation looks after both the legal aspects, i.e., the preparation of the legislation required for the installation of the various tourism services, dealing with such matters as the classification of hotels or the control of travel agencies, etc. It has various departments for planning, marketing, research, training, and legal and administrative services.

Tourist marketing and promotion

The final stage of the plan is concerned with the preparation of promotional activities aimed at launching the new tourist industry both within and outside the country. The main concern of tourists is having an enjoyable and pleasant experience rather than details associated with planning their journeys. Most of the tourists leave these details to travel professionals and intermediaries who look after all the details of the travel plans. Contacts with and support of travel professionals and intermediaries are among the most important factors for successful marketing and promotion of tourist destination. Facilities and specialities of travel professionals include national tourist offices, regional travel promotion organisations, airlines including other carriers, tour wholesellers, tour operators, travel agents, travel clubs and convention and conference organisers. The various channels of communication used to inform and stimulate include tourist literature in the form of catalogues, brochures and folders, direct mail, advertising, public relations and publicity. All these media are selected and organised into promotion campaigns aimed at selling to consumers and travel professionals and intermediaries. The media campaigns are timed in such a way that these correspond *with the* selling effort supporting a destination. It is very important to ensure that these activities match the level of tourist development aimed at.

Monitoring progress

Monitoring the progress periodically is very crucial to get the best results. Preparation of a plan document is not an end in itself. The task of the planner does not end when a plan for three years, five, years or seven years has been prepared. A system of constant revision and monitoring of the plan progress should be a part of the exercise of the planning. Targets must be revised continually in the light of changing resources and other circumstances. The error is to mistake a plan for planning. To use a more elegant vocabulary, a plan is static and planning must be dynamic. Plans are interesting mathematical or literary or technical exercises that can be formulated with a great variety of methods and degrees of perfection. Planning on the other hand is a diffuse but coherent process of making and revising decisions that must be closely attuned to the implementation of planned action. What is needed is a system of monitoring progress and mechanisms for constantly and rapidly adjusting to the changing conditions and circumstances.

The time factor

Time factor is a very important element. The main purpose of development planning is to move towards self-sustaining growth; that is to create a cadre of trained manpower, to increase knowledge of natural resources and their effective utilization and to create institutions for enterprising investment. All this takes time. The plan could be for 25 years, 10 years, 7 years or 5 years duration. Many planners are of the view that the first development plan should be a 10-year plan, as it requires an assessment of long-term perspective. Time is a fundamental factor in the preparation of the plan and in the identification of the objectives to be attained upon its termination. The medium-term plan ranges between three and seven years with five years as the most popular choice. The long-term range upwards from 10 years to 25 years. The short-term plan on the other hand is an annual plan. The annual plan is the controlling plan as it is the authorised document to check its possible achievements being matched by available resources year by year. It is governed by medium or long-term plan, which sets its direction, The annual plan is the operative document, while long-term or medium-term plans are merely a set of intentions. Thus the need for orienting the short-term plan budgets with the long-term or medium-term plan budgets is the core of planning process. Time factor is the main element in the planning including planning of tourism in any nation. It is vital to the prospect of achieving the economic and social expansion which is linked with tourism.

Tourism is receiving ever increasing attention from national governments and from international development agencies. It can generate much needed foreign exchange for financing other sectors of the economy of a developing country and also for bridging the trade gap. In its broadest sense, tourism can do more to develop understanding among people, generate employment and raise living standards than any other economic force known There is unlimited potential for tourism development. If properly conceived and executed such development will prove not only to be financially viable but will also prove to be of immense benefit to a country. Inadequate planning and development on the other hand, can increase probabilities of failure, resulting in great loss.

Some degree of planning is very essential. It is perhaps much easier to have planned development in countries where there is a potential which is only just beginning to be realised. However even in those countries having a long established and a highly developed tourist industry, some measure of planning is essential. Planning is essential for three main reasons : first, most countries, to a lesser or greater degree have planned economies and if tourism development is to be a part and parcel of national economic development, then this sector of economy also should be subjected to planning. Secondly, the success of tourism development depends very largely upon appropriate facilities being available in the right place and at the right time and these can only be provided by adequate research into national tourist assets and markets. Research has a very important part io play in the future planning of tourism development. Thirdly, planning is required to ensure that the natural and man-made assets are conserved and protected to maintain tourist appeal, for lack of care and coordinated development may impair and even ruin those assets upon which tourist industry is founded.

Environmental planning

Tourism is the world's largest industry. This fact has now been recognised all over the world. Although a 'smokeless' industry, it has environmental implications. Expanding tourism has the great capacity to pollute the environment as would any smoke-ridden industry. A few years back, the United Nations organised a conference in Stockholm on Human Environment. This conference symbolized the growing importance that the people of the world attach to maintaining and improving the quality of human life and to enrich the human environment. It is a fact that all over the world man has been using the natural resources without any thought of the future. it is the wrong use of these resources which causes problems. Today environmental pollution poses a serious threat to life on earth and this is true not only of the areas where there is a great concentration of industries, but also areas where there is a great concentration of tourists.

The disadvantages of haphazard and unplanned development of tourism are well illustrated by many areas in North America and Western Europe and also to a greater or lesser extent throughout large parts of Asia's tourism circuit. Yugoslavia's Adriatic coast and the Seychelles are other examples. Many of the world's finest resorts have become ugly. Sochi, Russia's popular Black Sea resort, has proclaimed itself the world's first no smoking city.' New laws ban smoking in all restaurants, cinema theatres, public transportation, hospitals and on the beaches. In India there are many examples of uncontrolled growth of industries, shops and also slums near tourist spots creating problems of environmental pollution. Many of the beaches of North America and Western Europe bear a mute testimony to the havoc that can be wrought by uncontrolled development of tourism. Destinations once noted for their particular character are reduced to unattractive show pieces as many countries endeavour to keep pace with the visitor inflow. Despite a measure of governmental control during the development, the great increase in number of visitors to these areas resulted in rapid, unplanned construction of hotels and dwellings for tourists and for migratory service employees. These expansions threatened to destroy the very environment that is the tourist attraction. A prominent leader in the Seychelles objected to seeing his country become a nation of maitres d'hotel." These examples underline environmental threat both aesthetic and biological, from overcrowding of particularly attractive areas.

Tourism development germinates special ecological problems not encountered in other types of economic activity. The environmental resources 'exploited' for tourism attract tourists because of their outstanding beauty, recreational possibilities or educational and cultural interest. The modem tourism's most paradoxical trait is its capacity to destroy those attributes which attracted the visitor in the first place. The well-known economic analyst and futurologist, Herman Kahn, described the rapidly expanding tourism as "... next only to atomic power in its potential for environmental destruction..." Mass tourism has brought in its wake certain ecological and environmental pollution problems.

The environmental amenities which attract tourists have tended to be taken for granted. Preservation of their quality has only recently begun to concern tourism development planner. For tourism the quality of the environment is the basis for attracting visitors and needs to be conserved. Tourism development can become a positive factor for improving, the environment, if certain amount of intelligent basic planning is done. In fact the quality of the tourism product depends upon a high quality natural environment. The inter-relationship was pointed oat by International Union of Official Travel Organisations (IUOTO), predecessor of the World Tourism Organisation, as long ago as the 1950s. It was reiterated during the 1960s in the face of growing interest in environmental conservation.

It has been seen that major social benefits accrue to tourists, themselves. But tourism also has valuable spillover benefits for tourist receiving countries. Notable among these is the contribution of tourism to the preservation of historic sites and cultural values. Careful cleaning and beautifying ancient monuments, clearing the areas around the monuments and improving them, for tourism purposes is a case in point where, through tourism development, the environment is not degraded but in fact can be improved. So great has been the national and international demand for tourism and recreational facilities that governments have increasingly to face up to the choice between extending public access and availability of sites, and conservation and protection against over-development Governments are increasingly aware that future growth of the industry will necessitate careful management and avoiding overdevelopment of regions of natural beauty. Moreover, saturation in principal destination areas will require a more active policy of diversification and redistribution of tourist flows.

Regional planning considerations

The potential of a region for tourism may be so great that its development will be central to economic go Is and plans. However, regional planning for tourism more often will be considered as a separate and distinct planning effort, aimed primarily at determining the best location of facilities like hotels, resort facilities and transportation networks. Such planning views tourism primarily as a source of foreign exchange earnings. This approach would recommend development to accommodate maximum possible number of projected visitors and to design facilities to generate the maximum possible spending by the tourists. However this approach of profit maximising to tourism development can result in deterioration of fragile environment and attractive landscapes through over-building and excessive number of visitors. The aims of conserving the environmental amenities of a region and of advancing regional development through tourism are interdependent. The more local people benefit from tourism the more they will benefit from a commitment to preserve the environmental features which attract tourism. Consideration of the region's ecological characteristics are essential to provide adequate criteria for the development of facilities and viable plans for the use and management of resources for tourism.

In every tourist spot there is a carrying capacity for tourists, as well as for any other type of use, which will vary with the fragility of the area concerned and the nature of the tourist activity contemplated. For example, an island rain-forest is a fragile environment which could be endangered by excessive numbers of people. Enjoyment of such an environment by visitors necessitates a degree or restraint. By contrast a recreational beach is not easily damaged by sun-bathers or swimmers. Planning facilities for tourism development in the first case would require limitations on hotel and similar other installations in the region concerned, in order not to encourage excessive numbers of tourists, whereas in the second case high density accommodations for tourism might well be tolerated. International tourism by definition draws persons from diverse cultures. Regional resource inventories and evaluations for the development of tourism should therefore attempt to take into account diverse recreational preferences. The travel preferences of tourists from different cultures should also be considered in the layout and design of tourist facilities. Particular attention is needed for cultural preferences in the total environment destined for tourism use. Such considerations will again assist in assigning specific values to different landscapes and natural resources.

Of all the modern industries, tourism has the greatest need to protect the environment of the places of natural and cultural importance--be it a monument, a beach resort or a wild life sanctuary. The planners must consider the environmental process wherever large investments are made in tourism development. The tourist has a strong desire to see and experience places of wonder and beauty in areas where nature remains essentially unspoiled. Destinations noted for their particular character and beauty should not be reduced to innocuous urban jungles in order to keep pace with the visitor inflow. Wild life which is deteriorating and vanishing so rapidly can be safeguarded. The environment in which various animals live can be properly preserved. Similarly many other tourist areas can be safeguarded against forces which are responsible for their degeneration. Tourism must be used as a positive factor in environmental improvement.

Physical planning and area development are therefore very essential for environmental improvement. Tourism development can become a positive factor for improving the environment if certain amount of basic planning and aesthetics are applied in the entire process. Whenever there is any major tourism development, environmental planning should be made part of that development. Any development without some controls, without any thought given to the environmental factors can in fact prove to be disastrous and ultimately will be counterproductive for tourism itself.

As many agencies are involved in tourism development, coordination is i therefore very necessary among various segments responsible for environmental development and improvement. With a view to preserve the unique character, atmosphere and natural setting of monuments and other places of tourist interest, a coordinated approach needs to be evolved to exercise environmental control of tourist centres. In countries where there are Town and Country Planning Acts, these should be made effective enough and their provisions should cover legal protection to control environmental balance in tourist and development areas. In order to ensure that the Act is properly enforced, it would be desirable to involve all those agencies which are responsible for tourism development. In countries having federal set up, the authorities responsible for governing should carefully study the impact that the opening of a new area to tourists is likely to have on the cultural and social environment of the area. Master Plan or Area Development Plans should be formulated before permitting the tourists access to these areas. Concerned local authorities should be consulted at the time of working out of the proposals for area development with tourist potential. In order to ensure the implementation of the environmental control, it may be desirable for various regions to appoint coordinating committees consisting of various interests and departments to implement effectively environmental policies.

The United Nations Conference on the Human Environment, held few years back in Stockholm recommended evolving a conservation policy within the framework of the resolution of the 'World Cultural Heritage'. There was a unanimity of opinion that something radical had to be done to save the quality of human life and to enrich human environment. The conference was of the opinion that any development scheme of the particular area should be determined by the absorption capacity of the area, otherwise the environment would deteriorate and may in the long run create more complications than actually serve the purpose. This is true in the case of development of monuments, new tourist areas and resort towns.

A modem concept of conservation is that of science and ecology. The premise is that of man-environmental balance. The only way of striking this balance is to define conservation as protection of natural resources. Conservation means the exercise of rigid controls to prevent habitat destruction, habitat homogenization, reduction of species and natural resources pollution. Conservation, in the sense of preservation of the cultural heritage is popularly supported today. Many man-made artifacts have a scarcity value that becomes as important to society's well being as do the natural resources. Therefore, conservation means their protection, restoration and interpretation.

Today the relationship between tourism and the environment has been receiving a growing level of attention from both public and private sector organisations all over the world. During the last decade various international bodies have cooperated in the production of great number of studies, programmes, plans and activities on tourism and environment. The degree of importance of the relationship between tourism and environment is cited in the Manila Declaration on World Tourism during World Tourism Conference held in Manila in October, 1980. The Declaration states:

> "Tourism resources available in various countries consist at the same time of space, facilities and values. These are resources whose use cannot be left uncontrolled without running the risk of their deterioration, or even destruction. The satisfaction of tourism requirements must not be prejudicial to the social and economic interests of the population in tourist areas, to the fundamental attraction of tourism, and historical and cultural sites. All tourism resources are part of the natural heritage of mankind. National communities and the entire international community must take the necessary steps to ensure their preservation. The conservation of historical, cultural and religious sites represents at all times, and notably in time of conflict, one of the fundamental responsibilities of states."

The importance of the relationship between tourism and the environment is also stressed in the letters of agreement exchanged between the United Nations Environment Programme (UNEP) and the World Tourism Organisation. The letters of agreement state:

> "The protection, development and improvement of the various constituents of the environment of Man are among the basic conditions for the harmonious development of tourism. Similarly, intelligent tourism management can contribute in large measure to the protection and development of the physical environment and cultural heritage of mankind as well as the improvement of the quality of human life. It is therefore, advisable that tourism development and sound environmental management should be integral concerns of national development policies."

WTO environment committee

The growing importance of this subject of tourism's

impact on the environment led the WTO Executive Council to form the Environment Committee. This committee held its first meeting at Madrid in May 1981. The representatives of various countries who attended the meeting attempted to define the relationship between tourism and the environment, and formulate guidelines and activities to be implemented by the World Tourism Organisation in the future in the areas of the environment. Much of the discussion of the Environment, Committee Meeting centred on the theme: "Tourism Development and its effects on the Environment."

Tourism development can bring positive results to the countries that succeed in establishing an effective programme. It is important that the damage which can be done to the environment through a misuse of natural and cultural resources be avoided through the implementation of proper policies. Possible negative effects could then be checked such as: ecological deterioration in areas of good environmental quality, especially in mountain and coastal regions and in areas surrounding places of historical, architectural or artistic interest; speculative pressure on special sectors with the ensuing destruction of the landscape and wastage of natural environment, destruction of the traditional values of the domestic architecture and deterioration in the latter when the human dimensions of existing localities are exceeded; saturation and overcrowding of the urban microcosm with consequent deterioration in the quality of the environment in these areas.

Various positive steps have been taken with a view to preserve the natural environments. In the national and regional tourism plans compiled by World Tourism Organisation there is evidence of one or more of the following aspects receiving attention:

(a) Creation of natural reserves and national parks;

(b) preservation of historical towns;
(c) alignment of roads and highways so as to minimise environmental nuisance;
(d) restrictions on the encroachment of the town into the countryside;
(e) zoning of industry;
(f) restrictions on dumping at sea, inland and in fresh water of household or industrial residues.

The formation of the Environment Committee by WTO Executive Council is the step in the right direction. The Environment Committee has adopted the following goals:

(a) to identify clusters of closely related touristic environmental issues specifically including: carrying capacity, ecosystem solvency, protection of cultural elements, protection of the built environment;
(b) to systematize field information;
(c) to define ways to involve tourists in the preservation of the environment;
(d) to develop and disseminate guidelines for use by governments in assessing, controlling and minimizing adverse environmental effects in tourist activities.

With a view to achieve the above mentioned goals, the Environment Committee recommended a programme of work that includes the evaluation and updating of existing studies and methodology and the general understanding of touristic environmental problems, cooperation between public and private institutions at the national and international levels aimed at developing touristic environmental guidelines and standards and finally, action by WTO and other international organisations to apply guidelines.

8

International Tourism

The growth and development of any discipline depends to a large extent on the manner in which it associates itself with those pursuing similar disciplines. The world bodies or the international organisations provide a platform where ideas are exchanged and problems of mutual interest discussed. The subject specialists of various disciplines *be it* arts, science, commerce, etc., meet together on a common platform and discuss areas of mutual interest. This results in growth, development and promotion of the discipline. For any industry or discipline to develop, an organisation is an essential prerequisite as it plays a vital role in its proper planning, development and growth. Organisation consists of individuals whose primary role is the achievement of the objectives for which it has been set up. The aim of the organisation is to deploy staff into working groups, associating those with similar functions or purposes so as to move efficiently to obtain a desired result from their combined effort. In other words, organisation means combination of a group of individuals whose main purpose is to achieve through group action the objectives for which it has been set up.

Association of an organisation with a particular discipline with similar such organisations becomes a combined effort to develop the discipline. This association can be at various levels--local, regional, national and international. The international tourism organisations emerged with the objective of developing and promoting the subject of tourism. The role of international tourism organisations in strengthening tourism by way of combined efforts is therefore of vital importance.

The increasingly international character of modem tourism and the growing influence of international agencies in various fields are reflected in the growth and development of international cooperation and organisation in tourism. Organisers, and the providers of various tourist services whether in private or public sector come together at various forums at the international level to discuss and share common problems and arrive at certain conclusions. The providers of tourist services sometimes meet as individuals or as individual firms, but more often when their national sectoral organisation is a member of a particular international body which has been set up for general or specific purposes.

There are numerous international organisations existing today. Some of these organisations are specifically concerned with development and promotion of tourism at the international level while others deal wich the development and promotion of tourism in a particular region. There are other international organisations which do not concern themselves specifically with tourism but with fields indirectly connected with tourism like airlines, travel agents and the hoteliers.

Early history of cooperative endeavour

The history of cooperative endeavour in tourism can be traced back to the year 1908. Three countries--France, Spain and Portugal felt the need of pooling their resources in the interest of promoting tourism and founded the 'Franco Hispano-Portuguese Federation of Tourist Association'. This might perhaps be considered as the first international tourist organisation. Although started in a modest way and limited to a small region in Europe, this association made a beginning in cooperative endeavour in the field of tourism and paved the way for future such endeavours on a very large scale.

The need for international collaboration in the field of tourism found favour with many countries in the years following World War I. This need found its expression in setting up in the year 1924 of the 'International Union of Official Organisations for Tourist Propaganda'. The first congress of the Organisation was held at The Hague, Holland, in 1925, and, was attended by delegates from national tourist organisations of fourteen European countries. The aims of this congress were to exchange information on tourist publicity, to obtain international customs concessions for the export and import of tourist publicity material and to alleviate frontier formalities or other obstacles to free international tourist traffic. This organisation functioned with a considerable degree of success until the eve of the last World War. The International Union of Official Organisations for Tourist Propaganda was the forerunner of the International Union of Official Travel Organisation. In the year 1946, the representatives of various national tourist organisations met in London and the following year, in 1947, the International Union of Official Travel Organisations (IUOTO) was founded.

Although cooperative endeavour in the field of tourism began as early as in the year 1908 and the international organisation formed in the year 1924, the vital encouragement however, came from the United Nations in the year 1963. The importance of the work of the international organisations in the field of tourism was recognised by the United Nations Conference on International Travel and Tourism held in Rome in the year 1963. The conference recommended that "the United Nations should consider the International Union of Official Travel Organisations (IUOTO) as its main instrument for the promotion of tourism". The encouragement given by the United Nations to IUOTO paved the way for greater cooperation at international level in the field of tourism. India's first contact with the international tourism organisations was, however, established in the year 1950 when it joined the International Union of Official Travel Organisations.

International union of official travel organisations

It was in 1925 that the international cooperation in tourism development' had its beginning. The growth of international tourism in the 'twenties, and the consequent need for cooperation between national tourist bodies, led to the holding of an international conference in 1925 called by the National tourist Office of Holland. Representatives of fourteen countries took part in the conference. Further conferences led to the setting up of the International Union of National Tourist Propaganda Organisations (IUNTPO) at The Hague. This body sought to promote facilitation and overcome the obstacles to free international tourist traffic; such obstacles having come about as a result of the 191418 World War. IUNTPO, whose general aims were more streamlined than its title, established close contact with the Economic Committee of the Old League of Nations.

With the advent of the second World War, IUNTPO had to discontinue its practical activities. It was with the object of contributing to postwar reconstruction that one of its members, the Travel Association of Great Britain and Northern Ireland, decided in the spring of 1964 to call a World Conference of National Tourist

Organisations to discuss the restoration and reconstruction of travel facilitation destroyed by the war. The conference took place in London in October 1946 and the following year, in 1947, International Union of Official Travel Organisations (IUOTO) was founded. The Organisation represented over one hundred national tourist offices of various countries as full members and about eighty-eight national and international organisations, of both public and private sector, as associate members. It was at that time the only organisation whose activities related to every aspect of tourism throughout the world. One of its major tasks was the stimulation and coordination of tourism development. The category of full members was restricted to national tourist organisations or other organisations set up to promote the development of tourism established or recognised by the governments of the countries. The category of associate members was confined to international or national organisations, either commercial or noncommercial, representing tourist interest or interested in promotion of tourism.

The IUOTO was the only international organisation which grouped together the governmental or official tourist organisations of all parts of the world on the basis of one for each country and territory. The principal aim of the organisation was to stimulate and increase the free flow of persons in the interest of economic development and to strengthen social and cultural relations. This it tried to do by way of resolving the problems arising in the field of tourist movements and in the adoption of a common policy amongst the members for all questions dealing with international travel. The organisation tried in various ways, to develop the tourist industry in the member countries, and particularly by promoting measures on a national as well as on an international level aimed at reducing travel barriers and stimulating the movement of travellers.

A technical and specialised organisation, IUOTO was granted consultative status by the United Nations. The supreme body of the IUOTO was the General Assembly which held its meeting once a year. It had various committees and commissions which were assigned different subjects. The executive committee consisted of full members, while the Regional Commissions covered specific areas. The technical commissions aimed at examining all problems on a universal scale. The Secretariat General, whose headquarters were located at Geneva in Switzerland, was responsible for ensuring liaison between the members.

The general assembly

The General Assembly which consisted of full and associate members, was a sovereign body of the IUOTO. It met once a year. It elected the President and the Vice-President of the IUOTO, the members of the executive committee and the Auditors and decided upon the applications for new membership. Laying down general policy of the organisation and the actions to be carried out was another important function of the General Assembly.

The executive committee

The Executive Committee consisted of eighteen full members, representing the various geographical areas and, in an ex-officio capacity, the presidents of the Regional and Technical Commissions. Presided over by the President of the IUOTO and assisted by the Vice-Presidents, the Executive Committee was responsible to the General Assembly for the direction of the affairs of the IUOTO.

Regional commissions

Following Regional Commissions were created by the IUOTO:

(a) *The Regional Travel Commission for Europe* included the countries of western and eastern Europe. The countries of Western Europe were also grouped in the European Travel Commission which was an independent body responsible in particular for the collective publicity campaigns carried out in the United States of America.

(b) *The African Travel* Commission was responsible for tourism in African areas which had vast possibilities for growth.

(c) *The Regional Travel Commission for the Pacific and Fast* Asia. The members of this Commission were also members of the Pacific Area Travel Association (PATA) which had accepted to act as the regional commission for the Pacific and the East Asian areas.

(d) *The South Asian Travel Commission* was responsible for developing modern travel facilities in a very extensive area which had become travel conscious.

(e) *The Middle-East Travel Commission* was responsible for developing travel facilities in the Area. It had also created subcommissions of the Arab and non-Arab countries.

(f) *The Regional Travel Commission for the Americas* was created following the acceptance of the Inter-American Travel Congress to act as regional travel commission of the IUOTO for the American continent as a whole.

Technical committees

IUOTO had the following technical committees:

(1) *Committee on the Elimination of Travel Barriers* was concerned with the easing up of passport and visa requirements, frontier formalities including restrictions on the free circulation of publicity material, health regulations, taxes borne directly or indirectly by the tourists and tourist industry, currency controls, and other matters which slow down travel.

(2) *Research Committee* was charged with studying international travel statistics as well as carrying out other special studies with the assistance of the Advisory Committee.

(3) *Travel Plant Committee* was responsible for studies on hotels as well as motels, hotel accommodation and classification, standardization of hotel guides, state aid to the hotel industry, the training of hotel personnel and additional means of accommodation.

(4) *Committee on Travel Development* offered assistance to member countries in the field of travel, counselled national tourist offices *on* publicity activities, dealt with social tourism and youth and credit travel. The Committee also dealt with travel films, which came to be regarded as one of the most important means of tourist publicity.

(5) *Transport Committee* was responsible for examining the existing conditions in the field of rail, road, sea and air transportation and suggesting better facilities and improvements. It studied and recommended measures to improve the conditions and facilities available at airports, seaports *and* land frontier entry points.

The secretariat general

The Secretariat General which was located in Geneva was

the principal executive body for the decisions of the Assembly and the Executive Committee as well as the Presidency. It ensured the liaison between the members of the IUOTO, carried out the studies entrusted to it by the IUOTO members and was charged with the administration. It maintained contact with other international organisations. It produced various IUOTO publications and ensured the functioning of the Tourist Documentation Centre.

IUOTO had closer cooperation with the United Nations Economic and Social Council (ECOSOC), the World Health Organisation (WHO), the International Labour Organisation (ILO), the International Civil Aviation Organisation (ICAO) and the Inter Governmental Maritime Consultative Organisation (IMCO). It also had permanent links with the regional commissions of the United Nations.

The Organisation was set up with the following objectives:

(i) *To promote* the economic development of countries through tourism.

(ii) *To enhance* the social and cultural role of tourism in the life of nations.

(iii) To further the vital contribution of tourism to international trade.

(iv) To foster the steady expansion of international tourist flow.

(v) To supply its members with the results of the permanent tourist market research to enable them to keep abreast of development in this field.

(vi) *To protect* the interests of tourists and the tourist industry.

(vii) To gain recognition of the value of tourism as a means of prompting international understanding and world peace.

In order to achieve its objectives the organisation undertook various activities like monitoring and identifying trends in world tourism, studies on travel demands, market trends, tourist motivation, surveys of environmental effects of travel expansion and formulation of recommendations for the protection of natural and cultural resources. Other activities included acting as clearing house for tourist information, keeping its members informed of tourism development and its economic and social, aspects, publication of material, fostering research in the field of tourism, organising vocational training programmes and promoting the implementation of international agreements.

IUOTO's dynamic activities resulted in countless significant achievements. Some of the achievements were undertaken jointly with other organisations. These included preparation and participation in the United Nations on Customs Facilities and Tourism, initiation, preparation and participation in the United Nations Conference on International Travel and Tourism in Rome and initiation and realization of International Tourist Year. Besides establishing the Tourist Documentation Centre, the IUOTO has been responsible for organising various international travel research seminars and workshops. Another significant achievement of IUOTO has been the establishment of the International Centre for Advanced Tourism Studies at Turin, Italy and organisation of interdepartmental or specialized seminars on marketing, management, physical planning and promotion. It had also organized correspondence courses for the staff working in the field of tourism. Annual compilation and publication of official international travel statistics is yet another significant achievement of the IUOTO.

The IUOTO was the only non-governmental organisation whose activities covered every sector of tourism throughout the world. The organisation made a pioneering effort in the stimulation and coordination of tourism development at the international level. This pioneering task of the organisation is now being carried out by the World Tourism Organisation. The World Tourism Organisation came into existence as a result of the transformation of IUOTO on January 2, 1975. It was called upon to succeed IUOTO.

India joined the International Union of Official Travel Organisations in the year 1950.

World tourism organisation

The World Tourism Organisation (WTO), an inter-governmental technical body dealing with all aspects of tourism, began its legal existence on January 2, 1975. It was born of the International Union of Official Travel Organisation (IUOTO). The swift expansion of travel had created the need for a world body able to deal with tourism problems at the government level, and this led to the transformation of IUOTO into WTO.

Like its predecessor (IUOTO), the WTO has a very emphatic technical character, essentially creative and dynamic, performing a well defined service for its member states. The aims of the organisation, its *raison d'etre,* are defined with clarity in Article 3 of the statute which is divided into three sections:

(i) The fundamental aim of the Organisation shall be the promotion and development or tourism with a view to contributing to economic development, international understanding, peace, prosperity, and universal respect for, and observance of, human rights and fundamental freedoms for all without distinction to either race, sex, language or religion. The Organisation shall take all appropriate action to attain this objective.

(ii) In pursuing this aim, the Organisation shall pay particular attention to the interests of the developing countries in the field or tourism.

(iii) In order to establish its central role in the field of tourism, the Organisation shall establish and maintain effective collaboration with the appropriate organs of the United Nations and its specialised agencies. In this connection the Organisation shall seek a cooperative relationship with and participation in the activities of the United Nations Development Programme, as a participating and executing agency.

The World Tourism Organisation was originally conceived as an inter-governmental organisation in a UN General Assembly resolution--Number 2529--on December 5, 1969. This resolution called for establishment of WTO to play a "central and decisive role" in the field of tourism and to maintain effective collaboration with the appropriate organs of the United Nations and its specialised agencies.

At Torremolinos, in June 1977, the second General Assembly of WTO approved an Agreement with the United Nations for Cooperation and Relationships. On December 20, 1977 the 32nd General Assembly of the UN approved this Agreement which is now in force. In immediate implementation of this Agreement, the UN General Assembly in December 1977 a so approved a resolution sponsored by the Philippines with 24 cosponsors, including India, requesting the WTO "to intensify its efforts to promote tourism, particularly in developing countries, through international cooperation and to report to the General Assembly at its 33rd session on action taken". The WTO became an executing agency of the UNDP in May 1976. A few months later, UNDP Resident Representatives throughout the world became WTO representatives for all matters concerning technical cooperation in the field or tourism. The WTO has already completed its first project in Jordan and is now processing many more requests from member states, including Asian members, for both national and regional assistance programmes and projects.

There are three categories of members: full members, associate members, affiliate members. Full members are the sovereign states. Associate members are the territories or groups of territories not responsible for their external relations but whose membership is approved by the state assuming responsibility for their external relations. Affiliate members are international bodies, both inter-governmental and nongovernmental concerned with specialised interests in tourism, as well as commercial and noncommercial bodies and associations whose activities are related to the aims of WTO.

The activities of the organisation include: (i) clearing house for all available information on international and domestic tourism including statistical data, legislation and regulation and special events and its systematic collection, analysis and dissemination; (ii) making travel easier by reducing and simplifying frontier formalities and removing barriers to the free movement of tourists; (iii) organising and convening international conferences, seminars, round tables and technical meetings oil all aspects of tourism; (iv) preparation of draft international agreements on tourism, and; (v) examining vocational training problems with a view to contributing to the establishment of suitable teaching programmes tailored to specific needs, especially in the developing countries.

The permanent activities of WTO include the collection and updating of available information on training needs. Special activities include participation in technical cooperation projects for vocational training. There are three organs through which WTO functions:

(i) *General Assembly:* This is the supreme organ and sovereign body of WTO composed of delegates representing full members, associate members and representatives of affiliate members. It meets every two years and may consider any question and make recommendations on any matter within the competence of WTO. The General Assembly has created six *Regional Commissions.* The regions covered are, Africa, the Americas, Europe, Middle-East, the Pacific and East Asia, and South Asia. The Regional Commissions ensure the implementation, within their respective regions, of the~,, decisions and recommendations of the General Assembly and the Executive Council. They function and operate within the framework of the Organisation. There are the *Regional Secretariats* which are an integral part of the WTO Secretariat and help the Regional Commissions in organising and covering their conferences and meetings.

(ii) *Executive Council:* It consists of full members elected by the Assembly at the ratio of one member for every five fall members of WTO organisation with a view to achieving fair and equitable geographical distribution. The Executive Council!, among other matters, takes all necessary measures in consultation with the Secretary General, for the implementation of the decisions and recommendations of the Assembly, and reports thereon to the Assembly. The council meets at least twice a year.

(iii) *The Secretariat:* The Secretariat consists of the Secretary General and such staff as the organisation may require. The Secretary General is responsible for carrying out the general Policy and work programme of the organisation in accordance with the directions of the General Assembly and Executive-Council. The Secretary General ensures the legal representation of the organisation.

By the decision of the first General Assembly of WTO in May 1975 the headquarters were set up in Madrid (Spain) in January 1976. The activities of the Organisation cover all sectors of tourism on a worldwide basis. WTO works in cooperation with all international organisations, the United Nations in particular, as well as with commercial and noncommercial bodies involved in tourism.

The Organisation is performing extremely useful service of concrete and creative character by facilitating the exchange of technical information, the making of specialised studies, the holding of special seminars adapted to world regional requirements and advanced vocational training courses.

The essentially practical nature of its work programme, tailored as it is to regional requirements, takes full cognizance of the problems peculiar to countries and regions in all stages of development, such as investments, financial questions, physical planning and area development, economic analysis, marketing and market surveys all this not only with a secretarial approach but with a comprehensive concern from the point of view of the state.

The creation of WTO coincided with the universal

recognition of tourism as an important instrument of economic and social development and its consequent ascendancy to full government responsibility. An inter-governmental body of tourism officials--such as the WTO is empowered to act in the name of their governments and speak in terms of the impact of tourism on the balance of payments. The creation of WTO thus is not only a proof that the states are fully conscious or their own responsibilities in the field of tourism, but also of the establishment of tourism to its rightful ranking at international level.

India is a full member of the World Tourism Organisation.

Pacific area travel association

Pacific Area Travel Association (PATA) was founded in the year 1951 as a nonprofit corporation to stimulate interest in the Pacific region as a vacation land, and to develop, promote and facilitate travel to and among the many Pacific destinations. The Association had 44 founder members. The founder Lorrin Thurston, a leading newspaper publisher in Honolulu had an idea to organise all travel from the Occident to the Pacific area in a consistent, cohesive and systematic manner so as to ensure maximum benefit from existing opportunities and the creation of fresh opportunities through multimedia publicity. PATA's first conference was held in January 1952 in Honolulu and its headquarters established in San Francisco USA in 1953. PATA has its own Director for Europe who is based in London and works to promote traffic from the European markets into the, Pacific region. PATA's first Asian office was opened in Manila, Philippines in 1976.

PATA is a non-profit organisation set up with the objective, of developing, promoting and facilitating travel to and within, the Pacific area and South-East Asian region including India. It primarily operates in the United States market which is the world's biggest travel market. The organisation provides the meeting point for the people involved in all aspects of the travel trade from a large number of countries. It focuses attention on travel opportunities in member countries and builds up great awareness and specific contacts among the travel trade in countries from where the tourists originate. The underlying philosophy of PATA is that the entire travel industry must work together to develop an ever-increasing flow of pleasure travel from which each member will derive a fair share of the total business.

The activities of the PATA include assisting small and up-and-coming destinations to develop their infrastructure, providing expertise, planning group travel schemes, destinations, hotels operations and discounts. It provides up-to-date information and practical and theoretical experience in the field of tourism. The annual conferences of the PATA and its workshops provide greater scope to its members to share their ideas and exchange views about promotion of tourism in their respective regions. PATA staff are outstanding experts in their respective fields of marketing and research and regularly exchange with others, information on latest techniques and practices in their respective areas. All members benefit directly or indirectly from the continuing programmes of PATA, which include travel research, marketing, training programmes, and the development of visitor plants and services.

Promotion occupies a major portion of PATA's total effort. The PATA publication, Pacific *Travel News,* is relied upon by wholesale and retail travel agents as an important source of authoritative material on the Pacific. Recently, PATA has produced the first edition of the

Pacific Area Destination Handbook which compiles in a single volume all the data that is required for the planning and sale of travel and is the world's most authoritative and comprehensive handbook on 31 Pacific destinations. PATA also publishes its *Hotel Directory* and *Travel Guide* listing the hotels, resorts and travel services in Pacific area.

PATA Membership

PATA has nine categories of membership: Active Government, Associate Government, Active Carrier, Associate Carrier, Active Industry, Allied, Affiliated Allied, Associate and Sustaining. Active *government* members consist of the primary official organisation designated by the government of any nation, territory, or political division, wholly or partly in the Pacific area. *Associate government* members consist of any organisation charged with the responsibility of the domestic or overseas promotion of tourism as designated by the government of any nation, territory, or political division either situated outside the Pacific area, or situated within the Pacific area but not being the primary official organisation designated for the overseas promotion of travel, or not meeting other criteria as might be required for Active government membership. *Active carrier* members consist of any government recognised, registered or certified air or steamship line operating vehicles having individual passenger capacity in excess of twelve passengers and providing regular scheduled common carriage passenger service to and within the Pacific area.

Associate carrier members consist of any government recognised passenger carrier operating vehicles (a) each having a passenger capacity of twelve or fewer passengers and providing regular scheduled common carriage passenger service or having a passenger capacity in excess of twelve passengers but not providing passenger service on the regular common carriage basis as prescribed for Active carrier members. Active industry members consist of hotel organisation having management authority as distinguished from mere sales, advertising or reservations direction, over one or more hotels with a total of one thousand or more guest rooms in one or more Pacific areas, tour operator organisations excluding air or ship transportation. Allied members consist of travel agencies, tour operators, hotel representatives and firms serving as general agents of or representing various segments of the Pacific travel industry. Affiliated allied members consist of branch offices of an Allied member travel agency or tour operator. Associate members consist of individual operating organisations and firms such as communication media, media representatives, advertising, public relations and research agencies having definite interest in Pacific travel. Sustaining members consist of those organisations, firms or individuals whose commercial or cultural interests in the judgement of the Board of Directors, will further contribute to the aims of the Association.

The control of PATA is vested in the Active government, carrier and industry members. The organisations qualifying for Active government or Active carrier membership have the right to membership. They require no sponsorship and are requested merely to provide the Board of Directors with certain pertinent information. Membership in all other categories is at the discretion of the Board of Directors, and requires not only that the organisation comply with certain guidelines for eligibility, but also that certain categories of PATA members must sponsor the new applicant and vouch for its stability and professionalism.

Presently PATA has over 2193 members with 47 national and state governments, 54 airlines and 554 hotels amongst them. Every year a PATA conference is held where the participation exceeds over a thousand delegates. PATA has a membership drawn from as many as 50 countries.

India which was an Associate Member of PATA since 1957, became a full-fledged Active Member in 1964.

List of active members

(i) Active Governments

American Samoa Office of Tourism; Australian Tourist Commission; Bangladesh Parjatan Corporation; China, Tourism Bureau of the Republic of; Cook Islands Tourist Authority; Fiji Visitors Bureau; Guam Visitors Bureau; Hawaii, Department of Planning & Economic Development; Hong Kong Tourist Association; India, Department of Tourism; Indonesia, Directorate General of Tourism; Japan National Tourist Organization; Kiribati, Ministry of Natural Resource Development; Korea National Tourism Corporation; Macau, Department of Information & Tourism; Malaysia, Tourist Development Corporation of; Mexican National Tourist Council; Micronesia, Department of Development Services; Nepal, Department of Tourism; New Caledonia, Office du Tourisme; New Zealand Government Tourist & Publicity Department; Pakistan, Ministry of Culture and Tourism; Papua New Guinea, Office of Tourism; Philippines, Ministry of Tourism; Singapore Tourist Promotion Board; Solomon Islands Tourist Authority; Sri Lanka, Ceylon Tourist Board; Tahiti Tourist Development Board; Thailand, Tourism Authority of; Tonga Visitors Bureau; United States Travel Service; USSR, Intourist; Vanuatu Tourist Information Bureau.

(ii) Active industry

American Express Company; Hilton International; Hotel Indonesia International Corporation Ltd.; Unitours.

(iii) Active carriers

Aeronaves de Mexico; Air-India; Airlanka; Air Nauru; Air New Zealand; Air Niugini; Air Pacific; All Nippon, Airways; Aloha Airlines; American Airlines; Ansett Airlines of Australia; Bangladesh Biman; Bouraq Indonesia Airlines; British Caledonian Airways; CP Air; Cathay Pacific Airways; China Airlines; Condor Flugdienst; Continental Airlines; Delta Steamship Lines; Deutsche Lufthansa; Finnair; Garuda Indonesian Airways; Gulf Air Company; Hawaiian Air; Indian Airlines; Japan Air Lines; KLM Royal Dutch Airlines; Korean Air Lines; Malaysian Airlines System; Merpati Nusantara Airlines; Mexicana Airlines; Northwest Orient Airlines; Pakistan International Airlines; Pan American World Airways; Philippine Airlines; Qantas Airways; Royal Nepal Airlines; Royal Viking Line; Scandinavian Airlines System; Singapore Airlines; Sitmar Cruises; Thai Airways International; Transamerica Airlines; Trans-Australia Airlines; Trans World Airlines; UTA French Airlines; United Airlines; Western Airlines; World Airways.

(iv) Associate carriers

Ansett-Pioneer Road Passenger Group; Japanese National Railways; Mid Pacific Air.

(v) Associate Governments

Anaheim Visitor & Convention Bureau; Australian Standing Committee of Tourism; Bali Government Tourism Office; California Office of Tourism; Canberra Tourist Bureau (Australia); Central Java Provincial Tourist Office; East Java Regional Tourist Development Bureau; Gangweon-do Provincial Government (Korea);

Hawaii Visitors Bureau; India Tourism Development Corporation; Jakarta Metropolitan Tourism Board; Kementerian Tenaga Rakyat (Malaysia); Long Beach, Convention & Tourism Bureau; Korea Bureau of Tourism, Ministry of Transportation; Marianas Visitors Bureau; Melbourne Tourism Authority; New South Wales Department of Tourism; New Zealand National Travel Association; Northern Territory Tourist Commission; Pahang State Development Corporation (Malaysia); Penang State Government;

Philippine Convention Bureau; Philippine Tourism Authority; Queensland Tourist & Travel Corporation; Sabah Tourism Promotion Corporation; Sarawak Tourist Development Commission; Seoul Metropolitan Government; Travel Alberta; Victoria Government Travel Authority; West Java Regional Tourism Office.

PATA chapters

To assist in the fulfilment of the objectives of the Pacific Area Travel Association, the Board of Directors is empowered to encourage the development and to authorise establishment of PATA Chapter at any place in the world. The Chapter concept implemented in the year 1960 is unique with PATA among travel organisations. The primary purpose of a Chapter is to conduct continuing education programmes to keep PATA members abreast of the changes in Pacific travel. The Chapters also do considerable promotional work, and several times each year stage social events for the members. Specific objectives of the Chapters are as follows:

(i) To bring together representatives of PATA members at regular intervals to develop a closer working relationship and a better understanding of travel matters as such that relate to the Pacific area.

(ii) To obtain uniformity and combined action by members in pursuing national and local policies within the framework of PATA.

(iii) To implement specific PATA objectives and projects.

(iv) To pass to appropriate government and official organisations such matters approved by PATA, and to obtain action thereon as and when required.

(v) To process generally and to obtain opinions of members of the Chapters on any PATA requirement or objective.

(vi) As appropriate, to provide a forum which will enable the individual Chapter members to conduct their various assigned responsibilities for selling travel, and providing services to visitors to the Pacific in a more effective manner.

There are two types of Chapters viz: (i) Area Chapters, (ii) Promotional Chapters. *Area Chapters* were conceived as of the 8th Annual PATA Conference by a number of Allied and Associate members, as a means of keeping PATA members and their representatives in the Pacific better informed on happenings throughout the Pacific travel industry and on Association activities. Some of these Chapter activities include programmes involving matters of facilitation, staff training, improving visitor plants and services, and promotions aimed at developing regional tourist traffic and other marketing activities. Promotional Chapters were authorised by the 9th Annual PATA Conference as a means of furthering the promotion of visitors from priority market areas to Pacific destinations. Activities of these Chapters are all designed to increase the sale of travel to the Pacific area and include regular meetings of the PATA membership/travel trade with programmes on various Pacific destinations, providing up-to-date information on new developments, facilities, services, tours, educational seminars for travel trade, sales personnel and cooperation with PATA in the overall marketing programme, promotions and other PATA activities.

The Chapters are, however, not the branch offices of PATA. They are rather like local civic clubs working for the benefit of their respective communities. A Chapter is composed of the highest level of executives representing the local tourism industry who volunteer their services and their expertise to develop a constantly expanding overall business.

Presently, PATA has as many as 51 active Chapters. Two to three new Chapters are organised yearly to help more and more people keep abreast of the changes in Pacific travel.

Finances of the association

The administration and programmes of the Association are financed by way of membership dues and the marketing assessments paid by all members. The amount of dues however, varies with the category of membership. The marketing assessments of governments and carriers are calculated in accordance with a Stanford Research Institute formula. This formula take account, among other things, the growth in visitor arrivals and expenditures at member areas, and the growth in traffic volume of carrier members The Associations' financial position is, reviewed by the Board of Directors at their monthly meetings, and an annual audit is made by an outside accounting agency. In addition to membership dues and the marketing assessment amounts, there are additional revenues which come from Allied and Associate members, a portion of which is applied to various marketing programmes.

Pacific Area Travel Association performs a variety of

functions. These include:

(i) *Pacific Travel Conference and workshop.* During the first four months of each year, PATA sponsors and organises a conference of its members with the objectives of reviewing the progress, exchanging ideas and planning for future programmes. These meetings are held at different areas. The annual conferences attract a large number of delegates from all over the world. The conference also serves as a unique promotional tool for the host government providing it an opportunity to show to the travel industry from abroad what it has to offer in terms of tourist attractions and tourism plant to the foreign visitor.

(ii) *Marketing.* A long-range marketing programme coordinates all the promotional functions of PATA for a maximum impact in the consumer market and also among sales agents. The marketing programme includes: (1) Advertising, Publicity and Promotion. An extensive advertising programme schedule is carried in leading national magazines of North America with a view to increase interest in the Pacific region as a major travel area. The association prepares and distributes a wide selection of selling aids and sales promotion materials to travel agents, tour operators throughout the world. A strong trade advertising programme is directed towards travel agents in order to merchandise PATA's consumer advertising and sales promotion efforts Weekly news releases, special feature stories and photographs are provided to the various newspapers, magazines and radio and television networks by the Association's Pacific news service. Members may use Association's various materials including photographs for their own publicity purposes. (2) Marketing Research and

Development. The Association's research programme is designed to provide it with the marketing information needed to formulate its own marketing programme as well as to provide its members with information which will assist them in designing their own programmes. The Association organises research seminars, research presentations and technical assistance programmes for its members. Another important facet of the research programme includes the collection, analysis and dissemination of Pacific travel statistics and an effort designed to constantly improve and standardise the tourism statistics of the Pacific region.

PATA and India

India was admitted as an Associate Government Member of Pacific Area Travel Association in the year 1957. It was at the specific request of the Government that the Constitution of the PATA was amended suitably to enable India and other South Asian countries to become Associate Government Members. It was only in the year 1964 at Djkarta, Indonesia that India became an Active Member, of the Association. Basically, PATA was formed to promote traffic to Pacific countries only. However, the definition of PATA was somewhat enlarged to enable some of the countries bordering on the Pacific to join PATA. India was the first country to enter PATA from among the countries which bordered on the Pacific but were not in the Pacific region. Subsequently, a few other countries also joined the association from this region. Among these countries were Sri Lanka, Nepal and later Pakistan and Bangladesh,

It was not long before India realised the manifold benefits which this organisation had for promotion of tourism. India realised that PATA was one of the most active travel promotional organisations and that the country's association with it would not only benefit her from getting a share of the world's increasing tourist flow but also from the point of view of exposing it to the modern techniques of tourism marketing and promotion. During the 1964 annual conference at Sydney in Australia, PATA agreed to hold its annual convention in India in the year 1966. During the 1965 Conference in Korea, India's invitation to host the Annual Convention in 1966 was reaffirmed and accepted by the General Body of the PATA Conference. The decision regarding the venue of the conference is generally made three years in advance.

PATA '66 was the 15th Annual Conference of the Association. The five-days Conference and the Workshop which met in New Delhi was attended by over 500 delegates from a number of countries. India at that time was emerging as a new tourist destination with very little exposure in American and Pacific areas of its tourist attractions. The main objective in inviting PATA Conference to Delhi was to expose our facilities to a large; segment of foreign tour operators, travel writers, airline executives etc. The conference was a big success as, it resulted in a steady rise in tourist traffic to India during subsequent years. India enjoyed a continuous and uninterrupted growth till 1973 when the steep rise in oil prices followed by inflation in potential tourism markets led to a slight decline in the growth of tourist arrivals. However, during subsequent years the tourist arrivals increased. India after PATA '66 Conference is now a full-fledged member.

India was awarded yet another conference! PATA '78. India was unanimously chosen as the venue of the 1978 conference at the Sydney PATA Conference in 1975. The theme of the conference "Challenge of Change" became particularly significant in view of the fact that tourism was passing into a phase where there were no limits to its growth. The objective of hosting another PATA Conference in India after a period of twelve years was to expose tourist facilities to a large segment of tour operators, travel writers and airline executives etc. The conference was attended by over 1500 delegates and was the largest PATA Conference held in the history of PATA. The large number of delegates from all over the world provided an opportunity to India to expose its tourist plant to the international travel world. The Conference will go a long way in projecting India's image not only as a great tourist destination but also as a great host country.

PATA India Chapter. PATA (India) Chapter was organised in the year 1969 as one of the Area Chapters. This Chapter has 98 members with representation from Government (Central Department of Tourism), India Tourism Development Corporation, Indian Airlines, Air India and other international carriers, leading travel agencies in India, hotels, tour operators, advertising agencies etc. The Chapter undertakes promotional work specifically for promoting India.

In recent years there hag been rapid and continuous development of both national and international tourism. The international tourism organisations have played and are continuing to play a key role in the tourism development both national as well as international. India has regularly participated actively in the deliberations of international bodies which afford an opportunity to establish new contacts and renew old ties with persons from all over the world connected with tourism. These organisations also help the member countries to determine the general travel trends for proper channelisation of promotional activities. India's association with these bodies has definitely encouraged the flow of tourist traffic from international tourist generating markets to India.

International air transport association

As a result of the rapid expansion in the network of international airlines in the years following the Second World War, a need for worldwide regulation of air traffic and craft equipment was felt by many countries. Consequently an international convention was called by President, Franklin D. Roosevelt of the United States of America at Chicago from November I to December 7, 1944. The Convention constituted two permanent bodies, namely, the International Air Transport Association (IATA) and the International Civil Aviation Organisation (ICAO). Both these organisations are the leading international agencies looking after various aspects of world aviation industry including various problems and their solutions in the civil air transport.

But before reaching the position that it now occupies in the field of aviation, IATA passed through several stages in parallel with the spectacular development of commercial aviation. Its modest beginnings date back to 1919. Its predecessor, the International Air Traffic Association, was founded in that year in The Hague by half a dozen European airlines that had just been created. Right from the beginning they recognized the need to cooperate in setting up a network where everything needed to be rationalized.

The activity of the first, prewar version of IATA expanded steadily with the development of air services in the world. Among other things, it drew up the general formula for tickets and transport documents adopted in 1927. The innovations and improvements introduced by the Association progressively placed unique tools at the disposal of the industry.

In November 1944, as World War It hostilities were taking a final turn, 54 states met in Chicago to lay the first foundations of the new system that would soon be greatly needed by civil aviation. This Conference led to the creation of the International Civil Aviation Organisation (ICAO), the international body set up by governments to establish universal norms for the technical regulation of civil aviation. Indirectly, this Conference was also responsible for the foundation of the International Air Transport Association--a nongovernmental body officially set up in Havana in April 1945--which, in practice, carried on the task assumed by the former IATA. Both through its Organisation and its activity, IATA found itself closely linked to ICAO. International Air Transport Association's work became increasingly, diversified, specialized and extensive with the development of aeronautical technology and the expansion of the airline network. With the arrival of jets towards the end of the fifties, a whole series of new measures concerning technical matters, fares, procedures and Organisation was needed to replace regulations that no longer corresponded to the new conditions in the industry or to the growing potential of its market.

The International Air Transport Association (IATA) is the global organisation for virtually all the international carriers. The principal function of IATA is to simplify and speed the movement of persons and goods from any point on the world air network to any other by a combination of routes. This is accomplished by a single ticket bought at a single price in one currency. The ticket is valid everywhere for the same amount and quality of service. The same principles apply to the movement of freight and mail.

Under the provisions of its constitution, IATA must carry out a threefold task:

(i) encourage the development of reliable, regular and economical air transport for the benefit of the peoples of the world, foster air commerce arid study the problems involved;

(ii) provide the means for collaboration among the air transport enterprises involved directly or indirectly in international air transport services;

(iii) cooperate with the International Civil Aviation. Organisation and other international organisations.

Services provided

The IATA provides a wide range of services. The list of services provided is quite impressive and includes the following:

- the global planning of international timetables,
- the standardization of the inter-company communications and reservations systems,
- the international coordination of telecommunications networks and Computer Systems,
- the single formula for tickets and air waybills,
- the training of travel and freight agents,
- to regulate legal questions of genera, concern, to develop security measures,
- to examine and solve the problems raised by tourism and the flow of passengers and goods in the airports and to establish procedures and technical norms.

Organisation

IATA is a non-government organisation. There are three IATA traffic conferences--Western Hemisphere; Europe, Africa and the Middle East; Asia and Australia. The conference Areas are numbered in numerical order. Each

Traffic conference Area covers a number of countries. The IATA traffic conferences are, in effect, an important adjunct to government. Also, the rules which IATA formulates must be approved by the governments involved. IATA traffic conferences come in after governments have decided bilaterally upon the exchange of rights and after each government decides individually what air carriers are going to serve their area.

In order to be eligible for the membership of IATA and the conferences, an airline must hold a certificate for scheduled air carriage from a government eligible for membership of the International Civil Aviation Organisation. Airlines engaged directly in international operations are active members while on the the other hand airlines engaged in domestic operations are associate members.

Resolutions of the traffic conferences of International Air Transport Association standardise not only tickets but waybills, baggage checks and other similar documents. These resolutions also coordinate and unify handling and accounting procedures to permit rapid inter-line booking and connection. The resolutions also maintain a stable pattern of international fares and rates of over 100 member airlines all over he world. The standardization of air fares is the must significant part of IATA's work. In effect, this has resulted in permitting he linking of the routes of many individual international airlines into a single public service system for all nations of the world.

In order to carry out so many functions, IATA has a staff of over 450 people throughout the world and operates with funds provided in the form of annual dues paid by members.

Broadly speaking, IATA is the world association of

scheduled airlines within which they coordinate their efforts to serve their passengers, share their experiences and analyse their problems. Representing over 100 companies from 80 odd countries together provide the bulk of world scheduled air services. IATA plays a leading, role in three respects, on the basis of the aims defined in its statutes.

The Association provides machinery for the airlines for finding joint solutions to problems often beyond the resources of any single company. Through the Association, airlines have succeeded in standardising their operating methods and with their complementary routes they have created a worldwide public service network, despite the many differences in language, currency, legislation and regulations.

The Association is able to act as an intermediary between governments and its users. It is the world parliament of airline companies and their spokesman vis-a-vis various other international bodies. For governments it serves as a forum where proposals for international rates and fares are formulated in a neutral context for study and approval. For the general public--it symbolizes, because it monitors and encourages them, the uniform quality of services, the use of rational commercial methods by airlines and agents, the simplification of formalities and the lowest possible fares and rates consistent with sound economy.

International civil aviation organisation

The convention providing for the establishment of the International Civil Aviation Organisation was drawn up by the International Civil Aviation Conference held in Chicago from November 1 to December 7, 1944. A provisional International Civil Aviation Organisation (PICAO) functioned from 6 June, 1945 until the formal establishment of ICAO. The International Civil Aviation Organisation (ICAO) was formally established on April 4, 1947 as a specialized agency of the United Nations. ICAO has a membership of over 130 governments joined for the common purpose of promoting civil aviation on a global scale. The headquarters or the organisation are located at Montreal, Canada. The organisation has its regional offices in Mexico city, Lima, Paris, Dakar, Cairo and Bangkok. The International Civil Aviation Organisation representing over 130 governments of various countries throughout the world provides the machinery for the achievement of greater global cooperation in the matters of civil aviation. Over the years the organisation has achieved great success in various matters relating with civil aviation.

Objectives

The main objectives of the organisation are to develop the principles and the techniques of international air navigation and to foster the planning and development of international air transport with a view to:

(i) ensure the safe and orderly growth of international civil aviation throughout the world;

(ii) encourage the arts of aircraft design and operation for peaceful purposes;

(iii) encourage the development of airways, airports and navigation facilities for international civil aviation;

(iv) meet the needs of the people of the world for safe, regular, efficient, economical air transport;

(v) prevent economic waste caused by unreasonable competition;

(vi) ensure that the rights of contracting countries are fully respected and that every contracting country has a fair opportunity to operate international airlines;

(vii) avoid discrimination between contracting countries;

(iii) promote safety of flight in international air navigation;

(ix) promote generally the development of all aspects, of international civil aeronautics.

In addition to the above, the International Civil Aviation Organisation through its various proposals tries for the reduction of customs, immigration, public health and other formalities in order to facilitate air transportation. As part of the United Nations Development Programme, the organisation provides technical assistance to states in developing civil aviation programmes. Development of regional plans for ground facilities and services needed for international flying is another important function of the Organisation. The Organisation disseminates air transport statistics and prepares studies on aviation economics. It also fosters the development of air law conventions.

Organisation of ICAO

The principal organ of ICAO is an Assembly. The Assembly consists of all the members of the organisation and is the sovereign body of ICAO. It meets every three years and reviews in detail the work of the organisation. It sets the policy for the next three years. The organisation has a Council which is comprised of 30 states and is elected by the Assembly for a period of three years. While electing the states, the Assembly gives adequate representation to:

(i) member states of major importance in air transport;

(ii) those member states not otherwise included which

make the largest contribution to the provision of facilities for the international civil air navigation; and

(iii) those member states not otherwise included and whose election will ensure that all major geographical areas of the world are represented.

As a governing body, the council gives continuous direction to the work of the organisation. The main subsidiary bodies are: the Air Navigation Commission, composed of 12 members elected by the council; Air Transport Committee, open to council members; and the Legal Committee, on which all members of ICAO may be represented. India has been an elected member of the Council since it became a member of ICAO.

A close look at the range of activities and objectives of both International Air Transport Association and International Civil Aviation Oranisation indicates that they play a key role in the growth and development of international air transport. Their role since inception has been that of fostering the growth of air transport. Although not directly concerned with tourism, they have however, played an important role in its growth over the years by way or encouraging air transport.

The practice of corporate strategy, strategic management or business policy is an integrative procedure, which attempts to draw together all aspects of the organization's decisions into a coherent whole. Although these decisions are often taken at different levels in the organization and, in practice, are often uncoordinated, corporate planning is the responsibility of top management. It is only top management who can have the strategic vision necessary to take decisions on a company-wide long-term basis. This explains the difference between strategy that has a long-term aim and tactics that represent shorter-term contingent decisions aimed at implementing partial elements of the overall strategy.

Any company faces a variety of corporate and environmental pressures. Those pressures that impact on objectives may be termed stakeholders. These stakeholders, who can influence the firm, include: shareholders, management, suppliers, customers, employees and governments. In addition, objectives must take into account environmental change and, in the actions of competitors. The outcome of the process 'of setting objectives will represent a balancing of these interest groups.

Shareholders

It is frequently stated that the only objective of the firm is to maximize profits. As a long-run objective it is essential for survival that the assets of the company in the broadest possible sense earn a rate of, return superior to that which they could earn elsewhere. However, to give operational content to this and to achieve a balance between' the very long-term and shorter-term objectives, it is essential to set sub-goals and to satisfy other stakeholders. This is the essence of the, managerial theories of the firm, which propose a trade-off between profits and management satisfaction. Despite this trade off, and others, it is essential that shareholders remain content to hold shares, which represent ownership of the firm. If shareholders become dissatisfied, then it is open to them to dispose of their shares and thus to precipitate a change in ownership, with possible serious consequences for policy, including a change of management. Indeed, it may be managers themselves who own the company or, in the case of 'management buy-outs', who acquire a company from its existing shareholders.

In many countries, institutional shareholders are very important. These may include financial institutions, banks and intra-group holding. Where the proportion of shares held by powerful outside bodies is large, the influence of such bodies will be significant.

Similarly, the key form of ownership in many countries is the private company. This may be a family group, a cluster of related families or even a single individual. The owner/manager/entrepreneur will be a uniquely powerful figure in deciding corporate strategy, and the boss's word is final may be a sufficient explanation of strategy in these cases. Because financial institutions and the corporate framework differ so much between countries, private ownership does not necessarily only apply to small companies. In Germany, for instance, the private company can be become very large before there is any necessity to consider, change to a publicly quoted company.

For all private companies, however, corporate strategy influenced by the necessity to raise capital. Ibis is particularly for, rapidly growing private companies. The approach of p companies to the capital market is fraught with difficulties. The key, problem is the need to raise capital without losing control. Often, the competitive advantage of smaller firms rests in the possession of unique skills, products, technology or ideas. This compounds the problems when it becomes necessary to raise capital to exploit the idea without giving the idea away! Under these pressures many family-owned or closely held companies are constrained to issue shares, thus relinquishing total control.

The pressure then to earn a good (short-term) rate of return to prevent shareholder disquiet, takeover or buy-out provides a constraint on policy. Any policy that ignores the influence of the capital market in this way is bound to run into problems. Private companies are more able to withstand these pressures because they are insulated to some degree from the immediacy of returns required by a publicly quoted company. Indeed, in the leisure, tourism and travel field, it is noticeable that the entrepreneur Richard Branson brought his Virgin group of companies back into private ownership after being publicly quoted, so that they could concentrate on long-term policies by the exclusion of short-term earnings. The shareholder profile is thus a key influence on objectives.

Managers

Managers are the most important decision-makers in a company. In many cases, they will not be owners of the firm but will be professionals implementing, in theory at least, the wishes of the owners. In practice, it is an increasing trend that managers are given share-holdings in the firm for which they work in order to secure their loyalty, ensure that they work on behalf of all shareholders and to reward them for performance. However, we can separate the pure motivations of managers from managers as shareholders.

Models of managerial discretion suggest that managerial remuneration and discretionary income may well be traded off against increasing the net worth of the company (as measured, for instance, by the share price). In addition prestige, particularly among peer groups, may also be important. This may lead, for instance, to a desire for growth for its own sake or to becoming international. The objectives will be paid for by trading off other benefits.

The issue of ownership versus control has been a long-standing one in the corporate literature. The relationship between owners and managers is thus vitally important in the formulation of objectives.

Suppliers

Suppliers will be dependent on the company through purchasing behaviour. They will have a vested interest in the company's success as a buyer of products or services. In situations where the company is reliant (even dependent) on its suppliers, then it is important to take their interests into account. Examples include hotels being dependent on catering supplies and the famous network of sub-contracting that characterizes Japanese business. There is, of course, a tendency for the large and powerful to take over the small in purchasing chains, and such internalization strategies are as, characteristic of the tourism industry as elsewhere. However, control in a chain of supply can be exercised without ownership, as the retailing firm Marks and Spencers; have shown. Excessive dependence on key suppliers may, however, bias strategy and objectives.

Customers

Companies that forget customers in any part of the process of corporate planning, including the formulation of objectives, are doomed to failure. It is a truism that companies cannot ignore the market. It is through the medium of management that the impact of customers is felt. A key role of managers is to predict market demand. In an industry as fragmented, volatile and seasonal as tourism, this becomes an even more major task. Moreover, as a tourism company is involved in face-to-face transactions with people, contacts are vital and feedback is likely to be immediate.

Employees

The goodwill of employees is a *sine qua non* of successful operation in which human contact and personal skills are as important as in tourism. Often it is possible to regard the role and influence of employees as a constraint on the objectives of companies. Much more satisfactory is the view that the role of employees can contribute in a positive way to the establishment and achievement of company goals.

In many countries, notably the Federal Republic of Germany, In certain circumstances employees will, by statute, be equivalent to shareholders in being represented on the management board of the company. Their objectives can thus, in theory at least, be converted' into company policy. Although this relationship is not as direct in many other countries, an input from employees should certainly be considered in the formulation of objectives, as the employee, perspective can be most valuable, derived as it is likely to be in tourism from a direct interface with customers.

Governments

In international tourism, dealing with governments in the plural is a key fact of operation. For all but the most multinational of companies, the most important influence will be the government the home (or parent) country. Objectives will be constrained by the necessity to conform to the laws, directives, statutory requirements exhortations and ad hoc mechanisms of the country. Complicity matters of taxation, antitrust legislation, accounting practices, trade regulation, product liability and the Myriad other public policies of government is a crucial element of careful strategy formulation. However, when we deal with international operations, it is an unfortunate fact of life that the public policies of the host governments will conflict or at least not fully mesh with, those of the home government. This can involve heavy expenses, for example, in reconciling financial accounts of a conflict of objectives between different units of the firm and internal dissensions in management.

Setting objectives

It will be apparent from the review of stake-holder interests above that the process of setting objectives is essentially political in the sense of reconciling differences. The constraints on objectives are both internal and external, and the outcome will depend on the representation of those interests by the key actors, who will be in the main managers and owners. Despite these factors it is important that there should be a clear articulation of unambiguous objectives as a basis for policy choice, implementation and approval. Resistance to this process should not be ignored. It is essential to secure approval of objectives, and this can be done by consultation, attempting to achieve consensus, promotion of the objectives and linking incentives to the achievement of objectives.

The role of top management is crucial. But the process should not be confined to top management. Corporate objectives are long term and planning too must be long term. The length of time over which objectives are defined will vary over industry segments. Many firms find it useful to have long-term objectives (10 years) within which five-year rolling plans are defined.

Strategic appraisal

It is essential that firms in international tourism should have a clear, unbiased view of their internal and external position. It is important to know where the firm is, and where it is going. Inevitably, this will involve a view of where the firm has been. Strategic appraisal has two main components: internal and external.

Internal appraisal

An analysis of where the company is an appraisal of its strengths and weaknesses is a vital and continuous process. It is necessary to cover all aspects of the firm's operations: marketing' fin personnel, research and development, production, structure, systems and procedures.

Several techniques of internal appraisal are available. The appraisal can be conducted by insiders executives, managers directly meeting and discussing the position or surveys. It may be useful to employ outsiders, whose views more objective and detached but who may not have full information. Whoever conducts the analysis, it is i be systematic, unbiased and realistic. Evidence firms within and possibly outside the industry provides against which the position of the firm can be judged. The coherence past and projected strategy can judged against the position of the firm.

It is useful to place the information necessary for a strate appraisal in a framework like the Strengths Weaknesses Opportunities Threats (SWOT) approach. Debate can then take place among the relevant managers (an& possibly other stakeholders) regarding the realism and exactitude the entries. 'Harder' information, such as profitability, share, financial ratios and personnel audits, can then be brought bear in giving coherence to the appraisal.

External appraisal

Two levels of external appraisal may be distinguished: one is the analysis of the macro environment of the firm; the other a more micro and localized approval of the firm's particular industries, market a competitive framework.

Analysis of the macro environment is important because the longterm and overall framework in which the firm operates is not static and prediction of changes that have an immediate impact often, depends' on changes at the most fundamental level. For firm in international tourism, of particular importance will be: (1) changes in demand pattern, which depends on income levels, tastes, distribution of income; (2) changes in political circumstances, both in the firm's home country and worldwide; (3) changes in technology; (4) social changes, including the ageing of the population in the most advanced countries.

Each of these key factors will influence the internal organisation of the firm and the relative costs that face it in its own markets and in others that impinge on it. Consequently, the scale and scope of the firm must adjust in order to accommodate these external changes. A change in the taste from 'sea and sun' type holidays to 'cultural tourism' will affect the occupancy rates and, therefore, the profitability of hotels in different locations, the pattern of amenity provision and travel pattern. A revolution in Ruritania will deflect holidaymakers to countries that are close substitutes. Improvements in computer technology will allow worldwide centralized booking facilities for hotels and transport companies. Each of these changes will alter the size, scope and location of firms and their investment. They will also encourage or deter entry (and exit) into the industry. The firms that are most alert to changing opportunities will gain most.

Against this general backdrop, firms must attempt to appraise their more immediate environment. This will generally mean their competitors and potential competitors, their customers and suppliers and (potential) substitutes.

Congruence between internal and external appraisal

A crucial feature of a coherent corporate plan is that there must be congruence between the internal and external approval. If the internal appraisal has shown that a major strength exists in current product offerings, then we would expect this to be reflected in current market share. Putting the two analyses together should, reveal the extent to which internal perception is external reality.

Strategy choice

In examining the various frameworks available for strategy choice, several things should be borne in mind. First, these are merely frameworks. They enable choice to take place, based on the content put into the framework. If the content is wrong, the strategy will go wrong. If the internal and external appraisals contain errors of fact, perception and interpretation, no sophisticated framework of analysis will put it right. Second, the methods of structuring strategic choice will be more or less appropriate according to the strategic position and dynamics of the firm in its context. Some of these methods are appropriate to growing firms, others to firms wishing to arrest a decline. Some pay more attention to a rapidly changing environment, others are more suitable in situations closer to equilibrium. Third, none of the frameworks is a substitute for judgement. Managerial choice, entrepreneurial flair, careful planning are all required. The function of management is to adjust to change. These methods are an aid to that, not a substitute for it.

The Boston consulting group matrix

The Boston Consulting Group Matrix, often referred to in short-hand terms as the 'Boston Box', is a device relating growth rate to relative competitive position at product level. Like many models in the strategic choice area, it presents a 2 by 2 matrix and reduction to two dimensions raises serious questions about its ability to handle complexity. It also suffers from a number of restrictive assumptions that: the market can be defined, profitability and market share are positively related, there are no barriers to entry or exit in the market concerned, the stage of industry maturity" be defined and the market is still in the growth stage. Given these restrictions, however, the model still retains some heuristic value.

The two dimensions define four product categories high-growth products where the firm has a strong relative competitive position lower-growth products with a strong market share high-growth products without a strong market share and lower-growth products with a weak market share. By mapping products according to their business growth rate and relative market share a current audit can be obtained. Strategy choice should then proceed by exiting from 'dogs' unless there is a powerful reason not to and by converting question marks into stars by increasing market share. Stars will eventually become cash cows as the market rate of growth slows and then these can be reinvigorated by using the cash flow for reinvestment. The matrix points to the need for balance between high-growth stars, which are unlikely to generate cash flow, and cash cows, which provide the wherewithal to generate new products and find investment. The assumes that a portfolio of products can be generated. It to apply the concept to a narrowly focused single-product

General electric business screen

As a contrast to the over-simplistic approach of the Boston Box, the GE Matrix can become over-complicated. It includes, again, only two variables, but as these are industry attractiveness and competitive position, they break down into as many sub-variables as can be suggested to affect a firm's profitability. In truth, the blank framework allows many interpretations. Essentially, the positioning of a firm's business units can begin only a preliminary screening of its choices.

It is essential in these approaches to pay particular attention to constraints on movement. It is costly both to enter and to exit from an industry and an industry segment. Attention to these costs is necessary to augment the analysis of strategic moves as presented by these frameworks.

Strategic growth vectors

It is often appropriate to analyse strategies around the issue of directions of growth of the company. Growth vector components presented by Ansoff enable this to occur. Take first the simple division between existing and new products, existing and new missions. Thus, by examining the product market position it possible to delineate generic growth strategies.

Product cycle models

The product cycle model makes four basic assertions: (1) Products undergo predictable changes in production and marketing. (2) There is restricted information available on products and technology; in particular proprietary knowledge, owned and controlled by firms, is crucial in attaining competitive leadership. (3) The production of goods and provision of services change over time and economies of scale are prevalent. (4) Tastes differ, so patterns of demand can vary. In particular, tastes differ according to income. This provides an opportunity for firms to standardize their offerings according to income levels. Segmentation of the market thus occurs as products travel through a life-cycle.

The process has four stages, development, growth, maturity and decline. It is a notable weakness of product cycle analysis that the cycle is programmatic, not dynamic. In other words, the programme is set, but there is insufficient explanation of the critical variables that drive this development and their relationship with elapsed time.

Stage I of the cycle is the innovation stage where a new product is created. This new product will tend to be unstandardized, high-priced and the province of one or a few innovative firms. These firms will receive quasi-monopoly returns to reward the innovation. In Stage 11, the product becomes more standardized on both the demand side and on the supply side.

New competitors enter the market and drive the price down. The possibility of economies of scale (block booking, purchase of aircraft and hotels with assured full occupation) also drive down costs. Investment by established firms in this stage may well occur to forestall entry. In State 11 the product becomes mature and sells almost entirely on the basis of price. Attempts are made to secure niches within the market, but the primary imperative is to reduce costs. The product becomes susceptible to mass-marketing techniques.

There is a tendency for the market to become dominated by a few large oligopolists. In the decline phase, substitute 'new products' begin to erode market share. The necessary capacity begins to decline and the product becomes much more like a commodity.

This is not to say that the correct strategy is to leave mature product segments, because they are often capable of generating large cash flows. Strategies of product regeneration and segmentation can still earn a good return in such an industry. There is an imperative, however, to maintain strict cost control and this discipline may be beyond the capability of many operators.

Needless to say, there are many criticisms of the product cycle model as the basis for international corporate planning. It is over-deterministic and clearly does not apply to all products. It is also difficult to pin down exactly what constitutes a product.

In many ways the model is an industry cycle rather than a product cycle. There is also a great deal of evidence that product cycles are shortening, in many cases to the point where products are innovated, standardized and differentiated almost instantaneously rather than sequentially.

The use of the product cycle model in international tourism may still have validity. However, it should be borne in mind that it splits three strategic decisions which are interdependent: investment in product development and innovation, the method of approaching foreign markets and the optimum way of competing with new entrants. The major criticism that the model is outdated must be judged in the context of product development in particular industry segments.

Structured analysis and generic strategies

The analysis of industry structure, competitive behaviour and relative competitive advantages can be key factors in strategic choice. Porter's work has suggested three key generic strategies: differentiation, overall cost leadership and focus. The choice, determined by strategic target and strategic advantage, is driven by the degree of uniqueness as perceived by the customer and the cost position of the company.

Overall cost leadership rests on the ability of the firm to control costs. This means achieving economies of scale, gaining cost reduction through learning effects, tight control of overheads and reducing spending on sales costs. This strategy will tend to be linked to the achievement of high market share and maintaining a ruthless view of the product portfolio, eliminating products that do not conform to the strategy. Standardization of product and service is often the key to success in this strategy with mass marketing and advertising to maintain throughout. Examples in the tourist industry are basic package holidays and budget hotels.

A strategy based on differentiation requires that the firm's product be perceived as unique in the industry. This is usually but not necessarily a high-quality "aim at the top of the market' type of strategy. The firm thus attains a defensible position by creating an area of quasi-monopoly, giving it some price leverage. A strategy of building consumer loyalty and quality superiority are adjuncts to the strategy.

Some airlines, such as Cathay Pacific and Singapore Airlines, are in the enviable position of successfully following such a strategy. There is, however, often the necessity of sacrificing overall market share in order to differentiate successfully.

Finally, the strategy of focus is built on, aiming at a particular segment, geographical area or product line. The firm must be able to service this particular niche market more successfully than its broader-based-corapetitors.

It may, therefore, be lower cost or be perceived as superior by the key buyers in the niche. As there is an element of choice in this strategy, it can be used to secure niche positions that are least vulnerable to substitutes or where competitors are weak. Examples are companies specializing in safari holidays or specialists in particular destinations or hotels catering for minority needs.

Global planning —strategic alternatives

The issues of strategy choice do not differ when international aspects are considered, but the range of options and variables increase. International modes of operation and entry strategy in detail, and this should be reviewed at this point. The mode of foreign market servicing is a critical aspect of international strategic planning and should be included in the choice of strategy. As points; out, patterns of international competition vary widely across industries and a more flexible approach needs to be taken when planning on a global scale.

This will require organizational innovations to deal with increased complexity and may involve coalitions with other firms. The firm will also have more, and often conflicting, government regulations with which to deal, and will have opportunities arising from its inter national scope to generate and exploit competitive advantages.

Again, a two-dimensional table can be used to illustrate the key strategy choices in international competition. These are coordination of activities and configuration issues, which centre on the location of activities. This combination of internalization and location decisions across activities permits a great complexity of strategic choice.

In practice, however, in the international tourism industry, many decisions will be constrained: for example, the location of the destination, integration of key activities. Exporting also is impossible with location-dependent services. Combining the international competitive framework with the generic strategies. Porter is able to define a small number of strate alternatives where competition is global, as it is increasing becoming in large segments of the international tourism industry.

It will rarely be the that a firm follows one strategy exclusively from which the most appropriate strategy can be select as internal circumstances and environmental constraints dictate.

9

Managing Human Resources Development

This chapter discusses the importance of human resources development and the corresponding GTA role. It goes on to describe the steps taken in seeking to establish internationally agreed minimum working conditions.

The importance of human resources

The need to develop human capital is the starting point for all development. Nothing is possible without trained and skilled people. A human resources development policy can be split into two parts:

— To offer competitive employment conditions and career opportunities to ensure the adequate recruitment of all levels of personnel

— To provide educational and training opportunities for all occupations and specializations, at agreed and specified levels of skill wherever necessary in the country,

The responsibility for human resources development at the GTA is normally assigned to a separate department. This department should coordinate all aspects of a national tourism human resources development strategy.

Developed countries tend to have more money to spend on training initiatives. However, they often spend money on expensive training at the tertiary level; training which might be provided more cheaply in secondary schools or through on-the-job/work based training schemes.

They may also develop adult training schemes which only seem to Compensate for inadequacies in earlier education and training, or are merely a response to high rates of unemployment. Governments may also assume other training responsibilities, which are best left to the private sector.

The relative roles of the public and private sectors do differ from country to country. Much will depend on the stage of development of the private sector, and its capacity and willingness to tackle training effectively. This, in turn, may depend on the level of organization of the professional and trade associations.

The human resources development strategy

The human resources development strategy can also be published as a short document. It should cover the following main areas:

— The relationship of the tourism development policies to human resources.

— The current tourism product and the existing labour force this will summarize characteristics such as numbers of staff, geographical distribution, age, gender, educational level, staff turnover, length of employment, seasonal employment, training background and experience, occupation, and levels of skill. It will also assess the level of technology, operational standards, and occupational skill standards.

— The expected development of tourism and future workforce and training needs indicating the expansion in the number and category of hotels and other tourism enterprises.

— The current situation in the development of all training and education for tourism both for pre-employment and post employment levels. This will assess the adequacy of existing courses and programmes, location, capacity and output. As a result it will existing and future training gaps.

— The future development of all levels and types of education and training, located where it is needed and including the establishment any new public and/or private sector tourism training institutions. It may also propose measures to encourage the development of other new private sector training initiatives.

Tourism has developed steadily but conditions of work, worldwide, have not kept up. Workers, in many countries, have been forced to tolerate poor conditions. This has been mainly true of hotels, catering and similar establishments. The International Labour Organization's (ILO) Hotel, Catering and Tourism Committee is of fairly recent origin. The first meeting was held at the ILO in Geneva in December, 1989. A convention concerning working conditions in hotels, restaurants and similar establishments, ILO Convention 172, was not adopted until 1991. This convention applies to hotels and similar establishments which provide lodging, and restaurants and similar establishments providing food, beverages or both.

The convention, which is rather general in content, states that workers should be entitled to reasonable working hours, overtime provisions, and daily and weekly rest periods, according to national law and practice. They should also be given sufficient advanced notice of work schedules. Workers should be compensated in time or pay, if they work on public holidays, as determined by collective bargaining or in accordance with national law or practice. They should also receive annual leave with pay also as determined by collective bargaining or in accordance with national law or practice. If not entitled to full annual leave, they should receive leave proportionate to the length of service or payment of wages in lieu.

Regardless of any tips, the workers concerned should receive a basic remuneration that is paid at regular intervals, The sale and purchase of employment are prohibited. Although this is all the convention covers *it,* represents a step forward, *However, such* a belated and limited starting point gives an idea of the backward nature of the sector on a worldwide basis. Many of the more developed countries have already legislated far more comprehensive conditions for their tourism workers. Also the travel trade may often be more advanced in this area than the hotels, restaurants and similar establishments.

At the same time as the convention, the ILO also adopted a recommendation which goes further but lacks the teeth of a convention. It states that measures fixing hours of work and overtime should be the subject of consultations between the employer and workers or their representatives. Overtime work should be compensated by a higher rate of pay than normal. Working hours and overtime should be properly recorded, and each worker should have access to the records. Split shifts should be progressively eliminated.

The number and length of meal breaks should accord with local customs and traditions, and with whether the meal is taken in the establishment itself or elsewhere. Weekly rest should be not less than 36 hours which, wherever practicable, should be an uninterrupted period. The average daily rest period should be 10 consecutive hours. If the length of paid annual holidays is not four weeks for one year of service, it should be brought progressively to this level. Programmes of vocational education and training, and management development, should exist. They should be aimed at improving skills and the quality of job performance, and enhancing career prospects.

A GTA should encourage consultations between workers and employers to arrive at sound, fair and mutually acceptable working conditions. These are fundamental to the successful development of the sector.

Education and training

There are various definitions of the terms education and training. Education is about teaching ideas and knowledge; it's about understanding the world better. Training teaches specific skills; it's about how to do a job effectively.

In most cases students need some of both. 'This is particularly true when studying vocational subjects at an advanced level, for example, medicine, engineering, business, tourism and hotel management. The exact mix and balance between skill and educationally slanted subjects are questions of judgement.

The dividing line between education and training is often very fuzzy. The usage of each term also tends to differ from country to country. To avoid such difficulties, it is often best to link the two terms together education and training. Sometimes there is an aspect of elitism in the rejection of training. Superficial values often judge education as superior. As a result students are taught too few skills, and may be poorly qualified to take up many jobs.

A national council for tourism education and training

The GTA will look for ways to achieve the best possible coordination between the various agencies and organizations involved in human resources development. It is possible to establish either a national committee or council for tourism education and training,

This committee or council can be advisory and consultative, aimed at bringing together all the various interests: the government agencies responsible for tourism, tabour and education; the worker's organizations; and the profession at and trade associations. Also the association of the country's hotel and tourism schools, if it or a similar organization exists.

The committee or council provides for the active participation of the tourism sector itself, in setting standards and reviewing policies, objectives and results. It also monitors educational and training activities, watching for adjustments and improvements as they become necessary. The committee or council will be required to:

— Monitor, tabour market conditions, and all related trends.

— Keep under review the existing and future needs for management, supervisory, skilled and unskilled staff.

— Keep under review the existing education arid training institutions and centres arid their relevance to the identified needs, Liaise closely with the appropriate authorities and recommend any changes or modifications as considered appropriate.

— Recommend, based on the above, the development of

any new centres or programmes listing their proposed objectives and programmes.

— Liaise with the university system so as to promote the development of appropriate programmes and activities.

— Encourage the private sector to take initiatives in the provision of training facilities and programmes, and to recommend any tax and fiscal incentives.

— Advise, in particular, and encourage the sector in the development of inservice training programmes, establishing guidelines and organizing workshops.

— Keep under review a current database on the numbers and backgrounds of lecturers, instructors and trainers needed to meet existing and future needs.

— Set out guidelines as to the career development of vocational educators and trainers, and their recommended participation in intermediate and advanced programmes of further study.

— Promote the organization of seminars and workshops in management and supervisory techniques, and teaching and training techniques for trainers (train the trainers).

— Liaise with the relevant authorities in the development of occupational skill standards, and the testing and certification for agreed occupations.

— Enhance the image of the sector as an employer, and improve recruitment.

— Promote the effective teaching of foreign languages for tourism.

— Undertake all other activities which will assist in the

development of education and training for the sector, and the general improvement of standards.

Linking types and levels of training

Training should last a lifetime. One should build on what has gone before, adjust training to changing demands, and develop and upgrade People's skills. 'The links should exist between various stages and types of training. Each successive type of training should open up a further stage of personal advancement. These links are important. Training and education should not be categorized, and then sealed off within tight compartments. People should be able to transfer between different levels and types of course. The chef, for example, should be free to study management. The university graduate in management should be free to study cooking.

Surveys of the workforce

The first step in formulating a human resources development strategy is the study of the workforce. If adequate data do not already exist, surveys of the personnel currently employed in the tourism sector should be carried out. These will identify their characteristics, and training needs. They will also assess the level of technology, operational standards, and review the development of occupational skill standards for the sector.

Surveys start by identifying the number of hotels, tourist facilities and services in the country by size, category and geographical distribution. The methodology used to collect and analyse data should be discussed and agreed with the private sector itself.

Estimates of future workforce needs

The various employment ratios from the survey,

adjusting for trends, can be applied to the expected development of tourism to estimate future workforce requirements by occupation and level of skill.

The expected development of the tourism sector will cover growth of tourism traffic, number and location of new hotels and tourist facilities, and other future perspectives. These requirements for new staff should be reconciled against labour market conditions and the sector's current recruitment and selection policies.

The adequacy of existing education and training

The current situation in the development of all training and education for tourism—both for pre-employment and post-employment levels, also needs to be surveyed. As a result the adequacy of existing courses and programmes, location, quality, capacity and output, should be evaluated.

All educational institutions, centres, and training programmes should be identified and their curriculum, training materials and standards assessed for their current relevance and effectiveness. Post-employment training, including all in-service training, and train-the-trainer courses should also be assessed.

Future training needs

Future workforce needs should be translated into future training needs. These can be compared to the capacity of the existing educational and training facilities and programmes. As a result, shortfalls in this capacity to meet future needs can be identified. These are termed training gaps. They are gaps which will need to be filled.

One should develop a strategy to respond to all future training needs. It has to be developed according to all levels, all specializations and all parts of the country. It should cover as appropriate, universities, tertiary level vocational training institutions, and secondary schools. It will also cover a framework of minimum standards, inservice training, supervisory and management short course programmes, and foreign language training.

It will also recommend, if justified, the establishment of any new public and/or private sector tourism training institutions to interrelate appropriately with the national educational and vocational training framework. And it may also propose measures to encourage the development of other new private sector training initiatives.

Human resources information system

The human resources information system will form a part of the GTA's MIS, normally coordinated through the research department. It will monitor trends in employment, the profile of the labour force and labour market, the continuing trends in sectoral growth and development, future manpower and training needs and the capacity of existing education and training systems to respond to them.

To do this, it should input the results of the surveys described above. As a requirement in the annual licensing of hotels and other tourism enterprises, applicants may be asked to supply specific human resources data.

From time to time, other special surveys may be conducted to complement the information system. These may cover certain sections of the sector, or particular questions, or specific locations and provinces.

A framework of minimum standards

Occupational skill standards, trade testing and certification

Occupational skill standards are the minimum standards of knowledge and skills that a worker in a particular occupation, at a particular level, should possess. These are minimum acceptable standards staff can do better than the standards but nobody should fall short of them.

The emphasis of these standards is on employable skills. There is also a certain amount of knowledge needed with each skill. Standards for different occupations are agreed, and trade testing and certification are developed according to basic, intermediate and final levels of skill. Corresponding curriculum development and skills testing follow on. There are three steps:

— The standard specifies what people have to be able to do, where, when, how and under what conditions. It indicates both the skills and knowledge they should possess.

— Curriculum and teaching material which reflect the standard enable the trainee to reach the correct level of performance.

— The test validates that the trainee can reach satisfactorily this level of performance.

Skill standards help support sector-wide quality targets. They also assist employers in performance appraisal, career planning, recruitment and selection, and the development of training plans and targets. They create a basis for intercompany comparison, and they enable skills development to be monitored for the whole sector. National certification enables the quick recognition of levels of skill as well as the outputs of training institutions. 'Through the system of testing, all personnel can gain recognition for their level of skill.

Where classification schemes exist for hotels and other tourism enterprises, minimum training requirements may also be included.

At first glance, it may seem that industry-wide

occupational skill standards are very production oriented rather than market oriented. One starts by asking—what do workers do? One then asks what skills and knowledge they should possess to be able to do it. A marketing approach would start with what staff should be doing to meet the needs of the customers. Skill standards, however, are usually influenced by the major hotels, and tourism enterprises, many of which are operated by multinational companies, Usually these enterprises have already attuned their product to the mainstream market demands.

Regardless of which government agency is authorized to approve and license training institutions, minimum standards should also be established. Applications and submissions should include:

— A plan covering a period of at least five years. It will describe the needs and justification for the courses offered, and give details of student recruitment and links with the hotels and other tourism enterprises.

— Standards and curriculum describing their interrelationship with the relevant national skill standards and curriculum.

— The number of instructors and teachers, their qualifications and experience, and teacher/student ratios.

— The numbers of students enrolled or targeted, and the capacity of the programmes and their annual outputs.

— The financial structure including capitalization, projected operating results and sources of funds; government or any other grants and any proposed student fees.

— The facilities: land area, floor area ratio, range of

facilities, planning ratios, classrooms, offices, laboratories, library, student facilities, and other areas.

— The organization and the administrative staffing and systems.

— The employment expected to be obtained by students, on the completion of their education and training.

Pre-employment education and training

Vocational secondary schools

Some secondary schools may have, or should have, courses specializing in hotel, catering and travel subjects. This will keep this type of basic pre-employment course at the secondary level of education, leaving the tertiary level to concentrate on higher level courses. These basic courses will prepare school leavers for careers in the sector.

Tertiary level institutions of this kind are usually costly to build and equip and expensive to operate. Some countries have attempted to leave this level of training to the private sector. However, the private sector may not be sufficiently well developed to make this feasible. In such cases, the public sector will need to play a catalytic role setting up one or two key institutions to:

— Teach and develop management and supervisory level courses and programmes.

— Conduct research on employment trends, manpower and training needs, acting as a resource for the GTA, and assisting in the upkeep of the human resources section of the MIS.

— Maintain well-developed libraries, centres of documentation, and possibly computer Internet access.

— Act as a key resource in the development of national vocational skills standards and curriculum, and a system of trade testing and certification.

— Develop training material for all levels of tourism education and training.

— Train future vocational teachers for the country's secondary schools, as well as for private tertiary level hotel and tourism schools.

— Act as a major resource in the development of government tourism officials in tourism management and tourism development planning.

— Act as resource centres in certain specialized areas of tourism development, for example, in acting as custodian of the culinary heritage, or in acting as a resource centre in the promotion of small enterprise development in tourism.

In developed countries, without limitations of resources, there may be numerous tertiary level institutions offering hotel and tourism courses. Their contribution should be monitored by the GTA and any national committee or council,

Private sector tertiary level hotel and tourism educational and training institutions

Government, in close collaboration with the private sector, should encourage private enterprise to take appropriate training initiatives. Existing private sector schools should be encouraged to improve their physical facilities, teaching materials and equipment, as well as the standards of their teaching.

If there is a shortage of training programmes, the government may wish to encourage the creation of new institutions. It may therefore provide some guidelines for the location, size and student capacity for any new hotel training centre or centres, specifying the categories and levels of personnel to be trained. It may also offer incentives to set up such new institutions.

Universities

Universities generally have not all recognized tourism as a serious field for academic study and research and for assistance to the local community. Yet the universities play a key leadership role in the formulation of values related to overall socioeconomic development. In this sense they not only educate the future generation of technocrats, but condition attitudes to development options. For tourism to be viewed favourably, and for a wide range of graduates to have developed an awareness of its needs and potential contribution, the study of tourism should be included across a wide range of university programmes. This means not only full-time courses in various tourism specializations, but the inclusion of tourism in the social sciences, business studies, architectural, environmental and physical planning studies, and, language and communications studies.

The role of the universities in relation to tourism should be studied

— Identify and review current university programmes and activities, in support of the tourism sector

— Identify ways in which the universities can develop or improve this support.

Universities should be surveyed to review the following questions:

— University perspectives in developing postgraduate programmes related to various aspects of tourism, and particularly tourism development planning.

— The development of tourism options within the social sciences curriculum. Any MBA programme might have a tourism option, and even the possibility of a major in tourism.

— The intention and capacity to develop tourism as a subject for research, relating this to the specific university faculties and departments. The integration of tourism in any current university research programmes.

— Involvement with local government in studies related to the monitoring and development of the tourism sector, for example, the economic and employment impacts of tourism, the physical planning aspects, and the management and marketing aspects.

— The range of short courses in tourism-related subjects which a university might feel able to organize, related to the needs of a particular region.

— The links with community development and public awareness programmes, and the role of the university in these areas.

— The development of any programmes for small enterprises.

— The possibilities of using university resources in the training and upgrading of tourist guides.

— Any role that universities are able to play in foreign language teaching programmes, directed specifically at the needs of tourism.

University activities base themselves on the link between teaching, research and documentation and the concept of service, to the community,

Post-employment education and training

A supervisory and management development programme

The public and private sector training institutions should offer, often in collaboration with the trade associations, a variety of upgrading and recycling courses particularly for supervisors. However, these are often fragmented, and of varying standards, certification and scope.

A national committee or council, as described, can play an important part in identifying the precise needs for these types of course. It can then encourage their organization.

There may be a case for one centrally coordinated and controlled sector-wide management and supervisory development programme, endorsed by the appropriate government bodies. Such a scheme might best be organized by the professional and trade associations, under the auspices of any national committee or council.

In-service or in-house training programmes at the local level

A GTA should want to improve the operational standards of the sector. Inservice training will contribute significantly to this objective. The professional and trade associations should be encouraged to help organize this training working closely with its members.

Large enterprises should be encouraged to appoint specialized training personnel and develop in-house training departments and programmes. In many countries there is a need to cover basic skills training in the more remote parts of the country, and mobile training teams can be used. These teams will journey from area to area, organizing basic level training courses,

Specialized clubs and societies

The formulation of specialized clubs and societies among different hotel and tourism specialists, can greatly assist the objectives of human resources development. These may include, for example, one for marketing specialists, one for financial management specialists, and one for food and beverage specialists. Of particular importance will be one for the sector's personnel and training specialists, creating an additional forum for the discussion of all human resources development issues.

Training for small hotel and tourism enterprises

Small and medium-sized tourism enterprises offer an important source for new jobs and income generation in rural areas. New business activity of this kind can also create more opportunities for the employment of women.

Assistance will focus on those areas considered essential for successful business establishment and growth, namely:

— The identification of business opportunities.

— Technical assistance in project formulation and feasibility studies.

— Training in the basic skills and knowledge necessary for starting and running a business enterprise. Assistance in obtaining appropriate loan finance.

— Ongoing technical assistance and advice.

— Development of support networks for small businesses.

Cooperatives

The development of cooperatives also relates to the area of small and micro-tourism enterprises. There is a strong case for the creation of cooperatives among these operations, particularly small hotels, with a focus on marketing and training.

Other educational and training courses and programmes

Tourism documentation and publications

The tourism sector needs access to tourism texts, reference material, and teaching material. These needs may be met by private sector initiatives. If not, the GTA may promote and assist the production of various texts and material.

Vocational teachers

In many countries there is a shortage of qualified vocational teachers for hotel and tourism studies in both the private sector and public sector.

Some teachers can be drawn from senior personnel working in the sector, interested in becoming teachers. They can be given the teaching skills through specially organized intensive courses. However, where the sector is not as yet highly developed, this source of recruitment may be limited. Alternatively a number of hotel and tourism school graduates may be interested, after a few years of appropriate experience, in a teaching career. They will just need to acquire the necessary teaching skills.

Another course of action is to offer three-year courses at the tertiary level, designed to produce vocational teachers in tourism specializations.

Government tourism officials

Highly skilled technicians are essential to the effectiveness of a GTA. It is important that these personnel be kept up-to-date on various tourism management techniques and approaches.

Tourist guides

Many visitors form their impressions of a country through the tourist guide, The skills of these personnel are therefore a major influence on the quality of the overall tourism product.

Tourist guide standards may be developed for general tourist guides and tour leaders, with a separate category for various special interest guides. This latter category represents a guide specialized in one aspect of tourism or one tourism attraction. To designate the different categories, a system of badges can be introduced. A major problem affecting the standards of guides is the level of foreign language proficiency, and the proportion of guides available in each particular language. While English has become the major international language, its importance and widespread use has not replaced the need for proficiency in other languages; for example, in Japanese or Korean.

Tourist guide should be included among the occupational skill standards and national system of trade testing and certification.

Language training

The ability to communicate effectively with tourists is fundamental to a successful tourism sector. The introduction of specified standards for foreign language competence is essential, together with a range of comprehensive courses and programmes. A number of occupational skill standards for tourism should include a foreign language component.

Human resources development activities

Many of the activities have already been discussed and explained during the course of this chapter. The following summary can therefore act as a checklist. In accordance with the results planned, the first group of activities addresses the identification of existing workforce characteristics and future needs. It also assesses existing and future training needs. The second group tackles the planning and implementation of a programme to respond to these needs.

Result 1—Future workforce and training needs

The following activities, described earlier in the chapter, enable estimates of future workforce and training needs:

— Design surveys of the existing workforce; questionnaires, interviewing and survey methods employee.

— Conduct surveys of the existing workforce including profiles and characteristics, occupations held, levels of skill, and any training received.

— Analyse data and process the results.

— Incorporate survey results, on a continuing basis, within the MIS.

— Institute a system for the regular collection and updating of workforce statistics.

— Review the expected development and expansion of the sector, the number of hotels under construction and the addition of other tourism facilities and services.

— Prepare, on the basis of the above, forecasts for future workforce needs.

— Review the future workforce needs by occupation, level of skill, and area of the country and identify future training needs.

— Discuss the workforce characteristics, and future workforce and training needs with any national committee or council, or similar consultative body.

Result 2—Human resources development strategy

The following activities reflect the various components of the strategy discussed earlier in the chapter:

— Survey the existing education and training institutions and evaluate their contribution to human resources development; the quality of programmes and the capacity and output of trainees and students.

— Assess the capacity and quality of the existing education and training system and identify any training gaps.

— Prepare proposals for the improvement, expansion and development of the network of educational and training institutions and centres to meet future needs.

— Review inservice training programmes, and other Post-employment training, in relation to the identified needs.

— Identify future needs for specialized teachers and training staff, and formulate proposals for the necessary teacher training programmes.

— Formulate programmes for all specialized training, including, for example, government tourism officials, tourist guides, and planning and marketing specialists.

— Outline the proposals for the development of a comprehensive set of occupational skill standards for the sector.

— Consult with the universities on the development of their role in relation to both tourism studies and research.

— Review with the educational authorities the introduction of tourism-related education and training in existing educational institutions.

— Develop initiatives to assist the private sector in playing a more active part in training, including the development of more and/or better inservice training programmes.

— Integrate all proposals with other areas of the plan, namely, GTA management and organizational development, regulation and control, research, marketing, product development and public awareness programmes.

— Draft, review and finalize, or update and finalize as the case may be, the tourism human resources development strategy.

— Consult extensively with any national committee or council, or similar body, on all aspects of the strategy.

10

Managing Public Awareness Programme

The chapter goes on to examine local community involvement and the role of a local community tourism action group. It by explaining relations with the press, press releases and press conferences, advertising, tourist newspapers, television and radio, competitions, schools, a host' programme workshops and seminars and public awareness campaigns.

The role of public awareness

Listed among the tourism development policies was the need to keep the general public closely informed about the growth of tourism. This included giving explanations about its development and its contribution to the country's social and economic wellbeing. It also included the need to encourage the general public to support the development of both international and domestic tourism. Public opinion has to be informed and led. It has to respond to people's concerns. At the same Lime people themselves are a part of the tourism product, and should be able to make a commitment towards its success. The job of mobilizing public support on the side of tourism is first the GTA's. However, it is also the job of everybody who works in tourism.

For any local community a public awareness programme answers four fundamental questions:

— What is there positive to say about inbound tourism?

— About which issues should the local community be consulted?

— What help should be offered and to whom?

— Who are the inbound tourists and what are they like?

In answering these four questions a public awareness programme:

— Explains and signals.

— Explains, consults and involves,

— Explains and provides help,

— Explains and interprets,

A public awareness programme also explains to tourists important aspects of the local culture and how best to behave to get the most benefit from their visit.

Public awareness has many similarities to marketing. It is about communicating ideas, values and plans, and uses many of the same public relations, promotional, sales and advertising tools as marketing. It is trying to get across a point of view, to involve people, to inform them, to educate them, to benefit from their ideas and to win their support.

A public awareness programme will be coordinated at the national level by the GTA itself. It should cover mainly the contribution of tourism to national economic and social development and the perspectives for its future development. Other elements of public awareness should be organized at the local community level.

The GTA, however, should provide guidance, suggestions, resources and materials to local community action groups and visitor bureaus. The GTA may also coordinate nationally some other activities, for example country-wide competitions. An important part of public awareness addresses the concept of sustainable development. Not as an abstract idea but in concrete and practical ways This involves a commitment to maintaining high environmental standards through sensible controls.

This is a good question to pose to different groups, for example to groups of schoolchildren or groups from local clubs, societies and organizations. The question and the range of answers are exactly what public awareness programmes are designed to communicate. It is essential, as a starting point, to agree the message.

Ideas which people, given time to think and discuss the question, are likely to call out or list are as follows. These are some of the positive aspects which a public awareness programme should signal.

Inbound tourism:

— stimulates local economic development

— generates income

— creates new jobs and career opportunities

— creates new investment possibilities

— opens up chances for small enterprises

— earns foreign exchange

— creates an audience for local cultural performances

— stirs an interest in the local cuisine

— creates a market for local handicrafts and arts

— brings contacts with different cultures

— promotes an interest in foreign languages

— helps to improve the local environment
— triggers new infrastructural development
— enables the provision of new community services
— generates government revenue
— enhances the country's and the destination's image
— strengthens the sense of cultural identity
— assists local agriculture and manufacturing
— stimulates investment
— brings in students for educational programmes
— helps to make it a nicer place to live.

Nearly all of the above answers may involve both international and domestic tourism, and can serve as the basis for more detailed explanation and discussion. All of them can serve as the basis for news items and press releases.

About which issues should the local community be consulted?

The above list covers points about which people should be made more aware. They consist of the information which will expand people's understanding of tourism. There are a number of these issues which are not just a question of awareness and understanding, but of consultation. Many people may also have serious concerns and objections. They need a chance to voice these and to make their points of view known.

Tourism development plans, associated physical plans, and planning and zoning regulations need to be publicly aired, with sessions dedicated to public comments, questions, objectives and open discussion. Individuals and action groups should be aware of any rights they may have to register objections and appeals against particular developments,

In the presentation of new plans, the rationale, policies, strategies and objectives should be carefully explained. Objections and concerns often arise from misunderstandings.

Major issues are usually as follows:

— What are the perspectives for the development of tourism? How many tourists will be accommodated at any one time? Is this in keeping with the destination's carrying capacity?

— In land use planning and zoning, which areas are designated for what purpose? Where and how will tourism be allowed to develop and in what form?

— Where will new roads run, over what land, and to what purpose?

— Are there any new airports or extensions to existing airports planned? If so, where and on what scale?

— Is basic infrastructure adequate and will it be expanded, for example, water, power supplies and waste disposal?

— What specific planning regulations are to be applied to hotels and other tourism buildings building setbacks, height restrictions, floor area and site coverage ratios?

— How do these interrelate with other types of building and proposed zoning plans?

— In which areas will hotel and other types of tourist facilities not be allowed and why?

— Are there new plans to add car parking facilities, pedestrianize certain *streets and* control vehicular traffic?

People should be told where they can view the detailed plans involved, and what further meetings may be held to review the details of these plans. They should know where and how to ask their questions.

Many people will want to be informed about tourism not only to learn about it, but also to take particular action. For example, they may want to know how a son can train for a tourism career; or how they can rent a spare room to accommodate a visiting student; or how they can start a guest house.

— People will need answers to the following types of question:

— Where to go to learn more about tourism? Details of the following items should be provided: foundation and awareness courses; lectures and conferences; leaflets and publications.

— How to meet tourists? A possible programme might be organized by the visitors bureau whereby visitors and local citizens, with, similar hobbies or professional interests, are introduced so as to meet and spend a little time together.

— What jobs are available and careers open? The prospects, opportunities and training available, including details of courses and educational programmes.

— How to start a small tourism business? Details should be provided about the development of initial concepts and ideas. How to estimate capital costs, develop a business plan, and obtain loan finance.

— How to rent a room in one's house, for visiting students and members of youth groups? One should tell people where to find information about groups, times, prices, requirements and listings.

— How to clarify questions of planning permission? One should also tell people where they can view plans and future schemes, and obtain information and advice.

— Where to study foreign languages? Opportunities of using foreign language competence in tourism, including part-time jobs and training as a tourist guide. Details of language institutes, courses and programmes should also be given.

— How to design the products which visitors would like to buy? This may involve advice on menus and the choices to include. It may also include advice on handicrafts, souvenirs, or fashion items and jewellery design.

All of these answers will require liaison between the GTA or local visitors bureau and other agencies and organizations; for example, the educational authorities and secondary schools, the educational and training institutions, the planning authority, the local enterprise agency, the town hall or local government authorities themselves, the chamber of commerce and the local trade and professional associations.

Who are the inbound tourists and what are they like?

Most people have only a stereotyped image of visitors from abroad. This is true even in Europe where one country's understanding of another is still sketchy and full of mistaken ideas. One should explain the following principal characteristics of the culture which each major market represents:

— The country and its geography, climate, population, constitution, government and economy.

— Language and culture, ethnic arid tribal origins, historical influences, educational and social development.

— The arts: literature, theatre, music, painting, sculpture, architecture, handicrafts, etc. The impact of contemporary arts.

— Food and drink. National holidays. Religious practices. Codes of dress. Customs and traditions, Minorities and subcultures.

— The way of life, Lifestyles, values and attitudes. Behavioural characteristics and social norms. Regional differences. Sexual behaviour and consumption of alcohol and tobacco, Drugs and drug abuse,

These five areas sketch out the comprehensive profile of a given country and nationality. This profile provides for valuable understanding and insight when dealing with tourists from different countries.

Local community involvement

In every community there are groups of people with an interest in tourism and its development. They may be disparate groups representing different aspects of tourism; the local historical or archaeological society, for example, or an environmental group or the local hotel owners and travel agencies. Some may be directly involved with tourism, others less directly.

From these groups leaders will spring up; people with well-defined viewpoints prepared to give their time to prepare background notes and papers, call meetings, organize agendas, and contact other individuals, groups and organizations. These people will start to become aware of other people who share the same ideas. Eventually they will all come together, possibly through the chamber of commerce or similar body, as a committee or subcommittee set up for the purpose. Gradually a public forum on tourism is created, which may include tourism professionals, tourism businessmen, and people working on the fringes of tourism together with ordinary concerned citizens. This may take time and the leaders may change, but the initiative is maintained. It is often more likely to happen at the local level involving villages, townships, small resort areas and perhaps some cities. It represents the typical action of a small community anxious to influence future development.

The GTA should be sensitive to any local initiatives and assist in any way possible to get people working together. If, however, there are dynamic private sector people leading such initiatives, then the GTA should let them gel on with it—playing a supportive role only.

If the leaders and catalysts do not emerge and tourism is important, then the GTA should take the initiative. It can convene workshops or seminars to get people together for the first time arid stimulate their interest. Local individuals and organizations are then likely to continue by themselves.

The role of a local community tourism action group

As noted at the beginning of the chapter, the GTA should spearhead public awareness at the national level, It should maintain excellent relations with the press keeping it well informed on sectoral performance, tourism statistics, expansion in supply and other major trends and developments. There may be some other activities best undertaken by the GTA at the national level. For example, some radio and television programmes, the production of audiovisual and other material, and national competitions.

Some activities may also be undertaken at the regional and local levels. It is here that the close involvement of the community can be built up. A local community tourism action group can organize many activities. Depending on the community, different organizations may take the lead in organizing a group. This may also depend on the local GTA, or if the municipality has a tourism office or department, or whether an initiative to set up a visitor's bureau has been taken. Generally speaking, the role of the local community action groups is as follows:

— Maintain close links with the GTA receiving from it a newsletter, a constant flow of other current information on tourism, printed and audiovisual material, and notes, suggestions and guidelines on the development of the public awareness of tourism.

— Maintain close links with the sector's trade and professional associations, and any consultative organizations on tourism such as a council or committee on tourism education and training, or a joint marketing board or similar body.

— Organize a host programme providing basic foundation courses for tourism-related workers,

— Make the public aware of both the benefits and responsibilities brought by tourism.

— Make the public aware of the background and culture of the tourists. Stimulate public interest in the characteristics and requirements of tourism.

— Inform the public about new proposals and developments, reviewing their desirability and impact.

— Gain the commitment of both tourism workers and the population at large to the successful development of tourism.

— Provide education and training for all workers in direct contact with tourists.

— Develop on the part of visitors, some awareness of local cultural norms, practices and expectations.

— Maintain close relationships with the media enlisting their help and support in pursuing the above objectives.

— Organize a wide range of activities in pursuit of the above objectives including workshops, seminars, exhibitions, festivals, competitions and other special events.

— Advertise tourism public awareness messages through selected media.

If the local community action group is able to fulfil this role satisfactorily, the GTA may decide to offer financial support. For example the GTA may offer a fixed financial grant, or it may offer to match the funds provided through the local private sector and local government.

It is obviously in the interests of the GTA and tourism in general to build up effective and extensive local involvement.

Relations with the press

It is critical to maintain good relations with the press. This is a responsibility of the GTA's public relations staff. It is important not to fragment this activity, not to have different people talking to the press in an uncoordinated manner. The press should go through one centralized public relations office. Some flexibility has to exist on press contacts but people should always obey clearly established guidelines.

In public awareness the GTA should see that the press is kept informed:

— About trends in the growth of tourism, the numbers

of tourists, the average length of stay, the foreign exchange earnings, the jobs created, and the impact on GDP and government revenues,

— About the government involvement in shaping tourism—new public sector projects, improvements to community services, particularly health and education, and new infrastructural projects.

— About tourism's support for the arts and contemporary culture, e.g. film festivals, song festivals, successes of local bands and pop groups, singers, other musicians, writers, poets and artists.

— About the perspectives for improvement and expansion. What the sector is doing to try and maintain and improve quality levels. What new projects are to be developed; where, in what form and with what impact.

Press releases and press conferences

The fax machine now offers an excellent way of distributing press releases. They should be written on all items of interest and sent out immediately. It is better to give the media too much material than not enough. Although still designated as press releases they should be distributed to radio and television as well.

Personnel who write press releases should be trained accordingly, and write in the correct journalistic style. It is essential that releases are impeccable well written and with no spelling mistakes or errors of syntax.

Press releases have to be newsworthy. It is pointless to send out weak stories which have no interest. It is also important to follow stories up. Press releases need to provide updates on what happened or what is going to happen.

All of the media should be given information. It is short-sighted to start to work with only one or two favourite publications while neglecting the others. However, this does not prevent the selective distribution of some releases. Not everything interests everybody. A well-organized public relations office should know where to send and where not to send particular items.

Press conferences need to be worthy of the occasion. The news to be announced should be of some import, with the head of the GTA acting as spokesperson. For example, the sectors performance for the last year with a complete set of results. Or major new tourism developments or projects.

The press conference should be held in a suitable place with comfortable seating and good audiovisual equipment. The press should be given every facility, and coffee and refreshments should be served. It is a good idea for the GTA, depending on the topics to be discussed, to invite the participation of the trade and professional associations. The sector then presents a united front demonstrating that it is working in a well coordinated manner.

Advertising

The use of billboards can be effective in promoting public awareness. They represent a very direct form of advertising having both immediacy and impact. And they are seen by a large and random cross-section of society. The different space and locations have to be planned to form a network of coverage across a given city or area, for example, billboards might carry the following sorts of messages:

Courtesy Pays

Keep the Place Beautiful

Tourism Helps Us All
It's Nice to Come Back

Many different themes can be developed and used. Large billboards lend themselves to strong images and powerful messages.

Some local newspaper and magazine advertising can also be used. This need not be at the expense of the GTA. Tourism's private sector interests can be encouraged to sponsor some public awareness advertising. Radio and television stations can be encouraged to do the same.

Tourist newspapers

Tourist newspapers around the world are usually published in English on a weekly basis. English has now become the universally preferred second language. While 400 million people have English as a mother tongue, it is estimated that another 400 million speak it as a second language. Several hundred million more have some knowledge of the language, and are able to communicate at the basic level.

Most printed material used in marketing tended to mix three purposes information, education and promotion. This is also true of a newspaper although much of the information can obviously be categorized as news.

The newspaper is likely to feature the highlights of local news, items about tourism, about places, people and attractions of interest. Also about events, entertainment, where to eat and what to see, and about the characteristics of the country. It may carry a map of the town and the area, it may also run a lively letters to the editor section, and any number of other features. Editors should maintain close contact with the GTA. In turn the GTA should support and assist these newspapers in whatever way possible.

Television and radio

The use of television and radio will depend on the particular country and culture. There are many types of programmes that can use tourism as a theme, Radio !ends itself particularly to discussions on tourism and calling programmes, with listeners able to comment and ask questions.

The local stations ill tourist destinations can find many opportunities to support tourism. Programmes can be broadcast live from the hotels and resorts. Interviews with tourists and tourism workers can be featured, together with various types of quiz programme. A visitors of the week programme can be produced in which a tourist couple will talk about their holiday and choose favourite pieces of music. Programmes on the background and culture of various nationalities can also be produced.

Television also offers a variety of opportunities. A series of tourist dance competitions or talent competitions may make good viewing. Discussion programmes, tourist profiles, foreign language courses may all give wide exposure to various aspects of tourism. This all helps to build and develop public awareness.

Competitions

Skills competitions are preferable to competitions based on luck. Professionals may be invited to demonstrate their skills and knowledge. Or competitions may be based on ideas and insights about tourism in general. For example:

— Barman of the year, waiter of the year, chef of the year, etc.

— Hotel of the year, restaurant, travel agency of the year, etc.

— A national essay competition for tourist guides.
— Tourism essay competitions for schoolchildren.
— Most beautiful garden and most beautiful house.
— Best short story on tourism.
— A cookery festival, exhibition and competition.
— The most courteous police officer, immigration officer, customs officer, etc.
— Taxi driver of the year.
— Best newspaper article published on tourism.
— Best public awareness poster.

There are any number of other competitions which are possible. They should be tailored to the particular characteristics of the country's tourism. Some can be organized at the national level, others at the local level. Prizes should be organized with the collaboration of the sector itself, particularly with the help of the airlines and multinational companies. Some winning personnel can be sent on short study trips abroad with arrangements made to meet their counterparts in other countries. Other prizes may be more conventional.

Maximum media coverage should be arranged for all competitions. Their objective is to focus attention on tourism and to promote the opportunities which the sector offers. A number of tourism companies may be willing to sponsor selected competitions.

Schools

A special introductory text on tourism should be prepared for use in the secondary schools. It should cover tourism's overall characteristics; the product, the demand, tourism development planning and the environmental, economic and sociocultural impacts. It should describe the opportunities offered by tourism.

There are different possibilities as to where and how to slot tourism into school curriculum. For example, it could be a part of social studies, geography or current affairs.

Additionally the local community action group or GTA can organize talks and presentations on tourism, particularly related to careers. Students should be told about jobs, prospects and training courses. One can organize essays and other competitions designed to stimulate interest in tourism.

A host programme

The participants tor a host programme should be drawn from all occupations which have direct contact with tourism: for example, hotel and restaurant employees, shop assistants, taxi drivers, customs and immigration officials, travel and airline personnel and bank personnel. This programme can consist of a training module of perhaps 30 hours contact time which can be taught through either a full time or part-time course. The curriculum can be developed and tried with some test groups before being finalized. However, the programme will probably cover the following subjects.

— General knowledge about tourism. Of what does it consist? What makes it a success?

— Main aspects of the national cultural heritage. What is there to interest tourists? What can they see and visit?

— Other aspects of the tourist product. What else is there to see and do?

— Culture and background of visitors. Where do they come from? What are they like?

— Motivational and behavioural aspects of tourism. What do people want? What are their needs?

— Standards, environment and quality. Upkeep and conservation.

— Crime and the tourist. Warning and protecting tourists.

— Social and communications skills; how to deal with tourists. Making holidays memorable.

At the end there should be a test. On satisfactory completion of the course participants can be awarded a badge and a certificate. They become accredited hosts. They should be encouraged to feel proud of this achievement.

Workshops and seminars

The major objectives of public awareness conferences, workshops and seminars are to educate people, to involve them, to listen to then), and to join with them in the discussion of policies and future plans. One seeks a common understanding, a consensus of opinion, and a commitment to certain courses of action.

These activities call for well-illustrated presentations about the existing situation, the needs and opportunities, and the proposed sectoral expansion and development. Ideas about policies and strategies should be carefully explained. People should be split up into discussion groups. Panels should be used for the final feedback and discussion sessions. Workshops or conferences should allow the maximum possible participation, and use an ample cross section of speakers and panelists.

Campaigns

Some advertising may be best linked to a number of other activities to form a campaign. A campaign can include conferences, television and radio programmes, competitions and contests, and exhibitions and festivals.

It should be an intensive programme organized around a theme and running for a given period of time, for example, it can take the form of a tourism week.

A tourism week can be planned as an integrated programme highlighting all aspects of tourism. It can be opened perhaps by the head of the government and feature other prominent personalities during the course of the week. Activities should be designed to attract wide press coverage.

Making the tourists aware

People need help in the discovery and enjoyment of a new culture. They should be advised as to what to expect, how best to behave and what to watch out for; situation were described where visitors of one cultural and religious background encountered strong religious beliefs of a different kind. The world's religions tend to know little about each other. One should explain to visitors the basic beliefs and practices of the principal local religions.

Most tourists, particularly when visits to religious sites are made, are to learn more. Printed material can help. Booklets and leaflets can summarize a religion's most important aspects. Books of a more substantial nature should be on sale. Posters can be used to alert tourists on how to dress and behave. In general tourists should be advised on how to dress. Tourist guides should do this. The use of posters can also be effective. Some destinations are very open and permissive, others are sensitive to dress judged as improper.

Hotels and resorts can organize a lecture programme on aspects of the country and its culture, although this is seldom done. Tourists generally welcome the opportunity, in relaxed and pleasant circumstances, to listen and learn about the country they are visiting. The

GTA should encourage hoteliers to take more initiatives of this kind.

All one can do is make tourists aware of local norms. It is impossible to restrain them completely. People on holiday are out to enjoy themselves. Some may drink too much. Some may be a little too noisy. Let groups enjoy themselves, it is seldom that behaviour will gel out of hand.

Public awareness objectives and results

Objective

Develop and execute integrated public awareness programmes, designed to improve the general public's involvement with tourism, as well as its general perception and understanding of it.

Result 1

An integrated public awareness programme using

— A range of media: for example, newspapers arid Magazines, television and radio advertising and bill board, and printed material.

— A range of complementary activities: competitions and awards, programmes for the schools, workshops and seminars,

Result 2

A tourism host training programme offered on both a full time and part-time basis for personnel having some contact with tourists, for example, hotel and restaurant employees, shop assistants, taxi drivers, customs and immigration officials, and travel and airline personnel.

Public awareness activities

Result 1 —An integrated programme

The following are the activities needed to formulate and execute a public awareness programme:

— Frame the precise objectives and content of the proposed public awareness programme.

— Assist in the development of any local community action groups or other local initiatives.

— Specify the various target audiences to be addressed the public in general, the business community, special interest groups, and schoolchildren.

— Plan the messages to be communicated and the media to be used.

— Integrate proposals with other areas of the plan; namely, management and organizational development, regulation and control, research, marketing, product development and human resources development.

— Develop relations with the national and local press, and outline the use of press conferences, editorial, and advertising.

— Formulate ideas for the use of television and radio, call-in programmes, discussion panels, special programmes, advertising, etc. and implement.

— Plan and implement the placement of other types of advertising, including the use of bill boards.

— Plan the use of various printed material, design and prepare the items, and produce and distribute or display.

— Develop and organize various competitions, and decide the participation and prizes. Organize any exhibitions and other surrounding events.

— Organize a specific programme for schools; career talks, talks on tourism, special days and events, and special projects.

— Organize a programme of workshops and seminars, developing objectives, targeting audiences, and organizing venues and speakers.

— Develop any comprehensive public awareness campaigns to run in connection with a tourism week or other similar special event.

— Lobby on behalf of tourism, to mobilize the support of both public and private sector organizations and agencies.

Result 2—A tourism host training programme

The following are the activities to be undertaken:

— Liaise with the various trade and professional associations at the national, regional and local levels, reviewing the needs for the host training course.

— Agree the duration of the course and its content.

— Draft the curriculum in modular style specifying and preparing the teaching materials.

— Agree the form of certification and any accompanying badge or other form of designation.

— Recruit and select part-time teachers for the course, and train and certify them accordingly.

— Agree the organization, venues, enrolment, fees, etc. for each particular location.

— Organize, advertise and implement the programme.

11

International Organisations and Tourism

Participation is the keyword. The growth and development of any discipline depends to a large extent on the manner in which it associates itself with those pursuing similar disciplines. The world bodies or the international organisations provide a platform where ideas are exchanged and problems of mutual interest discussed. The subject specialists of various disciplines *be it* arts, science, commerce, etc., meet together on a common platform and discuss areas of mutual interest. This results in growth, development and promotion of the discipline. For any industry or discipline to develop, an organisation is an essential prerequisite as it plays a vital role in its proper planning, development and growth. Organisation consists of individuals whose primary role is the achievement of the objectives for which it has been set up. The aim of the organisation is to deploy staff into working groups, associating those with similar functions or purposes so as to move efficiently to obtain a desired result from their combined effort. In other words, organisation means combination of a group of individuals whose main purpose is to achieve through group action the objectives for which it has been set up.

Association of an organisation with a particular discipline with similar such organisations becomes a combined effort to develop the discipline. This association can be at various levels--local, regional, national and international. The international tourism organisations emerged with the objective of developing and promoting the subject of tourism. The role of international tourism organisations in strengthening tourism by way of combined efforts is therefore of vital importance.

The increasingly international character of modem tourism and the growing influence of international agencies in various fields are reflected in the growth and development of international cooperation and organisation in tourism. Organisers, and the providers of various tourist services whether in private or public sector come together at various forums at the international level to discuss and share common problems and arrive at certain conclusions. The providers of tourist services sometimes meet as individuals or as individual firms, but more often when their national sectoral organisation is a member of a particular international body which has been set up for general or specific purposes.

There are numerous international organisations existing today. Some of these organisations are specifically concerned with development and promotion of tourism at the international level while others deal with the development and promotion of tourism in a particular region. There are other international organisations which do not concern themselves specifically with tourism but with fields indirectly connected with tourism like airlines, travel agents and the hoteliers.

Early history of cooperative endeavour

The history of cooperative endeavour in tourism can be

traced back to the year 1908. Three countries--France, Spain and Portugal felt the need of pooling their resources in the interest of promoting tourism and founded the 'Franco Hispano-Portuguese Federation of Tourist Association'. This might perhaps be considered as the first international tourist organisation. Although started in a modest way and limited to a small region in Europe, this association made a beginning in cooperative endeavour in the field of tourism and paved the way for future such endeavours on a very large scale.

The need for international collaboration in the field of tourism found favour with many countries in the years following World War I. This need found its expression in setting up in the year 1924 of the 'International Union of Official Organisations for Tourist Propaganda'. The first congress of the Organisation was held at The Hague, Holland, in 1925, and, was attended by delegates from national tourist organisations of fourteen European countries. The aims of this congress were to exchange information on tourist publicity, to obtain international customs concessions for the export and import of tourist publicity material and to alleviate frontier formalities or other obstacles to free international tourist traffic. This organisation functioned with a considerable degree of success until the eve of the last World War. The International Union of Official Organisations for Tourist Propaganda was the forerunner of the International Union of Official Travel Organisation. In the year 1946, the representatives of various national tourist organisations met in London and the following year, in 1947, the International Union of Official Travel Organisations (IUOTO) was founded.

Although cooperative endeavour in the field of tourism began as early as in the year 1908 and the international organisation formed in the year 1924, the vital encouragement however, came from the United Nations in the year 1963. The importance of the work of the international organisations in the field of tourism was recognised by the United Nations Conference on International Travel and Tourism held in Rome in the year 1963. The conference recommended that "the United Nations should consider the International Union of Official Travel Organisations (IUOTO) as its main instrument for the promotion of tourism". The encouragement given by the United Nations to IUOTO paved the way for greater cooperation at international level in the field of tourism. India's first contact with the international tourism organisations was, however, established in the year 1950 when it joined the International Union of Official Travel Organisations.

International union of official travel organisations

It was in 1925 that the international cooperation in tourism development' had its beginning. The growth of international tourism in the 'twenties, and the consequent need for cooperation between national tourist bodies, led to the holding of an international conference in 1925 called by the National tourist Office of Holland. Representatives of fourteen countries took part in the conference. Further conferences led to the setting up of the International Union of National Tourist Propaganda Organisations (IUNTPO) at The Hague. This body sought to promote facilitation and overcome the obstacles to free international tourist traffic; such obstacles having come about as a result of the 191418 World War. IUNTPO, whose general aims were more streamlined than its title, established close contact with the Economic Committee of the Old League of Nations.

With the advent of the second World War, IUNTPO had to discontinue its practical activities. It was with the object of contributing to postwar reconstruction that one of its members, the Travel Association of Great Britain and Northern Ireland, decided in the spring of 1964 to call a World Conference of National Tourist Organisations to discuss the restoration and reconstruction of travel facilitation destroyed by the war. The conference took place in London in October 1946 and the following year, in 1947, International Union of Official Travel Organisations (IUOTO) was founded. The Organisation represented over one hundred national tourist offices of various countries as full members and about eighty-eight national and international organisations, of both public and private sector, as associate members. It was at that time the only organisation whose activities related to every aspect of tourism throughout the world. One of its major tasks was the stimulation and coordination of tourism development. The category of full members was restricted to national tourist organisations or other organisations set up to promote the development of tourism established or recognised by the governments of the countries. The category of associate members was confined to international or national organisations, either commercial or noncommercial, representing tourist interest or interested in promotion of tourism.

The IUOTO was the only international organisation which grouped together the governmental or official tourist organisations of all parts of the world on the basis of one for each country and territory. The principal aim of the organisation was to stimulate and increase the free flow of persons in the interest of economic development and to strengthen social and cultural relations. This it tried to do by way of resolving the problems arising in the field of tourist movements and in the adoption of a common policy amongst the members for all questions dealing with international travel. The organisation tried in various ways, to develop the tourist industry in the member countries, and particularly by promoting measures on a national as well as on an international level aimed at reducing travel barriers and stimulating the movement of travellers.

A technical and specialised organisation, IUOTO was granted consultative status by the United Nations. The supreme body of the IUOTO was the General Assembly which held its meeting once a year. It had various committees and commissions which were assigned different subjects. The executive committee consisted of full members, while the Regional Commissions covered specific areas. The technical commissions aimed at examining all problems on a universal scale. The Secretariat General, whose headquarters were located at Geneva in Switzerland, was responsible for ensuring liaison between the members.

The general assembly

The General Assembly which consisted of full and associate members, was a sovereign body of the IUOTO. It met once a year. It elected the President and the Vice-President of the IUOTO, the members of the executive committee and the Auditors and decided upon the applications for new membership. Laying down general policy of the organisation and the actions to be carried out was another important function of the General Assembly.

The executive committee

The Executive Committee consisted of eighteen full members, representing the various geographical areas and, in an ex-officio capacity, the presidents of the Regional and Technical Commissions. Presided over by the President of the IUOTO and assisted by the Vice-Presidents, the Executive Committee was responsible to the General Assembly for the direction of the affairs of the IUOTO.

Regional commissions

Following Regional Commissions were created by the IUOTO:

(a) *The Regional Travel Commission for Europe* included the countries of western and eastern Europe. The countries of Western Europe were also grouped in the European Travel Commission which was an independent body responsible in particular for the collective publicity campaigns carried out in the United States of America.

(b) *The African Travel* Commission was responsible for tourism in African areas which had vast possibilities for growth.

(c) *The Regional Travel Commission for the Pacific and Fast* Asia. The members of this Commission were also members of the Pacific Area Travel Association (PATA) which had accepted to act as the regional commission for the Pacific and the East Asian areas.

(d) *The South Asian Travel Commission* was responsible for developing modern travel facilities in a very extensive area which had become travel conscious.

(e) *The Middle-East Travel Commission* was responsible for developing travel facilities in the Area. It had also created subcommissions of the Arab and non-Arab countries.

(f) *The Regional Travel Commission for the Americas* was created following the acceptance of the Inter-American Travel Congress to act as regional travel commission of the IUOTO for the American continent as a whole.

Technical committees

IUOTO had the following technical committees:

(1) *Committee on the Elimination of Travel Barriers* was concerned with the easing up of passport and visa requirements, frontier formalities including restrictions on the free circulation of publicity material, health regulations, taxes borne directly or indirectly by the tourists and tourist industry, currency controls, and other matters which slow down travel.

(2) *Research Committee* was charged with studying international travel statistics as well as carrying out other special studies with the assistance of the Advisory Committee.

(3) *Travel Plant Committee* was responsible for studies on hotels as well as motels, hotel accommodation and classification, standardization of hotel guides, state aid to the hotel industry, the training of hotel personnel and additional means of accommodation.

(4) *Committee on Travel Development* offered assistance to member countries in the field of travel, counselled national tourist offices *on* publicity activities, dealt with social tourism and youth and credit travel. The Committee also dealt with travel films, which came to be regarded as one of the most important means of tourist publicity.

(5) *Transport Committee* was responsible for examining the existing conditions in the field of rail, road, sea and air transportation and suggesting better facilities and improvements. It studied and recommended measures to improve the conditions and facilities available at airports, seaports *and* land frontier entry points.

The secretariat general

The Secretariat General which was located in Geneva was the principal executive body for the decisions of the Assembly and the Executive Committee as well as the Presidency. It ensured the liaison between the members of the IUOTO, carried out the studies entrusted to it by the IUOTO members and was charged with the administration. It maintained contact with other international organisations. It produced various IUOTO publications and ensured the functioning of the Tourist Documentation Centre.

IUOTO had closer cooperation with the United Nations Economic and Social Council (ECOSOC), the World Health Organisation (WHO), the International Labour Organisation (ILO), the International Civil Aviation Organisation (ICAO) and the Inter Governmental Maritime Consultative Organisation (IMCO). It also had permanent links with the regional commissions of the United Nations.

The Organisation was set up with the following objectives:

(i) *To promote* the economic development of countries through tourism.

(ii) *To enhance* the social and cultural role of tourism in the life of nations.

(iii) To further the vital contribution of tourism to international trade.

(iv) To foster the steady expansion of international tourist flow.

(v) To supply its members with the results of the permanent tourist market research to enable them to keep abreast of development in this field.

(vi) *To protect* the interests of tourists and the tourist industry.

(vii) To gain recognition of the value of tourism as a means of prompting international understanding and world peace.

In order to achieve its objectives the organisation undertook various activities like monitoring and identifying trends in world tourism, studies on travel demands, market trends, tourist motivation, surveys of environmental effects of travel expansion and formulation of recommendations for the protection of natural and cultural resources. Other activities included acting as clearing house for tourist information, keeping its members informed of tourism development and its economic and social, aspects, publication of material, fostering research in the field of tourism, organising vocational training programmes and promoting the implementation of international agreements.

IUOTO's dynamic activities resulted in countless significant achievements. Some of the achievements were undertaken jointly with other organisations. These included preparation and participation in the United Nations on Customs Facilities and Tourism, initiation, preparation and participation in the United Nations Conference on International Travel and Tourism in Rome and initiation and realization of International Tourist Year. Besides establishing the Tourist Documentation Centre, the IUOTO has been responsible for organising various international travel research seminars and workshops. Another significant achievement of IUOTO has been the establishment of the International Centre for Advanced Tourism Studies at Turin, Italy and organisation of interdepartmental or specialized seminars on marketing, management, physical planning and promotion. It had also organized correspondence courses for the staff working in the field of tourism. Annual compilation and publication of official international travel statistics is yet another significant achievement of the IUOTO.

The IUOTO was the only non-governmental organisation whose activities covered every sector of tourism throughout the world. The organisation made a pioneering effort in the stimulation and coordination of tourism development at the international level. This pioneering task of the organisation is now being carried out by the World Tourism Organisation. The World Tourism Organisation came into existence as a result of the transformation of IUOTO on January 2, 1975. It was called upon to succeed IUOTO.

India joined the International Union of Official Travel Organisations in the year 1950.

World tourism organisation

The World Tourism Organisation (WTO), an inter-governmental technical body dealing with all aspects of tourism, began its legal existence on January 2, 1975. It was born of the International Union of Official Travel Organisation (IUOTO). The swift expansion of travel had created the need for a world body able to deal with tourism problems at the government level, and this led to the transformation of IUOTO into WTO.

Like its predecessor (IUOTO), the WTO has a very emphatic technical character, essentially creative and dynamic, performing a well defined service for its member states. The aims of the organisation, its *raison d'etre,* are defined with clarity in Article 3 of the statute which is divided into three sections:

(i) The fundamental aim of the Organisation shall be the promotion and development or tourism with a view to contributing to economic development, international understanding, peace, prosperity, and universal respect for, and observance of, human rights and fundamental freedoms for all without distinction to either race, sex, language or religion. The Organisation shall take all appropriate action to attain this objective.

(ii) In pursuing this aim, the Organisation shall pay particular attention to the interests of the developing countries in the field or tourism.

(iii) In order to establish its central role in the field of tourism, the Organisation shall establish and maintain effective collaboration with the appropriate organs of the United Nations and its specialised agencies. In this connection the Organisation shall seek a cooperative relationship with and participation in the activities of the United Nations Development Programme, as a participating and executing agency.

The World Tourism Organisation was originally conceived as an inter-governmental organisation in a UN General Assembly resolution--Number 2529--on December 5, 1969. This resolution called for establishment of WTO to play a "central and decisive role" in the field of tourism and to maintain effective collaboration with the appropriate organs of the United Nations and its specialised agencies.

At Torremolinos, in June 1977, the second General Assembly of WTO approved an Agreement with the United Nations for Cooperation and Relationships. On December 20, 1977 the 32nd General Assembly of the UN approved this Agreement which is now in force. In immediate implementation of this Agreement, the UN General Assembly in December 1977 a so approved a resolution sponsored by the Philippines with 24 cosponsors, including India, requesting the WTO "to intensify its efforts to promote tourism, particularly in developing countries, through international cooperation and to report to the General Assembly at its 33rd session on action taken". The WTO became an executing agency of the UNDP in May 1976. A few months later, UNDP Resident Representatives throughout the world became WTO representatives for all matters concerning technical cooperation in the field or tourism. The WTO has already completed its first project in Jordan and is now processing many more requests from member states, including Asian members, for both national and regional assistance programmes and projects.

There are three categories of members: full members, associate members, affiliate members. Full members are the sovereign states. Associate members are the territories or groups of territories not responsible for their external relations but whose membership is approved by the state assuming responsibility for their external relations. Affiliate members are international bodies, both intergovernmental and nongovernmental concerned with specialised interests in tourism, as well as commercial and noncommercial bodies and associations whose activities are related to the aims of WTO.

The activities of the organisation include: (i) clearing house for all available information on international and domestic tourism including statistical data, legislation and regulation and special events and its systematic collection, analysis and dissemination; (ii) making travel easier by reducing and simplifying frontier formalities and removing barriers to the free movement of tourists; (iii) organising and convening international conferences, seminars, round tables and technical meetings oil all aspects of tourism; (iv) preparation of draft international agreements on tourism, and; (v) examining vocational training problems with a view to contributing to the establishment of suitable teaching programmes tailored to specific needs, especially in the developing countries.

The permanent activities of WTO include the collection and updating of available information on training needs. Special activities include participation in technical cooperation projects for vocational training. There are three organs through which WTO functions:

(i) *General Assembly:* This is the supreme organ and sovereign body of WTO composed of delegates representing full members, associate members and representatives of affiliate members. It meets every two years and may consider any question and make recommendations on any matter within the competence of WTO. The General Assembly has created six *Regional Commissions.* The regions covered are, Africa, the Americas, Europe, Middle-East, the Pacific and East Asia, and South Asia. The Regional Commissions ensure the implementation, within their respective regions, of the~,, decisions and recommendations of the General Assembly and the Executive Council. They function and operate within the framework of the Organisation. There are the *Regional Secretariats* which are an integral part of the WTO Secretariat and help the Regional Commissions in organising and covering their conferences and meetings.

(ii) *Executive Council:* It consists of full members elected by the Assembly at the ratio of one member for every five fall members of WTO organisation with a view to achieving fair and equitable geographical distribution. The Executive Council!, among other matters, takes all necessary measures in consultation with the Secretary General, for the implementation of the decisions and recommendations of the Assembly, and reports thereon to the Assembly. The council meets at least twice a year.

(iii) *The Secretariat:* The Secretariat consists of the Secretary General and such staff as the organisation may require. The Secretary General is responsible for carrying out the general Policy and work programme of the organisation in accordance with the directions of the General Assembly and Executive-Council. The Secretary General ensures the legal representation of the organisation.

By the decision of the first General Assembly of WTO in May 1975 the headquarters were set up in Madrid (Spain) in January 1976. The activities of the Organisation cover all sectors of tourism on a worldwide basis.

WTO works in cooperation with all international organisations, the United Nations in particular, as well as with commercial and noncommercial bodies involved in tourism.

The Organisation is performing extremely useful service of concrete and creative character by facilitating the exchange of technical information, the making of specialised studies, the holding of special seminars adapted to world regional requirements and advanced vocational training courses.

The essentially practical nature of its work programme, tailored as it is to regional requirements, takes full cognizance of the problems peculiar to countries and regions in all stages of development, such as investments, financial questions, physical planning and area development, economic analysis, marketing and market surveys all this not only with a secretarial approach but with a comprehensive concern from the point of view of the state.

The creation of WTO coincided with the universal recognition of tourism as an important instrument of economic and social development and its consequent ascendancy to full government responsibility. An inter-governmental body of tourism officials--such as the WTO is empowered to act in the name of their governments and speak in terms of the impact of tourism on the balance of payments.

The creation of WTO thus is not only a proof that the states are fully conscious or their own responsibilities in the field of tourism, but also of the establishment of tourism to its rightful ranking at international level.

India is a full member of the World Tourism Organisation.

Member States of the World Tourism Organisation

1. Afghanistan
2. Algeria
3. Argentina
4. Australia
5. Austria
6. Bahrain
7. Bangladesh
8. Belgium
9. Benin
10. Bolivia
11. Brazil
12. Bulgaria
13. Burundi
14. Chile
15. Colombia
16. Congo
17. Costa Rica
18. Cuba
19. Cyprus
20. Czechoslovakia
21. Democratic Kampuchea
22. Democratic Yemen
23. Dominican Republic
24. Ecuador

38. India
39. Indonesia
40. Iran
41. Iraq
42. Israel
43. Italy
44. Ivory Coast
45. Jamaica
46. Japan
47. Jordan
48. Kenya
49. Kuwait
50. Laos People's Democratic Republic
51. Lebanon
52. Libyan Arab Jamahiriya
53. Madagascar
54. Malawi
55. Malaysia
56. Mali
57. Malta
58. Mauritania
59. Mauritius
60. Mexico

25. Egypt
26. Ethiopia
27. France
28. Gabon
29. Gambia
30. German Democratic Republic
31. Germany, Federal Re public
32. Ghana
33. Greece
34. Grenada
35. Haiti
36. Honduras
37. Hungary
76. San Marino
77. Senegal
78. Sierra Leone
79. Spain
80. Sri Lanka
81. Sudan
82. Switzerland
83. Syrian Arab Republic
84. Thailand
85. Togo
86. Tunisia
87. Turkey
88. Uganda
89. Union of Soviet Socialist Republics

61. Morocco
62. Nepal
63. Netherlands
64. Niger
65. Nigeria
66. Pakistan
67. Panama
68. Peru
69. Philippines
70. Poland
71. Portugal
72. Qatar
73. Republic of Korea
74. Romania
75. Rwanda
90. United Arab Emirates
91. United Republic of Cameroon
92. United Republic of Tanzania
93. United States of America
94. Upper Volta
95. Uruguay
96. Venezuela
97. Viet Nam
98. Yemen Arab Republic
99. Yugoslavia
100. Zaire
101. Zambia

Pacific area travel association

Pacific Area Travel Association (PATA) was founded in the year 1951 as a nonprofit corporation to stimulate interest in the Pacific region as a vacation land, and to develop, promote and facilitate travel to and among the many Pacific destinations. The Association had 44 founder members. The founder Lorrin Thurston, a leading newspaper publisher in Honolulu had an idea to organise all travel from the Occident to the Pacific area in a consistent, cohesive and systematic manner so as to ensure maximum benefit from existing opportunities and the creation of fresh opportunities through multimedia publicity. PATA's first conference was held in January 1952 in Honolulu and its headquarters established in San Francisco USA in 1953. PATA has its own Director for Europe who is based in London and works to promote traffic from the European markets into the, Pacific region. PATA's first Asian office was opened in Manila, Philippines in 1976.

PATA is a non-profit organisation set up with the objective, of developing, promoting and facilitating travel to and within, the Pacific area and South-East Asian region including India. It primarily operates in the United States market which is the world's biggest travel market. The organisation provides the meeting point for the people involved in all aspects of the travel trade from a large number of countries. It focuses attention on travel opportunities in member countries and builds up great awareness and specific contacts among the travel trade in countries from where the tourists originate. The underlying philosophy of PATA is that the entire travel industry must work together to develop an ever-increasing flow of pleasure travel from which each member will derive a fair share of the total business.

The activities of the PATA include assisting small and up-and-coming destinations to develop their infrastructure, providing expertise, planning group travel schemes, destinations, hotels operations and discounts. It provides up-to-date information and practical and theoretical experience in the field of tourism. The annual conferences of the PATA and its workshops provide greater scope to its members to share their ideas and exchange views about promotion of tourism in their respective regions. PATA staff are outstanding experts in their respective fields of marketing and research and regularly exchange with others, information on latest techniques and practices in their respective areas. All members benefit directly or indirectly from the continuing programmes of PATA, which include travel research, marketing, training programmes, and the development of visitor plants and services.

Promotion occupies a major portion of PATA's total effort. The PATA publication, Pacific *Travel News,* is relied upon by wholesale and retail travel agents as an important source of authoritative material on the Pacific. Recently, PATA has produced the first edition of the *Pacific Area Destination Handbook* which compiles in a single volume all the data that is required for the planning and sale of travel and is the world's most authoritative and comprehensive handbook on 31 Pacific destinations. PATA also publishes its *Hotel Directory* and *Travel Guide* listing the hotels, resorts and travel services in Pacific area.

PATA Membership

PATA has nine categories of membership: Active Government, Associate Government, Active Carrier, Associate Carrier, Active Industry, Allied, Affiliated Allied, Associate and Sustaining. Active *government* members consist of the primary official organisation designated by the government of any nation, territory, or political division, wholly or partly in the Pacific area. *Associate government* members consist of any organisation charged with the responsibility of the domestic or overseas promotion of tourism as designated by the government of any nation, territory, or political division either situated outside the Pacific area, or situated within the Pacific area but not being the primary official organisation designated for the overseas promotion of travel, or not meeting other criteria as might be required for Active government membership. *Active carrier* members consist of any government recognised, registered or certified air or steamship line operating vehicles having individual passenger capacity in excess of twelve passengers and providing regular scheduled common carriage passenger service to and within the Pacific area.

Associate carrier members consist of any government recognised passenger carrier operating vehicles (a) each having a passenger capacity of twelve or fewer passengers and providing regular scheduled common carriage passenger service or having a passenger capacity in excess of twelve passengers but not providing passenger service on the regular common carriage basis as prescribed for Active carrier members. Active industry members consist of hotel organisation having management authority as distinguished from mere sales, advertising or reservations direction, over one or more hotels with a total of one thousand or more guest rooms in one or more Pacific areas, tour operator organisations excluding air or ship transportation. Allied members consist of travel agencies, tour operators, hotel representatives and firms serving as general agents of or representing various segments of the Pacific travel industry. Affiliated allied members consist of branch offices of an Allied member travel agency or tour operator. Associate members consist of individual operating organisations and firms such as communication media, media representatives, advertising, public relations and research agencies having definite interest in Pacific travel. Sustaining members consist of those organisations, firms or individuals whose commercial or cultural interests in the judgement of the Board of Directors, will further contribute to the aims of the Association.

The control of PATA is vested in the Active

government, carrier and industry members. The organisations qualifying for Active government or Active carrier membership have the right to membership. They require no sponsorship and are requested merely to provide the Board of Directors with certain pertinent information. Membership in all other categories is at the discretion of the Board of Directors, and requires not only that the organisation comply with certain guidelines for eligibility, but also that certain categories of PATA members must sponsor the new applicant and vouch for its stability and professionalism.

Presently PATA has over 2193 members with 47 national and state governments, 54 airlines and 554 hotels amongst them. Every year a PATA conference is held where the participation exceeds over a thousand delegates. PATA has a membership drawn from as many as 50 countries.

India which was an Associate Member of PATA since 1957, became a full-fledged Active Member in 1964.

List of active members

(i) Active Governments

American Samoa Office of Tourism; Australian Tourist Commission; Bangladesh Parjatan Corporation; China, Tourism Bureau of the Republic of; Cook Islands Tourist Authority; Fiji Visitors Bureau; Guam Visitors Bureau; Hawaii, Department of Planning & Economic Development; Hong Kong Tourist Association; India, Department of Tourism; Indonesia, Directorate General of Tourism; Japan National Tourist Organization; Kiribati, Ministry of Natural Resource Development; Korea National Tourism Corporation; Macau, Department of Information & Tourism; Malaysia, Tourist Development Corporation of; Mexican National Tourist Council; Micronesia, Department of Development Services; Nepal,

Department of Tourism; New Caledonia, Office du Tourisme; New Zealand Government Tourist & Publicity Department; Pakistan, Ministry of Culture and Tourism; Papua New Guinea, Office of Tourism; Philippines, Ministry of Tourism; Singapore Tourist Promotion Board; Solomon Islands Tourist Authority; Sri Lanka, Ceylon Tourist Board; Tahiti Tourist Development Board; Thailand, Tourism Authority of; Tonga Visitors Bureau; United States Travel Service; USSR, Intourist; Vanuatu Tourist Information Bureau.

(ii) Active industry

American Express Company; Hilton International; Hotel Indonesia International Corporation Ltd.; Unitours.

(iii) Active carriers

Aeronaves de Mexico; Air-India; Airlanka; Air Nauru; Air New Zealand; Air Niugini; Air Pacific; All Nippon, Airways; Aloha Airlines; American Airlines; Ansett Airlines of Australia; Bangladesh Biman; Bouraq Indonesia Airlines; British Caledonian Airways; CP Air; Cathay Pacific Airways; China Airlines; Condor Flugdienst; Continental Airlines; Delta Steamship Lines; Deutsche Lufthansa; Finnair; Garuda Indonesian Airways; Gulf Air Company; Hawaiian Air; Indian Airlines; Japan Air Lines; KLM Royal Dutch Airlines; Korean Air Lines; Malaysian Airlines System; Merpati Nusantara Airlines; Mexicana Airlines; Northwest Orient Airlines; Pakistan International Airlines; Pan American World Airways; Philippine Airlines; Qantas Airways; Royal Nepal Airlines; Royal Viking Line; Scandinavian Airlines System; Singapore Airlines; Sitmar Cruises; Thai Airways International; Transamerica Airlines; Trans-Australia Airlines; Trans World Airlines; UTA French Airlines; United Airlines; Western Airlines; World Airways.

(iv) Associate carriers

Ansett-Pioneer Road Passenger Group; Japanese National Railways; Mid Pacific Air.

(v) Associate Governments

Anaheim Visitor & Convention Bureau; Australian Standing Committee of Tourism; Bali Government Tourism Office; California Office of Tourism; Canberra Tourist Bureau (Australia); Central Java Provincial Tourist Office; East Java Regional Tourist Development Bureau; Gangweon-do Provincial Government (Korea); Hawaii Visitors Bureau; India Tourism Development Corporation; Jakarta Metropolitan Tourism Board; Kementerian Tenaga Rakyat (Malaysia); Long Beach, Convention & Tourism Bureau; Korea Bureau of Tourism, Ministry of Transportation; Marianas Visitors Bureau; Melbourne Tourism Authority; New South Wales Department of Tourism; New Zealand National Travel Association; Northern Territory Tourist Commission; Pahang State Development Corporation (Malaysia); Penang State Government;

Philippine Convention Bureau; Philippine Tourism Authority; Queensland Tourist & Travel Corporation; Sabah Tourism Promotion Corporation; Sarawak Tourist Development Commission; Seoul Metropolitan Government; Travel Alberta; Victoria Government Travel Authority; West Java Regional Tourism Office.

PATA chapters

To assist in the fulfilment of the objectives of the Pacific Area Travel Association, the Board of Directors is empowered to encourage the development and to authorise establishment of PATA Chapter at any place in the world. The Chapter concept implemented in the year 1960 is unique with PATA among travel organisations. The primary purpose of a Chapter is to conduct continuing education programmes to keep PATA members abreast of the changes in Pacific travel. The Chapters also do considerable promotional work, and several times each year stage social events for the members. Specific objectives of the Chapters are as follows:

(i) To bring together representatives of PATA members at regular intervals to develop a closer working relationship and a better understanding of travel matters as such that relate to the Pacific area.

(ii) To obtain uniformity and combined action by members in pursuing national and local policies within the framework of PATA.

(iii) To implement specific PATA objectives and projects.

(iv) To pass to appropriate government and official organisations such matters approved by PATA, and to obtain action thereon as and when required.

(v) To process generally and to obtain opinions of members of the Chapters on any PATA requirement or objective.

(vi) As appropriate, to provide a forum which will enable the individual Chapter members to conduct their various assigned responsibilities for selling travel, and providing services to visitors to the Pacific in a more effective manner.

There are two types of Chapters viz: (i) Area Chapters, (ii) Promotional Chapters. *Area Chapters* were conceived as of the 8th Annual PATA Conference by a number of Allied and Associate members, as a means of keeping PATA members and their representatives in the Pacific better informed on happenings throughout the Pacific travel industry and on Association activities. Some of these Chapter activities include programmes involving matters of facilitation, staff training, improving visitor plants and services, and promotions aimed at developing regional tourist traffic and other marketing activities. Promotional Chapters were authorised by the 9th Annual PATA Conference as a means of furthering the promotion of visitors from priority market areas to Pacific destinations. Activities of these Chapters are all designed to increase the sale of travel to the Pacific area and include regular meetings of the PATA membership/ travel trade with programmes on various Pacific destinations, providing up-to-date information on new developments, facilities, services, tours, educational seminars for travel trade, sales personnel and cooperation with PATA in the overall marketing programme, promotions and other PATA activities.

The Chapters are, however, not the branch offices of PATA. They are rather like local civic clubs working for the benefit of their respective communities. A Chapter is composed of the highest level of executives representing the local tourism industry who volunteer their services and their expertise to develop a constantly expanding overall business.

Presently, PATA has as many as 51 active Chapters. Two to three new Chapters are organised yearly to help more and more people keep abreast of the changes in Pacific travel.

Finances of the association

The administration and programmes of the Association are financed by way of membership dues and the marketing assessments paid by all members. The amount of dues however, varies with the category of membership. The marketing assessments of governments and carriers are calculated in accordance with a Stanford Research Institute formula. This formula take account, among other things, the growth in visitor arrivals and expenditures at member areas, and the growth in traffic volume of carrier members The Associations' financial position is, reviewed by the Board of Directors at their monthly meetings, and an annual audit is made by an outside accounting agency. In addition to membership dues and the marketing assessment amounts, there are additional revenues which come from Allied and Associate members, a portion of which is applied to various marketing programmes.

Pacific Area Travel Association performs a variety of functions. These include:

(i) *Pacific Travel Conference and workshop.* During the first four months of each year, PATA sponsors and organises a conference of its members with the objectives of reviewing the progress, exchanging ideas and planning for future programmes. These meetings are held at different areas. The annual conferences attract a large number of delegates from all over the world. The conference also serves as a unique promotional tool for the host government providing it an opportunity to show to the travel industry from abroad what it has to offer in terms of tourist attractions and tourism plant to the foreign visitor.

(ii) *Marketing.* A long-range marketing programme coordinates all the promotional functions of PATA for a maximum impact in the consumer market and also among sales agents. The marketing programme includes: (1) Advertising, Publicity and Promotion. An extensive advertising programme schedule is carried in leading national magazines of North America with a view to increase interest in the Pacific region as a major travel area. The association prepares and distributes a wide selection of selling aids and sales promotion materials to travel agents, tour operators throughout the world. A strong trade advertising programme is directed towards travel agents in order to merchandise PATA's consumer advertising and sales promotion efforts Weekly news releases, special feature stories and photographs are provided to the various newspapers, magazines and radio and television networks by the Association's Pacific news service. Members may use Association's various materials including photographs for their own publicity purposes. (2) Marketing Research and Development. The Association's research programme is designed to provide it with the marketing information needed to formulate its own marketing programme as well as to provide its members with information which will assist them in designing their own programmes. The Association organises research seminars, research presentations and technical assistance programmes for its members. Another important facet of the research programme includes the collection, analysis and dissemination of Pacific travel statistics and an effort designed to constantly improve and standardise the tourism statistics of the Pacific region.

PATA and India

India was admitted as an Associate Government Member of Pacific Area Travel Association in the year 1957. It was at the specific request of the Government that the Constitution of the PATA was amended suitably to enable India and other South Asian countries to become Associate Government Members. It was only in the year 1964 at Djkarta, Indonesia that India became an Active Member, of the Association. Basically, PATA was formed to promote traffic to Pacific countries only. However, the definition of PATA was somewhat enlarged to enable some of the countries bordering on the Pacific to join PATA. India was the first country to enter PATA from among the countries which bordered on the Pacific but were not in the Pacific region. Subsequently, a few other countries also joined the association from this region. Among these countries were Sri Lanka, Nepal and later Pakistan and Bangladesh,

It was not long before India realised the manifold benefits which this organisation had for promotion of tourism. India realised that PATA was one of the most active travel promotional organisations and that the country's association with it would not only benefit her from getting a share of the world's increasing tourist flow but also from the point of view of exposing it to the modern techniques of tourism marketing and promotion. During the 1964 annual conference at Sydney in Australia, PATA agreed to hold its annual convention in India in the year 1966. During the 1965 Conference in Korea, India's invitation to host the Annual Convention in 1966 was reaffirmed and accepted by the General Body of the PATA Conference. The decision regarding the venue of the conference is generally made three years in advance.

PATA '66 was the 15th Annual Conference of the Association. The five-days Conference and the Workshop which met in New Delhi was attended by over 500 delegates from a number of countries. India at that time was emerging as a new tourist destination with very little exposure in American and Pacific areas of its tourist attractions. The main objective in inviting PATA Conference to Delhi was to expose our facilities to a large; segment of foreign tour operators, travel writers, airline executives etc. The conference was a big success as, it resulted in a steady rise in tourist traffic to India during subsequent years. India enjoyed a continuous and uninterrupted growth till 1973 when the steep rise in oil prices followed by inflation in potential tourism markets led to a slight decline in the growth of tourist arrivals. However, during subsequent years the tourist arrivals increased. India after PATA '66 Conference is now a full-fledged member.

India was awarded yet another conference! PATA '78. India was unanimously chosen as the venue of the 1978 conference at the Sydney PATA Conference in 1975. The theme of the conference "Challenge of Change" became particularly significant in view of the fact that tourism was passing into a phase where there were no limits to its growth. The objective of hosting another PATA Conference in India after a period of twelve years was to expose tourist facilities to a large segment of tour operators, travel writers and airline executives etc. The conference was attended by over 1500 delegates and was the largest PATA Conference held in the history of PATA. The large number of delegates from all over the world provided an opportunity to India to expose its tourist plant to the international travel world. The Conference will go a long way in projecting India's image not only as a great tourist destination but also as a great host country.

PATA India Chapter. PATA (India) Chapter was organised in the year 1969 as one of the Area Chapters. This Chapter has 98 members with representation from Government (Central Department of Tourism), India Tourism Development Corporation, Indian Airlines, Air India and other international carriers, leading travel agencies in India, hotels, tour operators, advertising agencies etc. The Chapter undertakes promotional work specifically for promoting India.

In recent years there hag been rapid and continuous development of both national and international tourism.

The international tourism organisations have played and are continuing to play a key role in the tourism development both national as well as international. India has regularly participated actively in the deliberations of international bodies which afford an opportunity to establish new contacts and renew old ties with persons from all over the world connected with tourism. These organisations also help the member countries to determine the general travel trends for proper channelisation of promotional activities. India's association with these bodies has definitely encouraged the flow of tourist traffic from international tourist generating markets to India.

International air transport association

As a result of the rapid expansion in the network of international airlines in the years following the Second World War, a need for worldwide regulation of air traffic and craft equipment was felt by many countries. Consequently an international convention was called by President, Franklin D. Roosevelt of the United States of America at Chicago from November I to December 7, 1944. The Convention constituted two permanent bodies, namely, the International Air Transport Association (IATA) and the International Civil Aviation Organisation (ICAO). Both these organisations are the leading international agencies looking after various aspects of world aviation industry including various problems and their solutions in the civil air transport.

But before reaching the position that it now occupies in the field of aviation, IATA passed through several stages in parallel with the spectacular development of commercial aviation. Its modest beginnings date back to 1919. Its predecessor, the International Air Traffic Association, was founded in that year in The Hague by half a dozen European airlines that had just been created.

Right from the beginning they recognized the need to cooperate in setting up a network where everything needed to be rationalized.

The activity of the first, prewar version of IATA expanded steadily with the development of air services in the world. Among other things, it drew up the general formula for tickets and transport documents adopted in 1927. The innovations and improvements introduced by the Association progressively placed unique tools at the disposal of the industry.

In November 1944, as World War It hostilities were taking a final turn, 54 states met in Chicago to lay the first foundations of the new system that would soon be greatly needed by civil aviation. This Conference led to the creation of the International Civil Aviation Organisation (ICAO), the international body set up by governments to establish universal norms for the technical regulation of civil aviation. Indirectly, this Conference was also responsible for the foundation of the International Air Transport Association--a nongovernmental body officially set up in Havana in April 1945--which, in practice, carried on the task assumed by the former IATA. Both through its Organisation and its activity, IATA found itself closely linked to ICAO. International Air Transport Association's work became increasingly, diversified, specialized and extensive with the development of aeronautical technology and the expansion of the airline network. With the arrival of jets towards the end of the fifties, a whole series of new measures concerning technical matters, fares, procedures and Organisation was needed to replace regulations that no longer corresponded to the new conditions in the industry or to the growing potential of its market.

The International Air Transport Association (IATA)

is the global organisation for virtually all the international carriers. The principal function of IATA is to simplify and speed the movement of persons and goods from any point on the world air network to any other by a combination of routes. This is accomplished by a single ticket bought at a single price in one currency. The ticket is valid everywhere for the same amount and quality of service. The same principles apply to the movement of freight and mail.

Under the provisions of its constitution, IATA must carry out a threefold task:

(i) encourage the development of reliable, regular and economical air transport for the benefit of the peoples of the world, foster air commerce arid study the problems involved;

(ii) provide the means for collaboration among the air transport enterprises involved directly or indirectly in international air transport services;

(iii) cooperate with the International Civil Aviation. Organisation and other international organisations.

Services provided

The IATA provides a wide range of services. The list of services provided is quite impressive and includes the following:

- the global planning of international timetables,
- the standardization of the inter-company communications and reservations systems,
- the international coordination of telecommunications networks and Computer Systems,
- the single formula for tickets and air waybills,
- the training of travel and freight agents,

- to regulate legal questions of genera, concern, to develop security measures,
- to examine and solve the problems raised by tourism and the flow of passengers and goods in the airports and to establish procedures and technical norms.

Organisation

IATA is a non-government organisation. There are three IATA traffic conferences--Western Hemisphere; Europe, Africa and the Middle East; Asia and Australia. The conference Areas are numbered in numerical order. Each Traffic conference Area covers a number of countries. The IATA traffic conferences are, in effect, an important adjunct to government. Also, the rules which IATA formulates must be approved by the governments involved. IATA traffic conferences come in after governments have decided bilaterally upon the exchange of rights and after each government decides individually what air carriers are going to serve their area.

In order to be eligible for the membership of IATA and the conferences, an airline must hold a certificate for scheduled air carriage from a government eligible for membership of the International Civil Aviation Organisation. Airlines engaged directly in international operations are active members while on the the other hand airlines engaged in domestic operations are associate members.

Resolutions of the traffic conferences of International Air Transport Association standardise not only tickets but waybills, baggage checks and other similar documents. These resolutions also coordinate and unify handling and accounting procedures to permit rapid inter-line booking and connection. The resolutions also maintain a stable pattern of international fares and rates of over 100 member airlines all over he world. The standardization of air fares is the must significant part of IATA's work. In effect, this has resulted in permitting he linking of the routes of many individual international airlines into a single public service system for all nations of the world.

In order to carry out so many functions, IATA has a staff of over 450 people throughout the world and operates with funds provided in the form of annual dues paid by members.

Broadly speaking, IATA is the world association of scheduled airlines within which they coordinate their efforts to serve their passengers, share their experiences and analyse their problems. Representing over 100 companies from 80 odd countries together provide the bulk of world scheduled air services. IATA plays a leading, role in three respects, on the basis of the aims defined in its statutes.

The Association provides machinery for the airlines for finding joint solutions to problems often beyond the resources of any single company. Through the Association, airlines have succeeded in standardising their operating methods and with their complementary routes they have created a worldwide public service network, despite the many differences in language, currency, legislation and regulations.

The Association is able to act as an intermediary between governments and its users. It is the world parliament of airline companies and their spokesman vis-a-vis various other international bodies. For governments it serves as a forum where proposals for international rates and fares are formulated in a neutral context for study and approval. For the general public--it symbolizes, because it monitors and encourages them, the uniform quality of services, the use of rational commercial methods by airlines and agents, the simplification of formalities and the lowest possible fares and rates consistent with sound economy.

International civil aviation organisation

The convention providing for the establishment of the International Civil Aviation Organisation was drawn up by the International Civil Aviation Conference held in Chicago from November 1 to December 7, 1944. A provisional International Civil Aviation Organisation (PICAO) functioned from 6 June, 1945 until the formal establishment of ICAO. The International Civil Aviation Organisation (ICAO) was formally established on April 4, 1947 as a specialized agency of the United Nations. ICAO has a membership of over 130 governments joined for the common purpose of promoting civil aviation on a global scale. The headquarters or the organisation are located at Montreal, Canada. The organisation has its regional offices in Mexico city, Lima, Paris, Dakar, Cairo and Bangkok. The International Civil Aviation Organisation representing over 130 governments of various countries throughout the world provides the machinery for the achievement of greater global cooperation in the matters of civil aviation. Over the years the organisation has achieved great success in various matters relating with civil aviation.

Objectives

The main objectives of the organisation are to develop the principles and the techniques of international air navigation and to foster the planning and development of international air transport with a view to:

(i) ensure the safe and orderly growth of international civil aviation throughout the world;

(ii) encourage the arts of aircraft design and operation for peaceful purposes;

(iii) encourage the development of airways, airports and navigation facilities for international civil aviation;

(iv) meet the needs of the people of the world for safe, regular, efficient, economical air transport;

(v) prevent economic waste caused by unreasonable competition;

(vi) ensure that the rights of contracting countries are fully respected and that every contracting country has a fair opportunity to operate international airlines;

(vii) avoid discrimination between contracting countries;

(iii) promote safety of flight in international air navigation;

(ix) promote generally the development of all aspects, of international civil aeronautics.

In addition to the above, the International Civil Aviation Organisation through its various proposals tries for the reduction of customs, immigration, public health and other formalities in order to facilitate air transportation. As part of the United Nations Development Programme, the organisation provides technical assistance to states in developing civil aviation programmes. Development of regional plans for ground facilities and services needed for international flying is another important function of the Organisation. The Organisation disseminates air transport statistics and prepares studies on aviation economics. It also fosters the development of air law conventions.

Organisation of ICAO

The principal organ of ICAO is an Assembly. The Assembly consists of all the members of the organisation and is the sovereign body of ICAO. It meets every three years and reviews in detail the work of the organisation. It sets the policy for the next three years. The organisation has a Council which is comprised of 30 states and is elected by the Assembly for a period of three years. While electing the states, the Assembly gives adequate representation to:

(i) member states of major importance in air transport;

(ii) those member states not otherwise included which make the largest contribution to the provision of facilities for the international civil air navigation; and

(iii) those member states not otherwise included and whose election will ensure that all major geographical areas of the world are represented.

As a governing body, the council gives continuous direction to the work of the organisation. The main subsidiary bodies are: the Air Navigation Commission, composed of 12 members elected by the council; Air Transport Committee, open to council members; and the Legal Committee, on which all members of ICAO may be represented. India has been an elected member of the Council since it became a member of ICAO.

A close look at the range of activities and objectives of both International Air Transport Association and International Civil Aviation Oranisation indicates that they play a key role in the growth and development of international air transport. Their role since inception has been that of fostering the growth of air transport. Although not directly concerned with tourism, they have however, played an important role in its growth over the years by way or encouraging air transport.